TALES

BY MARK DUGAN

Bandit Years: A Gathering of Wolves
(Sunstone Press, Sante Fe, New Mexico, 1987).

Knight of the Road
(Swallow Press/Ohio University Press, Athens, Ohio, 1990).

With John Boessenecker,
The Grey Fox: The True Story of Bill Miner — Last of the Old-Time Bandits
(University of Oklahoma Press, Norman, Oklahoma, 1992).

TALES

NEVER TOLD
AROUND THE

CAMPFIRE

True Stories of
Frontier America

BY MARK DUGAN

SWALLOW PRESS/
OHIO UNIVERSITY PRESS ATHENS

Swallow Press/Ohio University Press books are printed on acid-free paper ∞

Library of Congress Cataloging-in-Publication Data

Dugan, Mark, 1941–
   Tales never told around the campfire : true stories of frontier America /
by Mark Dugan.
     p.   cm.
   Includes bibliographical references.
   ISBN 0-8040-0954-6. — ISBN 0-8040-0955-4 (pbk.)
   1. Frontier and pioneer life—United States. 2. United States—History,
Local. I. Title.
E179.5.D93   1992   91-26183
973–dc20   CIP

01   00   99   98   97   96   9   8   7   6   5   4   3

TO JEAN
whose geniality is exceeded only by her ability

.

CONTENTS

ILLUSTRATIONS

CHAPTER I · TEXAS

CHAPTER II · NORTH CAROLINA

CHAPTER VIII · COLORADO

CHAPTER IX · MISSOURI

CHAPTER X · WYOMING

ACKNOWLEDGMENTS

ARKANSAS: John L. Ferguson, Arkansas History Commission, Little Rock; Ann Strother, Searcy; Donaly Brice, Texas State Archives, Austin; Gail Metcalf, Texas Department of Corrections, Huntsville; Linda Pansano, Bridge City, Texas; G. Clyde Lewis, San Augustine, Texas; Mary Alice Winborn, Houston, Texas; Drayton Speights, Hemphill, Texas; Helen Gomer Schluter, Fort Worth, Texas.

COLORADO: Dan Neeley, Federal Archives and Records Center, Denver; Catherine Engel, Colorado Historical Society, Denver; Sheri Pierce, Pagosa Springs; Alice Dalligen, Detroit Public Library, Detroit, Michigan; Tom Kruski, Federal Archives and Records Center, Chicago, Illinois; James S. Rush, Assistant Branch Chief of the Civil Reference Branch, Elizabeth Lockwood, and James Cassedy, National Archives, Washington, D. C.; James M. Whalen, Archivist, National Archives of Canada, Ottawa, Ontario.

ILLINOIS: Anna L. Vasconcelles and John Daly, Illinois State Archives, Springfield; Ronald J. Baker, Riverside City/County Public Library, Riverside, California.

MISSOURI: Patsy Leubbring and Jennifer Burlis, Missouri State Archives, Jefferson City; Kay Pettit, State Historical Society of Missouri, Columbia; Charles E. Hall and Betty Hively, McDonald County Circuit Clerks Office, Pineville; Zella Collie, McDonald County Library, Pineville; Robert D. Hubbard, Weir, Kansas.

NORTH CAROLINA: Jessie Williams, Foscoe; Sanna Gaffney, Boone; Bina Teague, Boone; Shirley Wayland and Evelyn Johnson, Watauga County Public Library, Boone; Rachal Rivers Coffey and Don Tolbert, *The Watauga Democrat*, Boone; Phyllis Foster, Recorder of Deeds, Watauga County Courthouse, Boone; John Heaton, Belk Library, Appalachian State University, Boone; Jean Joyner, Office of Senator Terry Sanford, Raleigh; Janice Mahaffey, Palatka, Florida; Karen Moll, State Historical Society of Iowa, Des Moines, Iowa; Wayne Brandt, Nebraska Game and Parks Commission, Fairbury, Nebraska.

NEW MEXICO: J. Richard Salazar, New Mexico Records Center and Archives, Santa Fe; Sherry Krukowski, Socorro Public Library, Socorro;

Edward M. Smith, Socorro; Donaly Brice, Texas State Archives, Austin, Texas; Shirley Wayland and Evelyn Johnson, Watauga County Public Library, Boone, North Carolina; Terry Harmon, Kansas State Historical Society, Topeka, Kansas.

OKLAHOMA: Kay Zahrai, Oklahoma Historical Society, Oklahoma City; Mary F. Manship, Osgood, Indiana; Terry Harmon, Kansas State Historical Society, Topeka, Kansas.

TEXAS: Ed Bartholomew, Fort Davis; Donaly Brice, Texas State Archives, Austin; Laura McGinty, Springtown Police Department, Springtown; Mark Warnken, *The Springtown Epigraph*, Springtown; McEvlyn Broumly, Weatherford Pubic Library, Weatherford; Barbara Rust, Federal Archives and Records Center, Fort Worth, Texas; Lois Fairman, Frederick, Maryland; Ellen Hockett, Sheridan, Oregon; Steve Hallberg, Oregon Historical Society, Portland, Oregon.

WASHINGTON: Joyce Justice, Federal Archives and Records Center, Seattle; Dave Hastings, Division of Archives and Records Management, Olympia; Jean Engerman, Washington State Historical Society, Tacoma; Janet Lowery, Bellingham Public Library, Bellingham; Eunice W. Darvill, Skagit County Historical Museum, LaConner; Dr. Roland DeLarme, Western Washington University, Bellingham; Dean DeBoer, Manager of Bay View Cemetery, Bellingham; Lorraine Peterson, Bellingham-Whatcom County District Department of Health, Bellingham; Forrest Daniel, State Historical Society of North Dakota, Bismarck, North Dakota; Linda M. Sommer, South Dakota Historical Society, State Archives, Pierre, South Dakota; Les Mobbs, Provincial Archives of British Columbia, Victoria, British Columbia; Paul Yee, City of Vancouver Archives, Vancouver, British Columbia; Art Downs, Heritage House Publishing Company Ltd., Surrey, British Columbia; James M. Whalen, Archivist, National Archives of Canada, Ottawa, Ontario.

WYOMING: Jean Brainerd, Cindy L. Brown, and Paula West Chavoya, Wyoming State Archives, Museums and Historical Department, Cheyenne.

Special thanks to John Boessenecker, San Francisco, California, and Bill Secrest, Fresno, California, for their help in securing photographs and bits and pieces of pertinent information necessary to complete this book.

FOREWORD

PROBABLY NO TOPIC OF AMERICA'S PAST has been so sorely neglected by academic historians as the criminal history of the Old West. Generations of scholars have turned up their noses at serious study of frontier crime and law enforcement, leaving the field open to a small number of dedicated avocational historians and to hordes of hacks and pulp writers. Many of the latter have produced books about frontier outlaws and lawmen that, while entertaining and full of western flavor, are sadly lacking in research and often contain more fiction than fact.

In more recent years a handful of scholars have rediscovered frontier crime, recognizing it as a rich field for study. Unfortunately, some of them write western history that is the converse of that written by the pulp writers: dry works that are heavy in statistical analysis and social interpretation, but devoid of the drama and color of the frontier.

With a few exceptions, it is the dedicated avocational historian who continues to produce the largest body of new and readable literature on western lawlessness. These works can be divided into two categories. First, there are those works that present fresh, previously unpublished data on well-known western outlaws and lawmen. Second, there is an ever-increasing number of books and magazine articles dealing with people and episodes in western criminal history which, though perhaps well known in the nineteenth century, are completely forgotten today. In either case this new breed of avocational historian forsakes the timeworn myths, dime yellowbacks, and oft-inaccurate secondary sources and instead delves into such primary sources as old newspaper files, court records, diaries, and journals. The result is a depiction of criminal justice and lawlessness in the Old West which is readable, entertaining, and highly reliable.

Mark Dugan is a writer and avocational historian who combines entertaining storytelling with such exhaustive primary-source research. An acknowledged expert on western outlaws, he is the author of *Bandit Years* (1987), a volume on the most noted of the Rocky Mountain stage robbers, and *Knight of the Road* (1990), a biography that resurrected the story of the once-notorious highwayman Ham White. Both books dealt with topics that had, for the most part, been forgotten for generations. The author flushed out his stories from pioneer newspapers, court documents, and government records.

In *Tales Never Told around the Campfire*, Dugan has put together an anthology that will please anyone who is interested in gunfighters, badmen, and western lawlessness. Some of the frontier characters who appear in these pages will be familiar to western readers: Sarah Shull, alleged paramour of Wild Bill Hickok; hired killer Tom Horn; and Oklahoma lawman Ed Short. But even die-hard western fans have never heard of Black train bandit Punch Collins or woman bank robber Cora Hubbard. For those who may think that the Pacific Northwest and Illinois did not produce frontier rogues, there are the stories of Jake Terry and William S. Ruby; for those who believe that women in the west were always treated with chivalry, the horrible lynching of the Hill family in Texas should disabuse them of the notion.

One of the enduring mysteries of the Old West involves the strange relationship between Wild Bill Hickok and his enemy and victim, David McCanles, and the beautiful Sarah Shull. Mark Dugan has managed to locate reams of new information on McCanles's flight from North Carolina and his romantic liaison with Sarah Shull, and recounts in detail the infamous Rock Creek fight in which Hickok killed McCanles. Working with newly found reminiscences of Sarah Shull and previously unused court records, Dugan demonstrates that Sarah Shull was not Hickok's paramour, despite the claims of many writers, and unearths the real reasons why David McCanles fled his home in North Carolina for the Nebraska frontier.

Like Wild Bill, Tom Horn was one of the most enigmatic figures of the Old West. He built an excellent reputation as an Army scout and trailer during the Apache Indian wars in Arizona in the 1870s and 1880s, and later did good service in Cuba as a packer during the Spanish-American War. An experienced cowman and top hand, he won top prize for steer roping at the Phoenix rodeo in 1891. During the early nineties Horn worked as a Pinkerton detective, tracking down outlaws and fugitives, but he found this line of work "too tame." He was already a well-known figure when he drifted into Wyoming in 1893. According to most authorities Tom Horn became a hired killer for the big cattlemen. He was suspected of ambushing reputed rustlers, including Fred Powell, William Lewis, Matt Rash, Isom Dart, and fourteen-year-old Willie Nickell, whose killer evidently mistook him for his father. Whether Horn was responsible for any or all of these murders has been a controversy that has raged for more than ninety years. In this volume Mark Dugan presents the first full accounts of the Powell and Lewis killings, and throws new light on the question of Tom Horn's guilt or innocence.

One of the most violent robber bands of the Old West was the Dalton gang of the Oklahoma and Indian Territories. In 1891 and '92, brothers Bob, Grat, and Emmett Dalton became the most wanted badmen in the American West during a bloodcurdling spree of bank and train robberies. Following the annihilation of the Dalton gang at thee hands of the peaceable townfolk of Coffeyville, Kansas, in 1892, a fourth brother, Bill Dalton, and gang member Bill Doolin became the leading lights in a new bandit gang. The story of these outlaws, and of the courageous Oklahoma lawmen who tracked them down, among them Bill Tilghman, Heck Thomas, and Chris Madsen, in one of the best-known and most exciting sagas of the frontier era. The first member of the Dalton gang to be slain was Black-Faced Charley Bryant, but the outlaw took with him Deputy U.S. Marshal Ed Short. The story of the Bryant-Short gun duel is known to all gunfighter aficionados, but the full story of Ed Short's career has never before been told. Once again Mark Dugan digs deep and uncovers the story of a controversial western hero.

The author has complemented each chapter with an excellent selection of photographs, many of which have never been published before. *Tales Never Told around the Campfire* should delight any history buff who thirsts for the real west.

John Boessenecker
San Francisco

[A San Francisco attorney, John Boessenecker is the author of *Badge and Buckshot: Lawlessness in Old California*, published in 1988 by the University of Oklahoma Press.]

INTRODUCTION

The Foundation of Legends

THROUGH THE YEARS, like many other western history buffs, I have collected bits and pieces of research, which, separate and apart, would not constitute a complete book. They certainly have historical value and should not be discarded. So, by compiling them into short stories, I hope they will expand the perception of this colorful yet distorted and sensationalized era of history.

Most people are familiar with Jesse James, Wild Bill Hickok, Billy the Kid, the Dalton Gang, Wyatt Earp, Bat Masterson, and Butch Cassidy and the Sundance Kid through books, films, or television. The lives of these frontier characters were colorful and full of hair-raising experiences, and the characters themselves have reached a plateau as folk heroes. However, many others, unknown and obscure, contributed to this legendary period in American history. In many cases, their lives were more exciting and graphic than those of their better-known contemporaries.

Here are ten factual stories of outlaws, killers, bandits, lawmen, and just plain individuals who happened to be pushed into the limelight. Some of these narratives are told for the first time, however none of them has ever been fully reported. They are the foundation upon which legends are made, and many of the persons whose lives are chronicled in this book are legendary in their respective regions. Now is their chance to join the ranks to compete with those who have attained so much notoriety and fame.

I. TEXAS

THE HILL FAMILY

The Day Chivalry Died in Texas

*T*HE ANNALS OF THE OLD WEST are literally riddled with accounts of swift justice being meted out by vigilantes and angry mobs. In several instances their victims were women, to wit: Ella "Cattle Kate" Watson in Wyoming, Elizabeth Taylor in Nebraska, and a young Mexican woman, Juanita, in California. But of all the lynchings and killings committed by vigilante groups, none was more brutal or more horrifying than the murder of Dusky Hill and her five daughters in the Texas counties of Parker and Montague during the summer of 1873.

The animosity that led to the killings had simmered for nearly twenty years, a period of time that has been shrouded in legend; a period of time that began prior to the Civil War and extended into the era of Reconstruction; a period of time when documentation and records were poorly kept and news was at a minimum. Although documentation is limited, examining and comparing records and histories that do exist leads to an essentially accurate account of what transpired.

It all began in 1854, when Allen Cash Hill migrated to Texas. Hill, born in Alabama in 1814, had moved to Tennessee before the mid-1840s and married twenty-year-old Luduska "Dusky" Brock around 1846. Their first child, Nancy, called Nance, was born in Tennessee in 1848. By 1852 the family was in Missouri, where a second daughter, Martha, was born. The next year they moved again, this time to Arkansas, where a son was born. Although the boy was listed as C. Hill on the 1860 Parker County, Texas, census, his actual name was Jackson, and he was known as Jack.[1]

One wonders if Allen C. Hill's questionable character, which plagued him in Texas, was the cause of his constant shifting from place to place.

In 1854 the Hills settled in what is now Parker County, Texas. After camping for two weeks, where a bridge would eventually stand in Springtown, they purchased a 160-acre tract of land about a mile southwest of the present town of Springtown, adjoining the Dunn and Matlock farms.

On December 12, 1855, Parker County was created from unorganized counties west of Tarrant County. In the same year, the town of Weatherford was founded and named for Senator Jefferson Weatherford, who had passed the bill creating Parker County. The Hills and other Parker County residents had to travel to Weatherford for supplies until 1859, when Springtown was founded by Joseph Ward of New Jersey. The town was so named by Ward because of the many springs abundantly scattered throughout the area. [2]

During the same year that the Hills moved to Parker County, their third daughter, Adeline, was born. In the next eight years Dusky gave birth to four more children: Allen Cash Junior in 1856; Eliza in 1857; Catherine, known as Kate, in 1858; and Isabelle, called Belle, on April 12, 1860. [3]

It was not long after the Hills moved to Parker County that hostility developed with their neighbors and the residents of Springtown. The basis for this rancor was threefold. One was Allen Hill's contempt and hatred toward everyone in the area; another was the family's support and sympathy for the Union cause. But the major reason was their complete disregard for law and order in using their home as a refuge for wanted criminals and fugitives. The atmosphere of malevolence finally erupted, sounding the death knell for all but two members of the Hill family.

Extreme acts of violence tend to create legends that are handed down from one generation to another. These legends, however, are usually based on fact, and a prime example is the tragic story of the Hills.

The earliest account of Allen Hill's antisocial nature reportedly occurred not long after the family's arrival in Parker County. Although Hill's reputation for hostility was widespread, a neighbor, Jim Dunn, did not believe Hill was entirely bad. He convinced his wife, Sophia, that an act of kindness might win the friendship of his new neighbors, so she baked an extra batch of sourdough biscuits for the Hills. Riding up to the Hill's front door, Dunn inquired if anyone was home. Hill came to the door and grumbled, "What do you want, reb?" Receiving the pan of biscuits, Hill took off the lid, spit tobacco juice on the biscuits, flung the pan to the ground, and kicked it contemptuously. Then he turned his back on Dunn and went back inside the house. Dusky Hill supposedly ran out on the porch with a kettle of boiling water, screaming, "Let me scald the damn bastard, Pa!" Without further ado, Dunn wisely retreated.

Dunn told the story to a large group of people gathered at the blacksmith shop. As Dunn was not one to exaggerate the truth, the residents made it a point to avoid the Hills from then on. Obviously, the conversation was only added color, because no one was referred to as "reb" in the mid-1850s.

A rather humorous story involving the Hills presumably took place in the fall of 1862. Several neighbors of the Hills' noticed that someone was stealing their firewood. While discussing the matter, Ben Morrel remarked that he could find out who the thief was and hid firecrackers in the stovewood. Several mornings later, the Hills' cookstove reportedly blew up.

Another incident that supposedly occurred centered on one of Allen Hill's daughters. A young man named Earl Davis wrote a note to Martha Hill, inviting her to a church box supper. Davis received no answer, but Allen Hill went looking for him, threatening to kill anyone who made overtures to his daughters. Although the incident probably occurred, it could not have involved Martha, for she was only ten years old when her father died in 1863. If the story is true, Nance Hill would have been the recipient of Davis' note, and Allen Hill had a right to be enraged, for she could not have been more than fourteen years old. [4]

The charge of the Hills' being Union sympathizers was likely circulated to cover Allen Hill's murder by vigilantes. It is rather hard to believe the accusation, when both Allen and Dusky Hill were born and raised and lived their entire lives in the South. However, because of his irascible and ill-tempered nature, Allen Hill could very well have expressed these sentiments for spite. In 1919 two citizens of Parker County came forward and made a sworn affidavit concerning the killing of the Hill family. They stated emphatically that Allen Hill was a Union sympathizer. [5]

The residents of the Springtown vicinity could overlook Hill's cantankerous nature and his so-called Union sympathies, but offering his home, for profit, as a haven for criminals was a major cause of concern. Although the Hills owned 160 acres of tillable land, they showed no inclination to work the soil. Instead, they turned their house into a refuge for the lawless, dug an escape tunnel from the house to a creek twenty feet away, and rigged a trapdoor at the entrance of the tunnel. There were several reported instances in which law officers trailed fugitives to the Hill homestead, where the hunted would suddenly disappear. Upon searching the house, the lawmen could find no trace of the wanted men. [6]

One account regarding the use of the tunnel involved a man who had just returned with his partner from a cattle-buying trip. The man, whose name possibly was Henry Chalk, had sufficient money of his own, but after learning his partner had six thousand dollars cash in his possession, he killed him, took his money, and headed for the sanctuary of the Hill homestead. A few days later a posse arrived at the house, and the man was forced to escape hurriedly through the tunnel. Legend has it that the man buried the money near the house but was never able to return for it. [7]

By the winter of 1863, the citizens of Parker County were fed up with the undesirable element that appeared on the streets of Springtown and with Allen Hill's continuing effrontery in sheltering them. Throughout Texas, attention was focused on the raging Civil War, and law enforcement was at a low ebb. The famed Texas Rangers were inactive throughout the war, and local law in Parker County could not or would not act on the situation. As a result, ten of the townsmen met in secret and agreed to handle the matter themselves.

Shortly after the meeting, one of the men received word that Hill was out riding alone several miles from his home. The others were quickly summoned, and all ten men left in pursuit of him. They soon located their quarry, surrounded Hill, and informed him he was under arrest. Within minutes, the vigilantes dropped their semblance of legality and told him he had better run for his life. All ten men fired their rifles at Hill the minute he started running. His body was left where it fell in the deep woods.

For about a year, Dusky Hill never knew what had happened to her husband and assumed he had deserted her. Sometime in 1864, she accidentally discovered his body. Although there was little left but bones, she identified her husband's remains by his wallet and shoes. As she gathered what was left of Allen Hill to take home for burial, a sliver of bone punctured one of her fingers. The finger became infected, and she had to have it amputated. Dusky Hill apparently never learned how her husband died but no doubt suspected he was killed by a mob.

Author John W. Nix adroitly summed up the reasons behind the murder of Allen Hill:

> Some have said that Allen Hill was murdered because he was a Union sympathizer; this we doubt, and rather think it was the accumulation of many acts of Allen Hill and his family that brought him into constant conflict, bitter wrangling and bickering with his neighbors and the people of the surrounding country. While we cannot and do not condone mob violence in any way, or any illegal act of any kind, there comes times in the history of all peoples when law enforcement breaks down and either is not or cannot be enforced. There is ample evidence from many sources that Allen Hill and his family harbored horse thieves, criminals, disreputable characters of many kinds, connived with and protected them, housed and fed them. [8]

The vigilantes disbanded after killing Hill, believing that Dusky and her family would either leave the area or refrain from committing any more acts of lawlessness. Time would prove them wrong on both counts.

Dusky Hill continued to use her home as a haven for horsethieves, desperadoes, and fugitives on the run. The aberrant lifestyle of Allen and Dusky Hill became firmly ingrained in the younger generation, and by the early 1870s, their home had evolved into a notorious bawdy house as well. As each daughter reached maturity, she took her place in line as a prostitute in the house. By 1873 all the daughters were ladies of pleasure, except twelve-year-old Belle Hill. Residents and passersby reported strange men arriving at the house at dusk and not leaving until dawn and the sound of music, gay laughter, and dancing throughout the night. Local folklore has it that the Hill women were fine fiddlers and dancers. [9]

Although the lawless traits of their parents profoundly influenced the future actions of the younger Hills, none took more to a life of depravity and degradation than the oldest daughter, Nance Hill. There are numerous stories handed down, citing her bold and heinous acts of violence, including the following account:

> Most of the family were vicious — so vicious that grown men feared even the women. One man said he was "as scared of Nance, the oldest daughter, as of an Indian." Another man, investigating the sound of a shot in the area of his hog pen, found Nance wrestling with one of his hogs. Her shot apparently only stunned the animal, which had revived, and Nance yelling and enjoying the fun, was finishing the job with a knife. The man, possessing more discretion than courage, quietly crept away. [10]

The following exploit credited to Nance Hill definitely did not endear her to the two hundred plus residents of Springtown. The town doctor sent out invitations for the double wedding of his twin daughters of the McQuade brothers. It was to be a big event, and everyone in Springtown contributed to it. The day finally arrived, and as the brides marched down the aisle, pandemonium broke loose. The ceremony was brought to an immediate halt by Nance Hill and several others, who came dashing around the church on horseback and began shooting out the windows while screaming at the top of their lungs. Needless to say, there was no wedding, and one of the bridegrooms reportedly fled in panic and never returned.

One tale, less believable, is of Nance coming home late one night and finding her lover in the arms of her sister Martha. In one report the man was train robber Sam Bass, and in another he was a soldier from Fort Richardson. Nance reportedly chased him to Jacksboro, shot him in the back, and was immediately caught, tried, and sentenced to hang by a Fort Richardson tribunal. Before she could be hanged, she managed to escape and flee back to Springtown. [11]

During the time period that Nance Hill was active, Sam Bass was working in Denton, Texas, for small wages and did not gain notoriety until 1877, four years after Nance's death. However, Bass very well could have frequented the Hill bawdy house, as Denton is only forty miles or so northeast of Springtown. No records have ever been located to substantiate the conviction of Nance Hill at Fort Richardson, and the newspapers that reported her actions made no mention of it.

More credence can be given to the writings of Judge Marvin F. London in his book *Famous Court Trials of Montague County*. Judge London took the time and effort to research many unknown facts that otherwise would be lost to history:

> Nancy Hill was a notorious horse thief of the 1860's and early 1870's. She operated along the frontier counties where police protection was hard to come by for the settlers. Civilization was moving westward. Already counties like Denton, Cooke, Wise, Parker, and Montague were being settled. She operated along this line of counties. She was usually accompanied by two or three men, who constituted her gang.
> She is known to have stopped occasionally at rural homes in Montague County in quest of food. She would always make her identity known. She was said not to have been unattractive. She was a woman

of ordinary appearance and looks; of average height and weight. She always wore men's cowboy style clothing, and carried two six-shooters. She was friendly, pleasant and always very generous in her payment for food. After receiving the food, and before officers could be informed of her presence in the county, she would be miles away.

Arriving in Montague County in June 1872, the Sam Atchison family was the recipient of one of Nance Hill's neighborly visits. One day their son, Charles, was dipping water from a creek when he was surprised by Nance. She asked him if he had ever heard of Nance Hill, and he said, "Yes." She then asked if he was afraid of Nance Hill, and he answered, "Naw." Lifting a skirt that hid her guns and the men's pants she was wearing, Nance revealed what seemed to the boy to be more than a hundred pistols. Awed by the female outlaw, young Charles took her to the house for a meal. Afterward, Nance remarked to Mrs. Atchison, "I couldn't harm such kind people." [12]

That Nancy Hill became infamous for her acts of prostitution and horse theft is confirmed by *The Dallas Weekly Herald*, dubbing her "the harlot ranger," a "notorious female horse thief." [13] However, her worst crime was not horse theft or prostitution.

There were many horse thieves lynched in the days of the early West, but as a female, Nancy Hill might have escaped that penalty (being a prostitute would not have warranted such action). What likely turn Springtown citizens into a mob obsessed with vengeance was Nance's depraved crime of infanticide. She committed this atrocious act at least twice and was jailed for it both times in Parker County, yet she was never tried and convicted. [14]

There is one account describing Nance's method of disposing of an unwanted baby, and since evidence shows that she was guilty of infanticide, this story is probably true, As she was riding her horse through the woods, she felt the beginnings of labor pains. She dismounted and tied her horse to a nearby tree. Soon she gave birth to the baby on her own. After a short rest, Nance picked up a rock and callously crushed the baby's skull. Her depravity soared when she threw the tiny body into a brush pile instead of burying it. After regaining her strength, she remounted and resumed her journey. [15]

This brings up the question of why members of the Hill family were never arrested, since they were all guilty of prostitution, harassment, horse thievery, infanticide, or harboring wanted criminals. It is evident that these crimes were openly committed, yet the law did nothing about it. The answer lies in the history of Texas politics and law enforcement.

Following the Civil War, Texas found itself under the misrule of Reconstruction, headed by Governor E. J. Davis. The period of 1870 through 1873 was marked by corruption and white disfranchisement. The Texas Rangers were no longer active and were replaced by Davis' hated State Police, who were granted extraordinary powers, for example, taking offenders across county lines for trial and operating undercover. No other comparable police force existed anywhere in the United States at this time.

However, the State Police were corrupt and ineffectual, favoring anyone who supported the Union cause, and the Hill family were known as Union sympathizers. Thus, this radical police force apparently looked the other way.

By 1873 lawlessness was rampant over most of Texas, dominated by organized gangs of outlaws and bloody feudists who carried on their own private wars. After defeating Davis for the governorship of Texas in 1873, Governor Richard Coke turned his attention to this lawless situation and reinstated the Texas Rangers in May 1874 through legislative action. But by this time the Hills had been eliminated by the Springtown citizens, who, because of ineffectual and indifferent law enforcement, felt compelled to take matters into their own hands. [16]

From the late 1860s through the early 1870s, the Hills continued their depredations and openly defied the citizenry of Parker County. It all ended in 1873, the year that would spell doom for seven members of the Hill clan. The first to die was nineteen-year-old Jack Hill. In January 1873 he was shot to death in Montague County by a man named Aaron Bloomer in a personal dispute. The chief justice and coroner, James M. Grigsby, held a two-day inquest over the body of Jack Hill. On September 29, 1873, the police court authorized the payment of $2.50 to James W. Morrow for serving as a juror during the inquest. It is probable that the family did not learn of Jack Hill's death in time to claim his body, and the county buried him in a pauper's grave in the cemetery at Montague. [17]

Before 1873, Nance Hill had organized a gang of horse thieves comprising Dugan McCormick, Dan Short, a young man from a reputable Parker County family named Dave Porter, and probably her brother Jack and one or more of her sisters. For several months after the death of Jack Hill, the situation remained tense, but the Hills did nothing to stir the wrath of the residents of Springtown until August, and then all hell broke loose.

On Friday morning, August 22, 1873, Nance Hill, McCormick, Short, and Porter rode into Springtown. Porter reportedly bought a bottle of whiskey at Bill Brazil's saloon, and the four then rode around the public square until they reached the northeast corner, where they shot and mortally wounded a Jacksboro resident named John Laird.

There are several versions describing the shooting. Mrs. Clyde Gear Beaty claims that Laird was a clerk in the Donathan, Culton, and Tarkington General Mercantile Store and was shot down because the store refused to let Porter have a pair of boots on credit. Robert C. Campbell, in Part 3 of his articles printed in *The Weatherford Democrat*, stated that Laird upbraided Porter about his choice of associates and was shot for his remarks. [18]

Author John W. Nix was likely closest to the facts when he reported:

> There is no dispute that they rode into Springtown one sunny morning, circled the public square and shot to death John Laird as he lay sleeping on the door of a cellar under the store building at the northeast corner of the square. [19]

More credence is added to the Nix version by *The Democrat* in Fort Worth:

On Friday, the 22 ult., Dave Porter, D. Short, and Dugan McCormick, accompanied by a woman of ill-fame named Nancy Hill, entered Springtown and without any known provocation, shot and severely wounded a Mr. Laird and fled the town.

In 1913 Mrs. Bill Brazil of Weatherford stated to *The Weekly Herald* that one of the men with Nance Hill shot Laird out of pure cussedness, just to try out his pistol. She said the information came from the youngest Hill daughter, Belle. [20]

Regardless how the shooting happened, it was a vicious act and the victim, Laird, lay in agony for three weeks before he died. It is not known who fired the fatal shot, but from all indications it was Dave Porter. Regardless, the four culprits realized the seriousness of their actions and immediately fled northward out of town.

It took little time for the Springtown residents to take decisive action. A body of men, reportedly headed by Thomas J. Tarkington, one of the proprietors of the mercantile store, quickly packed provisions, saddled their horses, and headed north after the fugitives.

In her haste to flee Springtown, Nance Hill either became separated from her three companions or deliberately split with them to throw off any pursuit. It was a futile move as the vigilantes had targeted Nance and doggedly followed her trail northward through Wise County and into Montague County. Around noon on Saturday, August 23, the vigilantes caught up with her on Denton Creek. Without ceremony, the enraged mob hanged her from a limb of a tree about one hundred yards from the iron bridge over Denton Creek on the Montague and Bowie Road. [21]

Late that afternoon, W. A. "Bud" Morris, who was out looking for cattle, found Nance's body still hanging from the limb of the tree. A two-day inquest was held under Chief Justice Grigsby, and the jury found that Nance Hill died by hanging at the hands of persons unknown. On September 29, 1873, the police court voted to pay Justice Grigsby six dollars for conducting the inquest. The police court, on December 12, approved payment of $16.60 to Constable William H. Slack for summoning witnesses and a jury for the inquest. Like her brother Jack, Nance was buried at county expense in the cemetery at Montague. [22]

The vigilantes never apprehended Porter, McCormick, or Short. They were probably satisfied just to run them out of the area. McCormick and Porter completely disappeared, but in 1886 a Dan Short was wanted in Brown County on two charges of cattle theft. Extradition papers were sent to the Indian Territory for his arrest in April, but apparently he was never caught. Short was reportedly living on a small ranch near Farmington, New Mexico in the 1890s, and supposedly gave shelter to train robber Grant Wheeler in the summer of 1895. [23]

The spirit of vengeance still burned in the residents of Springtown. The years of depravity, lawlessness, and acts of defiance had taken their toll, and only revenge and retribution would satisfy the enraged citizens. On the day Nance was hanged, a group of men went to the Hill homestead and seized twenty-one-year-old Martha Hill and her fifteen-year-old sister, Catherine. Taking into account the violent determination of the mob, it is evident that Dusky Hill and her remaining children either were not home or had fled when they saw the vigilantes approaching.

At first, the vigilantes could not decide what to do with the two women. In 1913 Mrs. Bill Brazil gave this account to *The Weekly Herald* in Weatherford:

> One Saturday afternoon in the summer of 1873, the vigilance committee passed her home twice with the notorious Hill women, who were hilarious and gibing, little suspicioning the tragedy awaiting them out in the hills that night.

The mob finally took the two women to a ravine, now known as Hangman's Hollow, approximately three miles southwest of Springtown. A vivid account of their fate was reported in *History of Parker County*:

> According to some versions of the story, these two were given a fair trial, though a somewhat speedy one, with a well-known lawyer present to defend them. Other versions say there was no trial. All, however, agree on the outcome. The men found a tree [oak], about fourteen inches in diameter, growing on the bank of a small creek and leaning so that it overhung the opposite bank. They tied ropes around the necks of the two women, who were sitting on their horses, led the horses under the overhanging trunk, and threw the ropes over it. When all was ready, the women were given a chance to say their last words, but they were defiant to the end. They never broke down and never asked for any consideration, showing no emotion except contempt. Someone slapped the horses sharply, and they bolted for home. The men separated and returned to their own homes.[24]

All remained quiet throughout Sunday, but it was just the calm before the storm. By Monday morning, August 25, the vigilantes who lynched Nance Hill had returned to Springtown and reportedly held a committee meeting to decide on a final solution. They agreed that their job would not be finished until old Dusky Hill and the rest of her offspring were eliminated.

That afternoon, the vigilantes rode again to the Hill's house. Dusky and her children saw them coming and escaped from the house before they arrived. Dusky, nineteen-year-old Adeline, and Eliza, aged sixteen, headed in a westerly direction while Allen Junior presumably took a different route with thirteen-year-old Belle.

Upon discovering that the Hills had fled, the vigilantes first set fire to the house, then hurriedly went after the fleeing women. Dusky Hill and her two daughters were run to earth near the little village of Agnes, about eight miles west of Springtown. They were taken to a clearing and promptly shot down and killed; however, other reports stated the mob shot into their bodies after they were hanged. *The Democrat* in Fort Worth reported they were taken to a swamp on Salt Creek and killed. The Springtown vigilantes had murdered six women in three days.[25]

All accounts reported that the mob also caught Allen Junior and Belle, but because they were the two youngest children, they were spared and sent back to Springtown, where they were turned over to a sympathetic family. This never happened, and the story was likely circulated to gloss over the actions of the vigilantes. In actuality, Allen Junior, at seventeen, was older than two of his sisters who had been killed. If the mob would hang a fifteen-year-old girl, they certainly would not hesitate to do away with a seventeen-year-old boy. Secondly, Belle Hill was never captured by the vigilantes but had hidden in fear somewhere near Springtown until the morning after the death of her mother and sisters. This is made clear by Mrs. Bill Brazil in an interview in 1913:

> On the morning following the hanging of the Hill women, a four-teen [sic] year old girl came to Mrs. Brazil's house, weeping, and inquiring for her mother and sisters. Asked why the lynching, she said a man companion of the Hill women shot and killed a man named Laired on the street in reckless cussedness, to try his pistol. A den of thieves and disreputable characters is about the way she put it. [26]

The Democrat in Fort Worth received the news of the killings from A. L. Thomas, one of the two men who came forward in 1919 and related the details surrounding the tragedy. He apparently released the information to the newspaper before he learned of Nance's fate. Their report shows not only the notorious reputation she bore but also their abhorrence of the killings:

> While the provocation may have been great, we can but feel a thrill of horror when we think of a mob of armed men deliberately taking the lives of defenseless females, no matter how low in the scale of degradation they may have sunk.
> Nancy Hill . . . is now at large, and fears are entertained that she will wreak a terrible revenge for the killing of her mother and sisters. [27]

The above statement also illustrates the nagging question of why the vigilantes would resort to so much violence when they could have easily burned the Hills out and run them out of the country. In Nance's case it is understandable, but to deliberately murder five defenseless women over a three-day period is enigmatical, unless there was an underlying reason that the vigilantes of Springtown wanted to cover up. In 1991, a probable cause came to light.

In March 1991, I contacted Mark Warnken of *The Springtown Epigraph* with a request for photographs of Hangman's Hollow and the Springtown Cemetery. Warnken complied and found that eighty-four-year-old Lonnie Lynch, who lives within a short distance from the Hill's former home, owned the land that contained Hangman's Hollow. In an interview with Lynch, Warnken found out that the Lynch family had lived on this land for several generations, and that Lynch's ancestors knew the Hill family and their history. Warnken reported in *The Springtown Epigraph*:

Lynch explained the incident of vigilante justice simply: The women of the Hill family — had been carrying on with some of the men in town. One daughter became pregnant, and the family began to threaten the men with extortion, saying they would spread their names around town if the men didn't give them money. The men decided that silencing the mother and her daughters forever would be the best answer, a decision that history says that ended in most of their deaths within a few days.

Lynch says that his uncle, Tom Clark, found the decaying leg of one of the women [Martha or Catherine], still clad in a stocking, in his pasture about a half-mile down the creek after a heavy rain a short time after the hangings.

"They got to looking then, you see. Some of them, I guess, looked here [Hangman's Hollow] and found where they were hung." [28]

This statement gives rise to the probability that the vigilantes also shot up the hanging bodies of Martha and Catherine, resulting in the severed leg of one of the women.

There were compassionate and charitable people in Springtown who thought the Hills should at least have a decent burial, but through intimidation by the vigilantes, they were afraid to bury the decaying bodies. One man decided to do something about it. Alexander "Al" Thompson was described as a rough, profane, and heavy-drinking former Texas Ranger who had definite ideas of right and wrong. About two days after the death of Dusky Hill and her daughters, Thompson decided to bury the bodies with the help of nineteen-year-old Columbus H. "Doc" Maupin, who the following December joined the Parker County Company of the Texas Rangers.

Daring anyone to interfere, Thompson and Maupin drove a sled pulled by two mules to the sites of the killings and gathered up the five bodies. It was a ghastly job, for the remains were in an advanced state of decomposition after several days of exposure to the August sun. But the two men were determined, and they placed the five bodies in a dry-goods box and returned to Springtown, where they found a man willing to dig a grave in the Springtown cemetery. Thompson and Maupin lowered the heavy box into the grave without benefit of a funeral ceremony. No stone or marker was placed over the grave, but the bodies were never disturbed after the burial. [29]

The lynchings had a sobering effect on everyone, and no further action was taken by the vigilantes. Allen Junior and Belle Hill were placed under the guardianship of the Reverend Pleasant Tackitt in October 1873. Tackitt posted a bond of $1,700 and was ordered by the court to make an annual statement of the conditions of the estate of Allen Junior and Belle Hill, minor heirs of Luduska Hill. On January 22, 1878, Tackitt was granted a discharge "from his trust as guardian of the Estates of Allen and Belle Hill" but his discharge was delayed until November 17, 1879, when both Hill children had "attained the age of majority." A final report on the condition of the estate was filed that showed that the balance for the estate was $76.62. As an aftermath, A. L. Thomas and G. W. Tackitt came forward on November 1, 1919, and gave a detailed account of the names, history, and events surrounding the killings of the Hill family in an affidavit to clear the title to the Allen Hill survey of 160 acres of land. [30]

Although never reported, there is more to the saga of the Hill family. Allen Hill, Jr., carried on the traits of his parents and harbored strong resentment for the killing of his family:

> The two small children were given to a kind family and raised by this family to maturity. The boy, it is said, displayed his "bad blood" by getting into trouble frequently and was eventually killed in a gunfight. [31]

Young Allen Hill did indeed get into trouble in Parker County. In 1880 he was indicted for assault to commit murder and fled to Palo Pinto County. It was not long before he was in trouble again, this time for the much more serious crime of murder.

In Mineral Wells, Texas, on October 30, 1881, Hill got into a personal dispute with Olanden Harris. In a rage, Hill pulled his pistol, deliberately shot and killed Harris, and fled before he could be apprehended. On March 10, 1882, the grand jury in Palo Pinto indicted him on the charge of murder, and the case was continued. On March 6, 1883, the following was entered in a criminal minute book:

> The whereabouts of the Deft being unknown it is ordered by the Court that this cause and Capias be retired from the Docket until Deft is heard of. [32]

The following is a description of Hill in *A List of Fugitives from Justice, Indicted for Felonies in the State of Texas*, which was issued to all Texas Rangers and became known as the "Ranger's Bible":

> Assault to murder, ind. 1880 [Parker County], wanted in Palo Pinto County for murder, is about 25, 5 feet 8, very dark complected, prominent teeth, dark hair and eyes, weighs about 130. [33]

The family of Olanden Harris was determined to bring Hill to justice and hired detectives to search for the fugitive. In 1888 Hill was reportedly located in Kansas, and extradition papers were sent to the governor of Kansas on May 17. Either it was a case of mistaken identity or Hill left the area before he could be apprehended. [34]

Harris' family did not give up their hunt for Allen Hill, Jr., and in January 1896 a deputy sheriff from Palo Pinto County reported he had located him in Guadalupe County, New Mexico Territory. On February 11, extradition papers were sent to the governor of New Mexico. Extradition was granted, and the man was arrested without resistance on February 29 near Endus, New Mexico, but Private Edward F. Connell of Company B, Frontier Battalion of Texas Rangers. [35]

Once in Texas, the prisoner was turned over to Captain A. F. McConnell. On the evening of March 2, the man was brought to Weatherford and handed over to Marshal Charles Harris of Mineral Wells, brother of the slain man. The next morning the prisoner was brought to Mineral Wells, adamantly insisting he was not Allen Hill, Jr. *The Fort Worth Gazette* reported:

WAS THE WRONG MAN
HE WAS NOT THE MURDERER OF ORLANDO [*sic*] HARRIS

The man said to be Allen Hill, brought from New Mexico this week, charged with killing Orlando Harris at Mineral Wells about fifteen years ago says that his name is John Keene and that he has one brother in New Mexico and two at Brownwood. The majority of those who knew Hill and who have seen the prisoner say that he is not the murderer.

Hill's mother and two sisters were lynched near Springtown, Parker County, in the 70's. [36]

Allen Hill, Jr., was never apprehended for the murder of Harris, and the case remains retired in the old *Court Docket* and *Minute Book* in Palo Pinto County. No one knows what happened to him, except the report in the *History of Parker County* that stated he was killed in a gunfight; however, there is no proof of this. Allen Hill, Jr., got his revenge by being the only criminal member of his family to escape retribution.

Reports of money and valuables buried by old Allen Hill were circulated in Parker County and have caused treasure hunters to search for it ever since. In one account, someone supposedly found a great deal of money buried in an iron pot:

Many decades later, someone found the buried treasure by solving a very intricate puzzle. He had to cut several inches deep into the trunks of several trees to find nails which Hill had driven into them to serve as some sort of code to give directions. How did the finder figure out what the nails meant? How did he even know where to look for them? These questions are apparently destined to remain unanswered, but obviously someone found the money. An empty hole with an old iron pot beside it gave mute testimony to this effect. [37]

This story just might be true, and, if so, the finder would have to have been an old member of the Hill gang of horse thieves or one of the criminal class that used the Hills' house as a hideout. It is extremely doubtful that any treasure is still buried on the old Hill property, for criminals and desperadoes of the Hill category were prone to spend money, not save it. But who knows, maybe old Dusky and her brood forgot where it was buried or never even knew it was there.

Belle Hill had none of the criminal characteristics of her notorious family and overcame the stigma attached to the Hill name. Unfortunately, tragedies would continue to dog her until her death. The *History of Parker County* reported that she lived our her life near Springtown in Parker County with her past completely hidden. [38] The following information provided by Belle's great granddaughters, Lois Fairman and Ellen Hockett, corrects this error.

Twenty-four-year-old John Calvin Vinyard of Greene County, Illinois, married Belle Hill in 1877, presumably in Parker County, Texas. Belle had jumped from the frying pan into the fire, for John Vinyard had a quick temper to match her father's, and it caused him serious trouble in Illinois at age sixteen.

On the evening of October 12, 1869, John Vinyard and his cousin John Wesley Vinyard attended a dance held in a hall over the post office in Walkerville, a little hamlet of no more than eight houses that already had a bad reputation. Earlier in the day, Vinyard and his cousin had been drinking heavily in White Hall, seven miles northeast of Walkerville. Upon approaching the hall entrance at Walkerville that evening, Vinyard accosted eighteen-year-old Edgar Yeager, for whom he held a grudge. The confrontation was reported in *The White Hall Register*:

> Vinyard said to Yeager in a threatening manner: "I understand you said that Johnny Gowens was a better man than me." Yeager replied, "I didn't say so. I said I wouldn't be surprised if he was." Then says Vinyard, "You're a damned liar. I'll shoot the . . . out of you." About that time the cousin says, "Go in." Yeager repeated his former statement and tells Vinyard he doesn't want to have any trouble. The cousin says, "Don't shoot John," but John does shoot, or attempts to, though merely snaps the cap without discharging the pistol. Yeager then turned to go off, and had retreated some three steps, when Vinyard again pulled the trigger, this time with effect. Poor Yeager reeled forward a pace or two, turned back for support, clutching the gate by which he'd been standing, cried "murder" and fell. He groaned heavily for a few moments and was dead, shot in the back. The boy-murderer walked off and disappeared without an effort on the part of anyone to arrest him.

In March 1870 John Vinyard was indicted for murder during the March term of Greene County District Court. The case dragged on for more than four years until stricken from the docket in March 1874 with leave to reinstate. Apparently John Vinyard fled west after the murder and was never apprehended.

Following their marriage, John and Belle Vinyard moved to Arkansas, where their first child, Joseph Allen, was born on September 2, 1878. By 1881 they had returned to Parker County. On March 12 Belle went before Justice of the Peace A. B. Horton in Pooleville and gave power of attorney to attorney D. O. Sullivan to sell and collect payment for her half of the Allen Hill Survey of 160 acres of land near Springtown. On October 12 she gave birth to twins, Mary and Martha. The family moved back to Arkansas in 1882, and another son, William, was born in August.

By 1885 the Vinyards had emigrated to Lake County, Oregon, and settled on a ranch near Adel, on Deep Creek, just north of where Oregon, California, and Nevada converge. Here four more children were born: Andrew on March 13, 1886; Reta J. on December 16, 1887; Alvin on September 14, 1890; and Sophia in 1892.

The family lived a typical pioneer life, toiling laboriously until they established a foothold in the raw frontier country. To shop for their needs, Belle personally blazed a twenty-six-mile trail from her home to Fort Bidwell in Modoc County, California.[39]

All went according to plan until 1894, when Belle suffered another catastrophe in her already tragic life. On October 4 John Vinyard was shot to death in Lake County, supposedly in a personal dispute over haying equipment. According to family members, Vinyard was a hard, tough, strong-willed man. The circumstances surrounding his death confirm this assessment; however the only version of Vinyard's killing was given by his killer and his witnesses. Their statements, true or false, were reported in this October 1894 article from *The Lake County Examiner*:

HOMICIDE IN WARNER COUNTY

TWO MEN GET INTO
A DISPUTE OVER
A HARNESS AND
ED DONOVAN KILLS
JOHN VINYARD

Donovan Gives Himself Up To The Sheriff And Circumstances All Point To Self Defense—Report Of Coroner's Jury.

Last Friday morning [October 5] about seven o'clock, Mr. Ed Donovan came into town and gave himself up to Deputy Sheriff Nelson, saying that he had killed a neighbor, Mr. John Vinyard in Warner Valley on the preceding afternoon. He then made a statement of the case to Coroner Joseph W. Howard, after which the coroner, in company with Deputy District Attorney L. F. Conn and M. D. Hopkins, proceeded to the scene of the shooting where a jury was impaneled and an inquest was held on last Saturday.

Mr. Donovan's statement was, in substance, about as follows; previous to the shooting, Donovan had been mowing some grass for Vinyard, and owing to the water on a portion of the land, did not cut all of the grass. Vinyard wanted more of the grass cut, and Donovan objected to cutting it at the time. . . . They had a few words over this, but nothing of serious nature.

It also appears that in changing work and implements . . . they had been working a set of hamestraps belonging to Mr. J. L. Morrow on Mr. Vinyard's harness. At the time of the tragedy, Ed Donovan, E. J. Garrett, and William S. Tower, were fencing a stack of hay on the J. L. Miles ranch. . . . On Thursday afternoon about three o'clock . . . John Vinyard rode up on horseback and dismounted. . . . Vinyard first spoke to Garrett and said:

"Are you going to Lakeview with me next week?" Garrett answered "Yes," and asked him if he was going to let Joe Morrow have his wagon, and he said "No, that he would rather have the pleasure of breaking his skull with his six-shooter than see him hitch on to it."

Vinyard then turned to Donovan and asked him about a singletree which he had been using. Donovan replied: "It is over there at Garrett's place, you can get it anytime you want it."

Donovan then asked about the hamestraps belonging to Morrow that were on the Vinyard's harness. Vinyard protested that there were no straps on the harness, and Donovan said:

"Why, I saw them on the harness yesterday afternoon." Vinyard then said:

"You _____ lying _____, I'll fix you." And with this he reached his left hand behind him and drew a revolver. Donovan who was unarmed, hardly realized what was transpiring until he saw the pistol in Vinyard's hand. He then jumped for a rifle which was leaning up against a [hay] stack, probably five or six feet from where Donovan was standing. They were twenty or thirty feet apart . . . Vinyard fired but missed his mark and then jumped behind Garrett. Garrett got out of the way in an instant and then the two both commenced firing and started towards each other. . . .

Garrett stated in his testimony that as soon as he jumped out of the way, Donovan fired and Vinyard fell to the ground . . . and then jumped to his feet and fired once more and snapped his pistol once. Donovan fired again and Vinyard fell to the ground, shot through.

Donovan's first shot grazed Vinyard's back, but the second plowed through his left hand, entered his side under the left arm, and exited out his right side. The men were so close that Vinyard's clothes caught on fire from the powder burns. Vinyard was dead when he hit the ground. Belle buried her husband in the cemetery at Fort Bidwell.[40]

There was more to the killing than either Donovan or Garrett would admit, and at least part of their testimony was suspect. On the preceding July 15, a haystack belonging to the Warner Valley Stock Company was deliberately burned. On November 13 three more stacks were burned. The prime suspects were William Sherman Tower and E. J. Garrett, and arrest warrants were issued for the pair on November 29. Tower was arrested, but Garrett had gone to Rogue River Valley and was not caught, although Lake County Deputy Sheriff Joe Lane was still on his trail in mid-December. On December 10 the case for the November hay-burning was dismissed on a technicality, but Garrett was subpoenaed as a defense witness for the July incident. Another subpoenaed defense witness was John Vinyard's slayer, Ed Donovan, who fled to Summer Lake, where he was taken into custody by Lakeview constable Cleland.

On the other side, the major witnesses against Garrett and Tower in the hay-burning cases were Belle Vinyard, her son Joseph, and John Vinyard, had he lived. This establishes a motive for the killing. Although the whole story will never be known, John Vinyard may well have been murdered.[41]

Following the death of John Vinyard, rumors that he was an unsavory character began circulating around Lake County. Belle Vinyard was as strong-willed as her husband and was determined that his name not be maligned. She wrote the following to *The Lake County Examiner* from Creswell, where the Vinyards had a contract business to cut hay:

A CARD FROM MRS. VINYARD,
WARNER LAKE, OREGON, MAY 2, 1895.

Editor *Examiner*:

Would you be so kind to publish the enclosed card and also the following statement for me, as I have heard it rumored that there are people who try to claim that Mr. Vinyard had a bad character, and I should like to have it published on account of my children.

"Creswell, Oregon, November 30, 1894

To whom it may concern. The undersigned doing business at Creswell, Oregon, can cheerfully say that during the residence of John Vinyard in our neighborhood, we each did more or less business with him and have no hesitancy in saying we found him honest and upright in all his dealings, and a straight forward, honest and upright citizen.

J. H. Whitiker, General Merchandise; L. D. Scarborough, M. D.; W. T. Lower, Blacksmith; W. M. Robinette, Shoemaker; and Ino F. Hilfrey.

Many friends of the Vinyards' realized that Belle was going through tough times after her husband's death and tried to help her monetarily. Although she was appreciative, her character was such that she was resolved to stand on her own two feet and added this statement to her letter to *The Examiner*:

> I hear that certain parties are talking of taking up a collection for me. I do not want the people to donate, and will not accept anything from that source. I want the people to feel that I shall ever feel grateful to them for their kindness to me already, and think I could get along now if I could get what is due me for work last haying season that my husband and son [Joseph] did, and which Mr. J. L. Murphy said he would see was paid. [42]

Apparently Belle held her own, for she remained on the ranch the rest of her life. However, she suffered one more misfortune: About 1914, her son William was reportedly indicted for cattle rustling. To escape punishment, he changed his name to Frank Howard and fled to Berkley Park, Essendorn, Australia, where he spent the remainder of his life.

Belle Hill Vinyard lived to be sixty-five years old, succumbing to carcinoma of the intestines at 2 a.m. on December 28, 1925, in Lakeview, Oregon. Funeral services were held in Fort Bidwell on January 1, 1926, and she was buried next to her husband. [43]

Not many women had suffered as Belle had, losing her husband and all but one member of her family to violence. It is hoped that her latter years were blessed with serenity and her mind never haunted by those horrifying memories of her childhood.

Above: Hangman's Hollow and the now dead oak tree (right center foreground) from which Martha and Catherine Hill were lynched on August 23, 1873. PHOTO TAKEN BY MARK WARNKEN OF *THE SPRINGTOWN EPIGRAPH*, MARCH, 1991.

Left: Purported photograph of Dan Short taken in New Mexico in the early 1890s. COURTESY JOHN BOESSENECKER, SAN FRANCISCO, CALIFORNIA.

Eighty-four-year-old Lonnie Lynch holding the limb from which Martha and Catherine Hill were lynched on August 23, 1873. Mr. Lynch, and his father and grandfather before him, have lived on this land within a stone's throw of the Hill's homeplace. His grandfather knew the Hills. Mr. Lynch also owns the land on which Hangman's Hollow is located.
PHOTO TAKEN BY MARK WARNKEN OF *THE SPRINGTOWN EPIGRAPH*, MARCH, 1991.

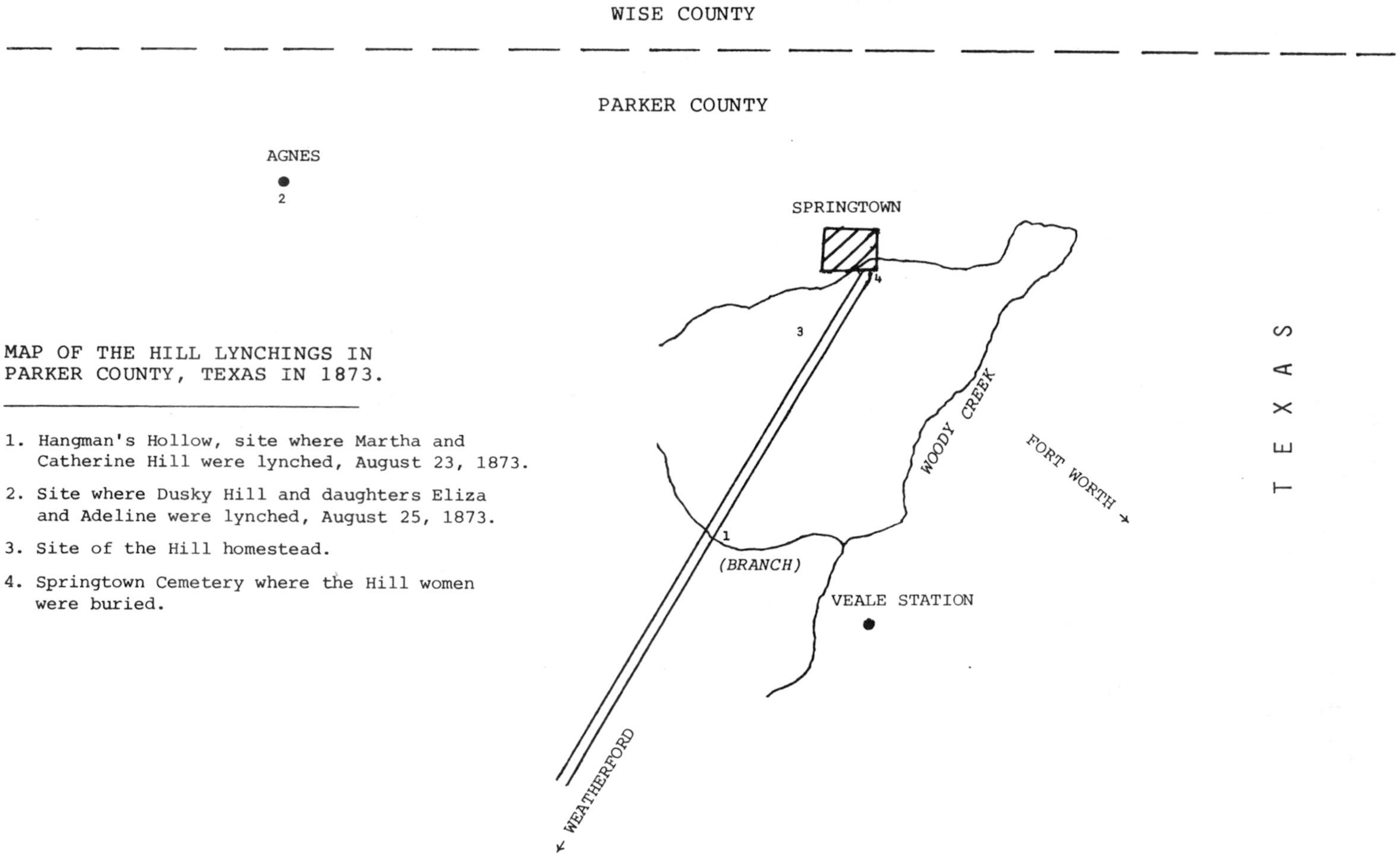

TEXAS

WISE COUNTY

PARKER COUNTY

AGNES
● 2

SPRINGTOWN

WOODY CREEK

FORT WORTH →

VEALE STATION ●

(BRANCH)

WEATHERFORD →

3

4

1

MAP OF THE HILL LYNCHINGS IN
PARKER COUNTY, TEXAS IN 1873.

1. Hangman's Hollow, site where Martha and
   Catherine Hill were lynched, August 23, 1873.

2. Site where Dusky Hill and daughters Eliza
   and Adeline were lynched, August 25, 1873.

3. Site of the Hill homestead.

4. Springtown Cemetery where the Hill women
   were buried.

THE GRAND JURORS of the County of *Palo Pinto* in the State of Texas, good and lawful men. duly elected, tried, empannelled, sworn and charged by the District Judge at the *March* Term. A. D. 18*87*. of the District Court of said County, to inquire into and true presentment make of all offences therein committed against the penal laws of the State of Texas, upon their oaths in said Court, do say and present, that heretofore, on. to wit: the *30th* day of *October* A. D. 18*81*. in the County of *Palo Pinto* and State of Texas. *Allen Hill in and upon Olander Harris feloniously willfully and of his malice aforethought did make an assault; and that the said Allen Hill a certain pistol then and there charged with gunpowder and leaden balls, which said pistol he the said Allen Hill in his hand then and there had and held, then and there feloniously willfully and of his express malice aforethought did discharge and shoot off to and against and upon the said Olander Harris; and that the said Allen Hill with the leaden balls aforesaid, out of the pistol aforesaid then and there by force of the gunpowder aforesaid, by the said Allen Hill discharged and shot off as aforesaid then and there feloniously, willfully and of his express malice aforethought did strike penetrate and wound him the said Olander Harris in and upon the body of him the said Olander Harris, giving to him the said Olander Harris then and there with the leaden balls aforesaid, so as aforesaid discharged and shot out of the pistol aforesaid by the said Allen Hill in and upon the body of him the said Olander Harris one mortal wound of which mortal wound he the said Olander Harris then and there instantly died. And so the Grand Jurors aforesaid, upon their oaths aforesaid do say and present that the said Allen Hill him the said Olander Harris in the manner and by the means aforesaid feloniously willfully and of his express malice aforethought did kill and murder —*

contrary to law and against the peace and dignity of the State.

W. D. Uchart Foreman Grand Jury.

Indictment against Allen Hill, Jr., for the murder of Olanden Harris in 1881 in Palo Pinto County, Texas. Palo Pinto District Court Case No. 543. PALO PINTO COUNTY DISTRICT CLERK'S OFFICE, PALO PINTO, TEXAS.

Executive Office

No. 175

APPLICATION FOR REQUISITION

on the GOVERNOR of *New Mexico*

for the Apprehension, Surrender and Return of

Allen Hill

Fugitive , Charge, *Murder*

Received *Feby 10th 1896.*

Applicant *C. M. Harris*

Address *Mineral Wells, Tex.*

Date *Feby 6th 1896*

Executive Office, Austin, Texas, *Feby 10 1896.*

Let Requisition issue,

O. L. York

appointed State agent to receive and return said
fugitive , without any expense to the State of Texas
under this appointment. (ACTUAL NECESSARY
EXPENSES not exceeding the sum of $
will be paid by the State upon delivery of said fugitive
to the proper officer inside the jail of
County, Texas, upon sworn item-
ized account and upon proper evidence of said delivery.)
By order of the Governor

J. W. Madden,
Private Secretary.

Mail delivered to *O. L. York*
Palo Pinto Texas 189

Above: The old section of the Springtown Cemetery where Dusky Hill and four of her daughters are buried. PHOTO TAKEN BY MARK WARNKEN OF THE *SPRINGTOWN EPIGRAPH,* MARCH, 1991.

Below: Springtown, Texas, in the early days. COURTESY. WEATHERFORD PUBLIC LIBRARY, WEATHERFORD, TEXAS.

Upper: Belle Hill Vinyard and family around 1896. Left to right: Andrew, Alvin, Joseph, Belle, Martha or Mary, and William. COURTESY, ELLEN HOCKETT, SHERIDAN, OREGON.

Lower: Twenty-six-mile trail blazed by Belle Hill Vinyard from her home in Lake County, Oregon, to Fort Bidwell. PHOTO TAKEN BY ELLEN HOCKETT OF SHERIDAN, OREGON.

Belle Hill Vinyard in July 1912. COURTESY, ELLEN HOCKETT, SHERIDAN, OREGON.

II. NORTH CAROLINA

SARAH SHULL

The Mystery of Sarah Shull

PART ONE: Controversies

SARAH SHULL WAS INDEED AN ENIGMA in the annals of the Old West. On one of the most controversial dates in this legendary period, she flashed into history and then faded into oblivion. Yet, she alone held the key to what happened that day. The date was July 12, 1861; the event was the death of David Colbert McCanles, the first man allegedly killed by Wild Bill Hickok. Some historians claim Sarah Shull was a witness to this killing, others say not. In 1925 writer Frank Jenners Wilstach went to North Carolina and interviewed Sarah regarding the incident, but she was reticent and evaded most of his questions, finally telling him whatever he wanted to hear to get rid of him.

Although more regional than the death of McCanles, there are two additional controversies that only Sarah Shull could resolve, Was D. C. McCanles guilty of stealing Watauga County, North Carolina, tax money when he headed west in 1859, and did Sarah leave with him? If anyone believes that these controversies dating back to the 1850s are dead issues in western North Carolina, they need to take a look at a full-page article on McCanles in *The Watauga Democrat* and two front-page articles about him in the Mountain Accent supplement of *The Tomahawk*, both published in 1988. [1]

Statements have been made that it was regrettable that Sarah Shull did not have a moment of truth before she died; but fortunately she did. Sarah lived to be ninety-eight years old and told her story to only a few close friends in Watauga County. One person in particular formed a warm relationship with Sarah in 1921 that lasted until Sarah's death eleven years later. She is Mrs. Jessie Williams, of Foscoe, North Carolina, who graciously related Sarah's story to the author. Through Mrs. Williams' exceptional memory, these controversies can now be resolved.[2]

Sarah Louisa Shull was born on Thursday, October 3, 1833, at Shulls Mill in what was then Ashe County, North Carolina, which in 1849 became a portion of newly formed Watauga County. In the highest elevations in the northern part of the Blue Ridge Mountains, this county is one of the most beautiful and picturesque areas in the United States. In the mid-1800s, however, it was a rugged, remote, and isolated section inhabited by only the most hardy pioneer families, one of which was the Shulls.[3]

The family can be traced to Fredrick Scholl (b. 1690), who emigrated from Bavaria to Pennsylvania and had at least one son, John Fredrick, who married Gertrude "Charity" Merchel. They settled on the Johns River in Lincoln County, North Carolina, where their son, Simon Phillip, was born on October 24, 1764. On March 29, 1790, Simon married Mary Sheiffer on Upper Creek of Catawba River, and on March 6, 1791, their first child, Elizabeth, was born on Johns River. The next year they moved to Valle Crucis on the Watauga River, which was first settled in 1779. They raised seven more children, one of whom was Sarah's father, Phillip, born February 15, 1797. By this time, the spelling of Scholl had changed to Shull.[4]

On October 3, 1820, Phillip Shull was married to nineteen-year-old Phoebe Ward by Justice of the Peace L. White in Carter County, Tennessee. Shortly after their marriage, carrying their belongings on their backs, they left Valle Crucis and moved approximately five miles southeast on the Watauga River and built a small log cabin. This area, which became Shulls Mill, was first settled in the 1790s. Among these settlers was Jesse Boone, the nephew of Daniel Boone, who built a cabin on a branch of the Watauga River known as Boone's Fork.

Within a few years, Phillip and Phoebe Shull built a larger house on a small hill nearby. In 1835 Phillip built a gristmill, which gave the area its name. The mill washed away in 1861 and was never rebuilt. In 1850, when Sarah was sixteen, they built the Shulls Mill Store on the west bank of the Watauga River. Although in a different location, this store is still standing and in operation at Shulls Mill. Here, Phillip and Phoebe reared thirteen children: Elizabeth (b. July 25, 1821), Matilda (b. 1824), Nathaniel Canada (b. 1825), Mary (b. 1827), Thomas (b. 1828), Rhoda E. (b. Janaury 5, 1830), Temperance (b. 1831), Sarah Louisa (b. October 3, 1833), William R. (b. May 17, 1836), Susan Caroline (b. 1838), Simon Phillip (b. July 8, 1840), Joseph Carroll (b. April 21, 1842), and Phoebe Sophina (b, 1846).

As the children grew to adulthood, they would help run the mill or work in the store. Following her arrival in Nebraska in 1859, Sarah reportedly kept books for McCanles and had undoubtedly learned this by working in her father's store. She could read and write well, indicating that she received sufficient schooling in her youth.[5]

Life was hard in the Blue Ridge Mountains, and big families like the Shulls' were common, giving the household a large work force. Most everything was made by hand: wool hats, shoes, tools, and bedding filled with cattails, oak leaves, or corn shucks, unless one was lucky enough to collect feathers to fill a tick. They made their own candles but often were forced to use saucers filled with tallow and a cloth wick, which were strangely called sluts. In place of sugar, molasses was used as sweetening, and once a year people would organize horse or ox teams and head for South Carolina or Georgia for staples such as salt and sugar. Since matches were extremely scarce, everybody had a firebox with live coals. Needless to say, everyone helped each other.

Each community had a mill to grind corn into meal, and Phillip Shull's mill served the area residents. It was a custom that for every turn of ground corn, the miller got a small measure, called a toddick. It was law that every man work one day a month on the roads. Most all the furniture was hand-made, walnut tables and chairs held together with hickory dowels.

Woman's work was extremely hard. Besides cooking and cleaning, they joined together in making quilts and coverlets; helped to plant, hoe, and gather crops; and even plowed and split rails, if needed. They made cider and molasses on shares and made all the necessary clothing on spinning wheels and looms. Today we call those times "the good old days."

For relaxation and social activity, the communities got together for corn shuckings and molasses pulls. The latter was designed to promote courtships, thus the origin of the phrase "stuck on a girl." Music was played on banjos or an adaptation of the German zither called a dulcimer, a plaintive oblong string instrument created in the Appalachian Mountains. [6]

It was also common practice to marry young and to quickly raise a family, and all of Phillip Shull's children followed this tradition, except Sarah, who had a will of her own. Jessie Williams remembers her as aristocratic and very intelligent, an attractive woman about five feet, two inches in height, with luxuriant thick gray hair, which was formerly brown. She stood straight, spoke well, was quiet and refined, and loved to ride horses. Frank Jenners Wilstach stated that a man who knew her in later years described her as "a neat, gray-headed little woman, slightly stoop-shouldered, with bright blue eyes. She is quick spoken, and with a mind of her own." William E. Connelley, an early biographer of Wild Bill Hickok, agreed with Mrs. Jessie Williams:

> Sarah Shull was voluptuous and beautiful. . . . She was very fair.
> She had fine blue eyes and a mass of dark hair. She was always neat and
> tidy, well dressed . . . she was reserved and somewhat shy in company.
> But she had decision and self-reliance. [7]

The only known photograph of Sarah, however, does not show her to be voluptuous, but her eyes seem to exhibit a faraway, wistful look. Despite her appearance, these are not qualities that a typical Blue Ridge Mountain man would look for in a woman. And Sarah Shull was definitely not looking for a typical Blue Ridge Mountain man.

Sarah had that rare, indescribable quality that attracts men, and throughout her life, her major fault would be her choice of men. It all began around 1855, when, at twenty-one, she attracted the attention of David Colbert McCanles. This association would alter the course of both of their lives.

David Colbert McCanles, known as Colb or Cobb in North Carolina, was a controversial figure to say the least, much like the fabeled Dr. Jekyll and Mr. Hyde. McCanles too had his roots deep in North Carolina. His great grandparents, James A. and Jane McDowell McCanles migrated from Scotland and settled near Hillsboro, Orange County, North Carolina, in 1770. Their youngest son, David McCanles, served in the Revolutionary War, married Catherine Wasson, and had a family of ten children.

David and Catherine's oldest son, James, was born October 30, 1796, in Salisbury, Rowan County. He married Rachael Salina Alexander on August 29, 1821, and settled on the southeast bank of the Yadkin River, five or six miles east of Statesville, Iredell County. They had five children, Mary C. around 1823; Julia Elizabeth about two years later; David Colbert on November 30, 1828; Emily Verdinia in 1833; and James Leroy in 1836. In the 1830s James McCanles moved his family to Shulls Mill and settled within a mile of the home of Phillip Shull. James was an educated man, an expert cabinetmaker, and fine fiddler who also taught school near Shulls Mill. He served as a justice of the peace after 1849.[8]

David Colbert McCanles was apparently showered with all the advantages his parents could give, attending private schools and finishing with a six-year education at an Episcopal academy. He excelled in a military training and tactics course and attained the rank of commander of general musters. On February 21, 1848, he married Mary Green, the daughter of prominent resident Joseph Green. Their first child, William Monroe, was born on January 26, 1849. The 1850 census shows D. C. McCanles and Phillip Shull living next door to each other. In 1852, about the time his second son, Julius C., was born. McCanles decided to run for the office of sheriff of Watauga County.[9]

McCanles ran a bitter race with opponent John Horton of Cove Creek. It was a hard-fought contest, with rumors of frequent fistfights between the contestants, who reportedly became inveterate enemies. This is apparently in error, because Howard Bingham, who witnessed the campaign, stated in The Watauga Democrat that although both candidates came close to fighting, the conflict remained verbal. The most heated debate occurred on Cove Creek when both men accused each other with complicity in the business of counterfeiting. In the end, the oratory powers of McCanles overcame his reticent opponent, and became the first elected Sheriff of Watauga County. McCanles served as sheriff for the next four years and fostered two more children, Clingman in 1854 and Elizabeth in 1856.

The question of who actually was sheriff between 1852 and 1856 has also been a minor dispute in Watauga County through the years. Writer John Preston Arthur states that it was Horton, and in 1894 Watauga County resident Howard Bingham claimed it was McCanles. A Watauga County tax receipt of Jesse Council for the year 1852, signed by Michael Cook as acting for Sheriff D. C. McCanles, clearly settles the issue. Cook had been appointed sheriff by the court in 1849 when Watauga County was organized, and apparently served as McCanles' deputy following the election.

Relatively unknown to most residents of the county; McCanles as sheriff was soon brought before the public eye. The following observations of his character were taken from early writings based on personal acquaintances. The complex characterization of this man clearly reveals the influence and effect of the indulgences of his childhood.

Overbearing and intolerant but well-informed and articulate, McCanles was a natural leader who would endure no interference with his plans. At around six feet in height and weighing more than two hundred pounds, he was a gregarious man who seemingly had no fear of danger and considered himself invincible, enjoying and excelling in the vigorous mountain sports such as foot racing, wrestling, and bare-knuckle fighting. McCanles loved to gamble on cockfighting, horse racing, and dog fighting and was what the mountaineers called a rough customer. Nebraska historian and writer Charles Dawson astutely wrote:

> He also had quite a reputation as an orator, and no early day gathering was complete unless McCanles had been called upon to expound his beliefs upon the issues of the day. Although many of his listeners did not agree with him, nevertheless he gained their respect and admiration by his sincerity and the able presentation of his beliefs. He was a man of many moods, capable of being stirred to the highest degree of action in anger or in mirth. He had original ideas of fun and punishment, and was wont to mix up the two, greatly to the discomfiture of his victims. He possessed a peculiar code of honor and manhood . . . hating above all things a man that would lie or attempt to deceive him. . . . He hated the man who would knowingly take advantage of a defenseless person, or would sneakingly steal, or do harm to another or to his property.
>
> When in a pleasant frame of mind he would greet each man in the most courteous manner, introducing himself to strangers and inquiring of their welfare. . . . He was keenly alive to his high qualifications and power over other men, making the best use of them to secure his desired ends.

In the flowery editorial writing of the day, Howard Bingham wrote in *The Watauga Democrat:*

> McCanlas [sic] was at least six feet in his stockings, with a large, massive frame slightly stooped, with a large head and very bushy hair which grew nearly to his eyebrows. His face and eyes indicated strength and determination and also that there pulsated within his Herculean bosom a warm and generous heart full of love and sympathy. His manners were very affable and his bearing superb. I have no hesitency in saying that he was by far the most astute electioneer I ever saw. [10]

In 1856 McCanles again ran a bitter campaign against John Horton for sheriff and, for the second time, won the election. Apparently neither man held a grudge, as Horton signed McCanles' official bond. [11]

It was during McCanles' first term as sheriff that he became involved with Sarah Shull. Although Sarah is never named, John Preston Arthur stated:

> McCanles [*sic*] was a strikingly handsome man and a well-behaved, useful citizen till he became involved with a woman not his wife, after which he fell into evil courses.

All the evidence together shows that this is not at all fair to Sarah Shull. Although she was an intelligent woman, she was still a naive, lonely mountain girl with no outside experience. How the affair started is not known, but it likely began in 1854 or 1855, when Sarah was clerking or keeping books in the Shulls Mill Store. The store offered the two a chance to slowly develop an inconspicuous relationship in a nonclandestine atmosphere. To Sarah, McCanles was a knight in shining armor, with his glib tongue and courtly manners. She was beguiled, and she conveniently overlooked the fact that he was a married man with three children. They both would pay for their mistake.

By mid-summer of 1855 Sarah was pregnant. In a small, isolated community like Shulls Mill the news quickly spread. In those days this was the ultimate sin, and the residents reacted with caustic comments and shunned the fallen woman. The pregnancy likely had the same effect on her family. Sarah made this comment in her later years: "I did something in my youth I regret; I had a baby." The child was a girl and was born May 4, 1856. Sarah named her Martha Allice Shull. If the shame was not enough, Sarah suffered another blow when her baby died a little over a year later on July 2, 1857. [12]

Although there is no documentation to prove that McCanles was the father, circumstantial evidence confirms it. In her later years, Sarah unhesitantly discussed her life history with close friends but refused to talk about her relationship with McCanles. This in itself is damning. Around the time Sarah's baby was born, Phillip Shull suddenly refused to grind corn for James McCanles, D. C.'s father. John Preston Arthur wrote:

> McCanlass [*sic*] went before a magistrate and got the usual penalty for such refusal to grind corn without good excuse. Shull still refused and McCanless still collected the penalty till at last Shull gave in.

After the death of Sarah's child, D. C.'s father wrote the following poem:

THE FAREWELL OF MARTHA ALLICE,
WHO DIED JULY 2, 1857

1. O mother dear, restrain thy tear
   Thy sorrow and thy grief:
   It wrings thy heart
   that we must part
   But gives me no relief.

2. On thee for help mine eyes I turn
   And make my feeble moan,
   Sure not for crimes
   that I have done,
   Or faults that were my own.

3. My little hands or heart or head
   No evil ever knew,
   And am I numbered
   with the dead
   A warning unto you.

4. Oh, if you love your Allice dear
   While health and time is given
   O parents dear,
   yourselves prepare,
   To meet your babe in heaven.

5. To you with open arms I'll fly
   On that great rising day,
   When earth and air
   and sea and sky
   In flames shall roll away.

6. Farewell, farewell, my parents dear
   I can no longer stay
   For Angels whisper
   in mine ear
   Haste thee, and come away.

7. Up to the Lord who in his arms
   took little babes like me,
   There to enjoy
   my Savoirs charms
   To all Eternity.

Why would James McCanles write such a heartrending poem with such feeling, along with the hidden meanings found in the second and third verses, for a child that was not his kin? Considering the character of D. C. McCanles and this period of Victorian austerity, would he have fled with a woman who had had an affair and bore a child that was not his?

Howard Bingham gave confirmation that David Colbert McCanles was indeed the father, when he wrote in *The Watauga Democrat:*

> But he [McCanles] became the devotee of wine and women and plunged into the deepest vortex of dissipation and debauchery and finally . . . fled the state and carried with him a beautiful mountain girl whom he had won and ruined. . . .[13]

There is no doubt that McCanles was a popular sheriff, but as the news of the scandal circulated, he must have considered his chances slim for reelection for a third term. He began making new plans for his future.

According to writer William E. Connelly:

> His family and friends have said that when intelligence of the discovery of gold at Pike's Peak trickled into the ranges of the Blue Ridge and the Great Smoky mountains, McCanles determined to leave the land of his birth and seek his fortune in the Great War.

Writers Wilstach and Dawson also reported that McCanles planned to head for the Colorado gold fields. Sarah Shull stated before they left Watauga County that McCanles had been out West and returned. If this is fact, he must have gone sometime during the summer of 1858, for it was in May that gold was first discovered near Denver by a party headed by William Russell, a former California forty-niner. [14]

Now comes the question of whether McCanles was guilty of absconding with the Watauga County tax money. The following account by John Preston Arthur in 1915, the only written record of what supposedly transpired, is quoted in full to eliminate misinterpretation:

> As sheriff he was tax collector and also had in his hands claims in favor of L. M. Weath [sic], a Frenchman, who sold goods throughout this section in job lots. As there was no homestead then, whatever an officer could find in a defendant's possession was subject to levy and sale. January 1, 1859, came and soon afterwards came also a representative from Weath for a settlement with McCanless.
>
> On the morning of January 6th "Colb" set out for Boone, accompanied by Levi L. Coffey, a near neighbor, then about twenty-seven years of age. "Colb" told Weath's man that he had made many collections for Weath, but had offsets against some of them and could settle the balance due only by an interview with Weath himself. Therefore, he would join Weath's man at Blowing Rock the following morning and go with him to Statesville. He and Jack Horton, who was on McCanless' official bond, then took a ride together, after which Horton sold his horse to one of the Hardins and McCanless immediately bought the same horse for the exact price Hardin conveyed certain real estate to his brother, J. Leroy McCanless. Subsequently, on the first day of March, 1859, J. L. McCanless conveyed the same land to Jack or John Horton, and on that day [sic: March 1, 1877] Jack Horton conveyed it to Smith Coffey. In a suit between Calvin J. Cowles against Coffey it was alleged and so found by the jury that these conveyances from D. C. and J. L. McCanless and from him to Jack Horton had been given to defraud the creditors of D. C. McCanless (88 N.C. Rep. p. 341). Horton is also said to have secured McCanless' saddle pockets with many claims in them against various people in Watauga County, these pockets having been left by McCanless in a certain store in Boone for that very purpose, thus securing Horton as far as possible from loss by reason of his liability on McCanless' official bond. McCanless also had the proceeds of a claim which as sheriff he held against Wilson Burleson, who then lived near Bull Scrape, now Montezuma, Avery County. This money was due to J. M. Weath also, and which, for safe keeping, had been placed by McCanless with Jacob Rintels in Boone, in whose store Col. W. L. Bryan was then clerking, then known as the Jack Horton Old Store. Late that sixth of January McCanless called on Rintels for the money, with the

request that as much as possible be paid in gold and silver. This was done. McCanless then started on the road to Wilkes County, where he claimed he was to pay the money over to Robert Hayes on an execution, having told Levi Coffey not to wait for him, as he was not going to return home that night. But instead of continuing on to Wilkes, McCanless went only as far as Three Forks Church, where he doubled back and went up the Jack Hodges Creek and through the Hodges Gap to Shulls Mills, where he was joined by a woman. They went together to Johnson City, where their horses, saddles and bridles were sold to Joel Dyer. They took the train to the west. [15]

How correct was Arthur? Did he rely on second-hand accounts that were unfounded, as some of McCanles' descendants claim? Their undocumented theory contends that McCanles went west in the spring of 1859 with his brother James Leroy and others, and did not leave with Sarah Shull. This theory is based on information passed down by their family and on their supposition that there was no railroad running from Johnson City, Tennessee, in 1859. [16]

The Watauga County Courthouse burned in 1865 and again in 1873, and many important documents were lost; however, the remaining records show that John Preston Arthur reported facts, not assumptions or hearsay. A large portion of the tax money in question was actually claims in the name of J. M. Weith, and the following document confirms that Weith was entitled to restitution from McCanles. According to a sheriff's deed proven in probate court in 1876:

> J. M. Weith Ashboro N.C. as of record doth appeared having levied said Execution on the lands and tenements of the said D. C. McCanles hereafter described on the 1st day of June 1859; and having made advertisement according to law, and sold said lands and tenements at public sale for cash on the 15th day of June 1859 at the Court House door at said County, when and where R. C. Miller assignee of W. F. Shull of the County of Watauga and the State of North Carolina became last and highest bidder, at the sum of one hundred and eighty Dollars which has been paid to the undersigned [Sheriff Sidney Deal] in accordance with the said terms of said sale. [17]

This land was located at Shulls Mill and was bordered by the Watauga River. Ironically, it was purchased by Sarah's brother William Shull.

Where John Preston Arthur erred was in the time sequence and proper names. The land that D. C. McCanles sold to his brother James Leroy for $350 was a 130-acre tract also located on the Watauga River at Shulls Mill; however, the date of sale was January 26, 1859, not January 6. This land was then sold by J. L. McCanles to John Horton for three hundred dollars on March 1, 1859. [18]

In Watauga County this same parcel of land was also sold at public auction for one dollar on November 16, 1859, to Calvin J. Cowles to satisfy one of two executions by Cowles against the properties of D. C. McCanles. For some reason Cowles did not procure the deed until 1876. Excerpted from the deed:

This Indenture made the sixth day of March in the year Eighteen Hundred and Seventy Six between S. Deal Esq. Former Sheriff of the County of Watauga and the State of North Carolina of the one part and Calvin J. Cowles of the County of Mecklenburg and the State of North Carolina on the other part, Witnesseth that Whereas, by virtue of ven. Ex. [*Venditioni Exponas:* Selling of property seized by an execution] issued from the County Court of Watauga Co. against the property of D. C. McCanles for a sum exceeding ten dollars which sum was recovered by Myer Myers and J. Councill of the said D. C. McCanles. [19]

Grounds for litigation arose on March 1, 1877, when John Horton sold the same land to Smith Coffey for $364.60. On March 22, Cowles brought suit against Coffey for title of the disputed land. Trial was held during the spring 1882 term of Watauga Superior Court under Judge J. Avery. The following are the arguments from both sides:

The plaintiff insisted that the deeds from D. C. to J. L. McCanless, and from the latter to Horton, were both made with the intent to defraud the creditors of the first grantor [D. C. McCanles]. This was denied by the defendant, who also insisted that, even conceding the deeds to have been fraudulently made, they still constituted color of title as against the plaintiff from the date of his purchase in 1859, and had ripened into a title under the statute of limitations. This, in turn, was disputed by the plaintiff, who contended that those deeds, being fraudulent, began to operate as color of title only from the time he procured his deed in 1876.

The jury decided in favor of Cowles, and Coffey appealed the decision to the North Carolina Supreme Court. During the February 1883 term, the case was held under Supreme Court Judge J. Ruffin. After review, the lower court decision was found in error on two points: First, Cowles acquired an inchoate title to the land in 1859, which his debtor and fraudulent grantee (D. C. McCanles) could not have defeated, and it was Cowles' duty to obtain title to the disputed land at the time of his purchase. Second, the judge failed to instruct the jury as to the time when the statute began to run in favor of Coffey. It was decided that Coffey was entitled to a venire de novo (retrial with a new jury). [20]

An earlier suit by Calvin J. Cowles and Josiah Cowles against D. C. McCanles, John Horton et al. was held in Yadkin County Superior Court on March 16, 1874. Judgment was found in favor of Cowles, and an execution against the property in the sum of two hundred dollars was levied. The property in question was a one-hundred-acre parcel of land owned by Horton on Howard Creek. Payment was ordered to be made in Watauga County Court House on Monday, April 3, 1876. [21]

Confusing to say the least, but these documents clearly confirm that McCanles did take Weith's claim money, and his indebtedness to Cowles was very likely due to either claim money paid by Cowles or money Cowles posted toward toward McCanles' sheriff's bond. The scenario surrounding John Horton's involvement in the scheme is unknown, he may have been only a pawn. However, he was elected sheriff of Watauga County in

1866, eight years before the Cowles' filed their suit against his land, and held that office until 1876.

The last bit of evidence against McCanles came directly from Sarah Shull. She unhesitatingly told at least two people that McCanles did take the tax money when she went west with him. Sarah told Jessie Williams' mother, "McCanles was sheriff, but he did not stand in such good favor with the people because of his taking the tax money. He left [Watauga County] because of trouble with the law." Bina Teague of Boone, who helped out at the Robbins Hotel where Sarah spent her latter days, also heard Sarah state that McCanles took the tax money.

Although the courthouse fire in 1865 destroyed all the indictment records, the old residents of Watauga County firmly maintain that many people suffered financially because McCanles took the tax money. In January 1990 C. D. Vance of Avery County wrote a letter to the editor of *The Mountain Times*, stating that his great great grandfather, Issac McClurd, was a victim of McCanles' actions. According to Vance, "My Great-Great-Grandfather signed his sheriff's bond. Issac had to sell off most of his farm to pay it. He barely saved his homestead."

Following D. C. McCanles' move to Nebraska, rumors spread that he had a large hoard of gold. Connelley reported:

> It was even whispered that he had so much money that he pur-
> chased a sufficient amount of gold to fill a large kettle, which he buried
> at some point near Rock Creek Station, and the legend of the "pot of
> gold" may be heard there to this day.[22]

Wilstach reported that McCanles buried ten thousand dollars in an iron kettle somewhere on the ranch, and after his death, people diligently looked for the cache but never found it. The most complete account was written in 1912 by Charles Dawson, historian of Jefferson County, Nebraska. He reported that McCanles allegedly brought a tidy sum of money from North Carolina and added to it from his income at Rock Creek. He buried the kettle of gold under the puncheon floor in the bedroom of his eastside ranch. When he sold the station, he reburied the gold near the house a few nights before he vacated the premises. He was gone only one hour and commented vaguely to his wife that it was marked by two boulders. Many have searched for this gold, but none have been successful.[23]

The descendants of D. C. McCanles maintain that Sarah Shull did not leave with him, claiming that Arthur erred when he reported there was a railroad running from Johnson City, Tennessee, in 1859. Again Arthur was correct; however, Johnson City was known as Johnson's Tank and then Johnson's Depot until 1869. Historian Ray Stahl of Johnson City confirms that the railroad began operations in Johnson's Tank two years before McCanles and Sarah Shull left North Carolina:

> In May, 1854, [Henry] Johnson bought a half acre of land from
> Abraham Jobe for fifty dollars. The land was along the proposed right-

of-way of the East Tennessee and Virginia Railroad and the north side of Stage Road (Market Street). Here he erected a dwelling and a general store and waited for the railroad and the town to come to him.

The railroad began operating between Bristol and Johnson's Tank (as the location of Johnson City was known then) in 1857. The railroad became operative between Bristol and Knoxville in 1858.

This is also confirmed by the 1923 history *Tennessee, the Volunteer State 1769-1923*. Sarah Shull validates that they took the railroad when she stated to Jessie Williams, "I left with McCanles in the night by horseback. I was young and frightened by the train."[24]

Only the question concerning the sequence of events subsequent to their flight from Watauga County is left to answer. Arthur wrote that the entire proceedings occurred on one day, January 6, 1859. This is incorrect as proven by the deed of sale from McCanles to his brother on January 26. Howard Bingham, who knew McCanles as far back as 1852 and was in a position to know the facts, stated in *The Watauga Democrat* that McCanles fled the state on or about February 9, 1859, with a young mountain girl he had ruined. This is more believable, adding credence that this was not a spur-of-the-moment decision but a well-executed plan of action.

Because of the scandal, McCanles realized that the stigma would forever stain his name and that of his family. He was a man used to having his way so it is quite possible he took the tax and claim money as retribution as well as for profit. In February 1859 his parents and relatives also left Watauga County and moved to Duggar's Ferry in Carter County, Tennessee. This was likely due to a combination of reasons: the pressures brought about because of the scandal and the missing tax funds, and the fact that the McCanles family were staunch Union sympathizers during this time of divided loyalties preceding the Civil War.

McCanles' immediate family and his brother undoubtedly had prior knowledge of his plans to leave Watauga County. It is inconceivable that his family were unaware that he had sold their homestead. Too, if he had abandoned his family without a word, they most certainly would not have followed him to Nebraska seven months later. Their thoughts and reactions regarding his flight westward with Sarah Shull can only be conjecture; that they had to know about it is unquestionable.[25]

Sarah stated she left because she could no longer stand being lonely, shunned, and treated as an outcast. Jessie Williams' mother, Nannie Elizabeth Garland, related, "If people had treated her different, maybe she wouldn't have left and gone west." Sarah was desperate and would have resorted to any means to escape Shulls Mill; McCanles offered her that opportunity, and she took it.[26]

PART TWO: Westward Flight

D. C. McCANLES AND SARAH SHULL arrived in early February in Johnson's Tank, where McCanles sold the horses to Joel Dyer, a Watauga County farmer. The two then took the train west. Traveling through Tennessee, Kentucky, and Illinois, they arrived in St. Louis and proceeded by steamboat to Fort Leavenworth, Kansas. Here, McCanles purchased one of the foremost outfits that ever set out for the Rocky Mountains.

Shortly after heading for the Oregon Trail, McCanles and Sarah met many disillusioned miners returning from the goldfields. The Pike's Peak bubble had burst. Diggers were earning less than two shillings a day, and those reaching Denver after a punishing trek across the plains were gladly willing to work for their board, but there was no work. Reaching the valley of the Blue River, McCanles decided to seek a different venture than digging for gold.

In late March, about seven miles across the Kansas line into Nebraska, the pair arrived at the Rock Creek Ranch, owned and built by Newton Glenn in 1856 as a small relay station on the Oregon Trail used by emigrants and freighters. Glenn was willing to sell the ranch, and McCanles immediately purchased it. Thus, Sarah became the first white woman to live in what is now Jefferson County, Nebraska.

The ranch was on the west side of Rock Creek but did not have a sufficient water supply. During the summer, McCanles built a house and some barns and dug a well on the east side of the creek. According to Charles Dawson:

> McCanles also built a toll-bridge across Rock Creek between the two stations, using the west ranch for freighters, emigrants, etc., and the East Station for the Overland Mail Stage and Pony Express business. The charge for crossing the toll-bridge ran from ten cents to one dollar and fifty cents per wagon outfit. This brought quite a daily revenue for McCanles. . . .

McCanles installed Sarah Shull as housekeeper of the westside ranch and soon leased it to the Rocky Mountain Dispatch Company. Connelley reported that McCanles prospered and his total income was one thousand dollars a month.[27]

In August 1859 D. C.'s brother, James Leroy, left North Carolina for Nebraska with his family, D. C.'s wife and children, a nephew of D. C.'s named James Woods, and an orphan named Billie Hughes, who would die of typhoid fever in the fall. While en route, they stopped in Tennessee, where D. C.'s wife gave birth to a son, Charles S. McCanles. They continued their trek by railroad, steamboat, and ox teams, arriving at Rock Creek on

September 20. The whole McCanles clan settled in at the East Rock Creek Ranch.[28]

With D. C.'s wife and family now in Nebraska, the question of what kind of relationship existed between McCanles and Sarah Shull is paramount. The following remembrances of Jessie Williams should leave no doubt regarding their intimacy. In answer to the question of whether McCanles and Sarah Shull continued their affair in Nebraska, Mrs. Williams responded, "Sarah Shull was a proud woman and very discreet. She valued Mama's friendship and seemed like she was apologizing for what she did. She left this to Mama's imagination. She knew that Mama could figure [this] out without her saying anymore. You see, Mother knew it. From just what Aunt Sarah had said. After she [Sarah] went out there, he [McCanles] went over the bridge just as much as he wanted to. He was welcome on that other side of the bridge."

Almost all who have written about McCanles and Sarah Shull claim that when Mary McCanles arrived at Rock Creek, she was enraged when she found Sarah residing at the westside ranch. Some allege that after several violent arguments, McCanles appeased her with halfhearted promises not to see Sarah anymore. Dawson likely was correct when he reported:

> Kate Shell [Sarah Shull] at the time of her arrival was described as . . . always carrying herself in a ladylike manner, and somewhat reserved in company. Underlying this quiet demeanor was a spirit of determination and self-reliance which became very evident to all persons attempting to trifle with her. Situated as she was, exposed to the advances of thousands of men, one cannot help but admire her steadfast allegiance to her accepted lover, despite all the wrongs she may have been guilty of, in the marital affairs of McCanles and his lawful wedded wife. . . .
>
> Both women, seemingly, were aware of the immoral relations, for it was but a continuation of that carried on in North Carolina. Although Mrs. McCanles was very much opposed too this, it was continued, despite her protests. McCanles even forced the two women to be friendly when they met in public, and to entertain each other, often exchanging dinner invitations back and forth.

This is substantiated by Sarah Shull's comments to Mrs. Williams that "the only people I saw were McCanles' wife and children." In the following words, Sarah confirms that she had no trouble with Mary McCanles: "McCanles' wife was a nice woman, and they had a nice family." Also take into consideration that McCanles' wife joined him in Nebraska, knowing that he left North Carolina with Sarah, and that the two women lived within walking distance of each other for more than one and a half years without any report of dissension.

Dawson's statement that Sarah Shull was a self-reliant and determined woman brings another perspective into this volatile situation, one that can be documented. Although she was McCanles' mistress, Sarah was not a fool and made the best of a bad situation by assuring her own financial security.

Sarah remarked to Jessie Williams that McCanles built her a warm house and an arched bridge across the creek and provided for her in

Nebraska. This agrees with all the written accounts, which reported that after the eastside ranch was built, Sarah worked as the housekeeper of the westside ranch and remained there after the arrival of the McCanles family. She was listed as a domestic in the household of D. C. McCanles in the 1860 territory of Nebraska census. Levi Bloyd, in an article in *The Fairbury Daily News* in 1965, wrote, "She was in the employment of David McCanles and kept books for him." Writer Joseph G. Rosa, through correspondence with Bloyd, furnishes corroborating evidence of Sarah's employment as bookkeeper, adding ". . . and he [Bloyd] told this writer at the time of his death McCanles owed her money."

Bloyd was correct; there is documentation to show that part of Sarah's association with McCanles was on a business level. Immediately upon reaching Nebraska in late March, McCanles signed the following note:

> $240 on or before the 3 day February Eighteen hundred and Sixty I promise to pay Sarah Louisa Shull Two Hundred & Forty dollars for value received. Witness my hand & seal this 29 day of March 1859.
> D. C. McCanles

Sarah received a second IOU from McCanles for $240 on March 26, 1861, without being paid for the first promissory note. The probate records from the estate of D. C. McCanles confirm that McCanles owed Sarah Shull $480 at the time of his death. This also helps to establish that Sarah and McCanles traveled together to Nebraska.[29]

In the spring of 1860, James McCanles moved his family to the mouth of Rock Creek on the Little Blue River, about three miles southwest of Rock Creek Station. He filed the first claim in Jefferson County when he purchased the land from the U.S. government on August 2, 1860. On December 17, 1860, D. C. McCanles sent an employee, Allen Ervin, to Brownville to enter a claim for the 160 acres of land at Rock Creek Station. The patent was issued April 1, 1861.

It was in the territory of Nebraska that the dual nature of David Colbert McCanles was brought to light. He was, in all fairness, extremely industrious and a forerunner in the settling and the advancement of southern Nebraska. He called a mass meeting of the citizens to organize the county so settlers might adjudicate minor criminal cases and controversies without having to travel fifty miles to settle them in Beatrice. An election for organization passed unanimously but was withheld by the Legislature because of limited population.

Around May 1861 McCanles built a small cabin near his ranch on the Little Blue River as the first schoolhouse in the county and hired a schoolteacher at his own expense. His reputation as a profound orator spread across the county, and no gathering was complete without his discourse on the issues of the day. At festive occasions, McCanles would invariably be called on to play the violin and banjo and sing popular songs in a rich, melodious voice. There is no doubt that McCanles was popular and well-respected by his fellow settlers in Jones County, now Jefferson County, Nebraska.

McCanles was also becoming prosperous. The ranch was a thriving business venture, and he employed as many as twenty men. Frank Helvey, an old resident of Jefferson County, stated that McCanles cursed his employees frequently and was hard on them but was never known to beat or injure any of them. In 1923 Robert Y. Shibley related that he worked for McCanles in 1860 and 1861 and was always well treated, adding that McCanles was a fine man and strictly honest in all his dealings. [30]

But there was a dark side to D. C. McCanles, which was reported by several of the old residents of Jefferson County. Dawson maintained that McCanles was a Confederate sympathizer, and there were claims that he had a gang of border ruffians who stole horses from the stage company for the Confederate army. The claim is ludicrous; the entire McCanles family were staunch Whigs and later Republicans. James McCanles belonged to the Republican party throughout his lifetime, which is attested to by his political career in Colorado. James stated that during D. C.'s terms as sheriff of Watauga County, he belonged to the party that opposed secession. In 1861 all of the residents in Jones County, Nebraska, were Republicans, and for the Fourth of July celebration that year, McCanles was selected orator and patriotically spoke against secession.

There is no doubt that McCanles was a rough customer, and several reports of his ruthless nature were likely true. One incident involved a band of Indians who often hung around the station and were notorious for their pilfering. In the spring of 1860, these Indians camped near the Rock Creek Station. Mary McCanles was cooking breakfast and had put a pan of biscuits near the window, and when the Indian reached in again, he pinned his hand to the table with a knife. The Indians took this as a great joke and gave McCanles no trouble.

There are several accounts of McCanles' vindictive abuse of other men. While McCanles was off on business, he left an employee, Harry Goff, in charge of the station, and the man drank himself into a stupor. Finding the man in a drunken sleep when he returned, McCanles poured a can of powder over his beard and set it on fire. Fortunately, some employees quickly threw him into a water trough and put out the fire. But Goff was now incensed and threatened to get his gun and kill McCanles. Unable to calm the man down, McCanles had him tied on the back of an un-broken horse, and he let it go until the horse was exhausted. Goff was still enraged, and McCanles threatened to give him the "third degree," a cruel measure in which a man is forced to climb a honey locust tree, whose trunks and limbs are covered with thorns up to eight inches in length. This punishment could put a man out of commission for several months, and Goff immediately calmed down and rarely became drunk afterward.

Another incident involved Joseph Holmes, the father of Jane Wellman, whose husband took over as manager of the East Rock Creek Station when McCanles sold it in the spring of 1861. In early July 1861 Holmes allegedly stole either a team, a wagon, and some farm supplies from McCanles, or a suit of clothing from one of McCanles' employees. On July 5 Holmes was apprehended by McCanles and taken to the Rock Creek Station, where he was hauled by rope to the roof of the station and then dropped to the ground numerous times. The unfortunate man was then given the third degree. His wounds festered and remained in this condition for some time. Mrs. Wellman was at the station during this time and possibly witnessed the torture of her father. This undoubtedly played an important part in the fate of McCanles a week later.

For some unknown reason, D. C. McCanles took a dislike to Mike Conley, who had lived in the territory several years before the coming of the white man. One evening as McCanles was passing James Shumway's ranch, he spotted Conley drinking with others in the ranch house. He entered the house and, pretending not to see Conley, invited everyone to have a drink with him while expounding on the character of Conley. McCanles then drew and fired his revolver into the fireplace behind Conley, who leaped through the window and fled to Joel Helvey's ranch. McCanles claimed it was the best joke he played on anyone since coming to Nebraska.

Another of McCanles' jokes involved a preacher who was with a party of emigrants camped near Joel Helvey's ranch one Sunday and had received permission to hold services at the ranch house. Unaware of the church service, McCanles strode in and invited everyone to have a drink. Realizing his blunder, McCanles apologized and attended the services. Sighting the preacher's glass of water, McCanles substituted it with a glass of clear moonshine whiskey. When the preacher took a healthy gulp of the fiery liquid, he commenced gagging and coughing, all to the amusement of the crowd. The preacher turned the tables on McCanles, when he quietly requested a glass of water, stating that gentlemen usually took a chaser after their drinks. McCanles good-naturedly complied, and the two men became friendly. On his departure, the preacher told McCanles that he was a man with natural gifts and should not be wasting his life. McCanles replied, "I appreciate your kindly feeling toward me, but my life was destined to be along different lines—I cannot change it. Good-bye."

There are also reports of McCanles' crossing the line into Kansas and engaging in drinking bouts and the sport of rough-and-tumble fighting with former South Carolinians in the border ruffian town of Palmetto, now part of Marysville.

The following incident, also undocumented, is the most savage act attributed to McCanles. After establishing the Rock Creek Station, McCanles opened another ranch at Little Sandy Station, fifteen miles east of Rock Creek. He put his most trusted employee, Charles Stockwater, in charge. Stockwater found a yoke of strayed oxen and returned them to the owner. Under estray law, they would have belonged to McCanles after a period of time. When he found out what Stockwater had done, he became enraged and gave his employee a savage tongue-lashing. Stockwater, also a rough-and-tumble fighter, had no fear of his employer, and he refused to take McCanles' abuse. A violent quarrel ensued, and soon the two went at it tooth and nail.

When McCanles began gaining the upper hand, Stockwater went for his gun. McCanles quickly pulled his own weapon and shot his opponent in the forehead, the ball penetrating the skin and following a course to the back of the head. McCanles was now out of control. He roped his victim around the shoulders and dragged him along the frozen road. Stockwater refused to give in, so McCanles tied the rope to the pommel of his saddle and drove the man all the way to the East Rock Creek Station, where he continued his persecution until the man's spirit was broken. When Stockwater finally admitted he had erred, McCanles tended his wounds and forgave him but the man had enough and left the area after his recovery. McCanles abandoned the Little Sandy Station shortly afterward.

Although the above incidents show a vicious streak in McCanles' character, this report illustrates his strong sense of right and wrong. The freighting firm of Farrell and Furbush became indebted to McCanles, and he confiscated its cattle and oxen to settle the debt. Mixed up in the herd were cattle belonging to a man named Bill Babcock. He was warned that he was begging for trouble if he asked McCanles to return them. Not heeding the warning, Babcock confronted McCanles, who acknowledged the mistake and allowed Babcock to take out his cattle from the herd. In a trial over this matter at Beatrice, McCanles gained lawful possession of the freighter's cattle. [31]

However, there is one brutal incident credited to McCanles that is documented in a deposition dated December 13, 1861, in the probate records of D. C. McCanles. John P. Shumway, who was running another station for the Overland Stage Company, stated that on October 6, 1860, McCanles made a verbal agreement with him for the premises of Rock Creek Station but would not sign any document until he was paid for the hay on the property he had stacked for the Overland Stage Company. Shumway made improvements at the ranch, but McCanles never signed the document. He also kept a wagon belonging to Shumway for the next four months, at which time Shumway retrieved it. When McCanles sent men to take the wagon back, Shumway went to the Rock Creek Station and asked if McCanles could do without it. In a rage, McCanles told him no, and Shumway said, "It was a hard case if a man could not control his property part of the time." McCanles told him that he controlled things about him and viciously kicked him under the chin. McCanles continued to kick his hapless victim as he attempted to flee from the house. That night, McCanles went to Shumway's house and threatened to kill him if he said anything detrimental to the agent of the Overland Stage Company.

The next afternoon, McCanles again went to Shumway's house and asked him if he was going to leave and, if so, did he intend to pay damages. The beleaguered man replied that he was the one who was damaged but, out of fear, agreed to give McCanles his store for a peaceful settlement. This did not appease McCanles, and the desperate man offered his hogs to pacify his tormentor. When Shumway said he had to stay and honor his contract, the enraged McCanles struck him with a two-pound weight, breaking his nose. Leading the battered man into the house, McCanles forced him to sign over his store and all his oxen, hogs, and hay.

Fearing that McCanles would kill him, Shumway contacted a man who had a team and wagon and had him stay the night. The next morning, Shumway and his family left, taking with them only what property McCanles had allowed him to keep. On December 12, 1861, Shumway filed a claim on the estate of D. C. McCanles for $215 for items taken by McCanles and three hundred dollars as damages for being driven away and for threats upon his life. Undoubtedly McCanles' vicious reputation would be the underlying factor that led to his death. [32]

PART THREE: That Fatal Day

DAVID COLBERT McCANLES' TROUBLES can be traced to the spring of 1860, when he began making improvements on the East Rock Creek Ranch in order to rent it as a relay station to Russell, Majors, and Waddell of the Central Overland California and Pikes Peak Express Company, commonly known as the Overland Stage Company. On April 3, 1860, the firm had organized the Pony Express and began establishing stations fifteen miles apart from St. Joseph, Missouri, to Sacramento, California, a distance of two thousand miles.

McCanles added a twelve-foot-wide lean-to on the south side of the house and built a bunkhouse, which he rented to the Overland Stage Company later in the season. The company had a policy to personally operate all of its stations and sent Horace G. Wellman and his wife or common-law wife, Jane Wellman, to take charge as keepers. The firm also employed J. W. "Dock" Brink as stock tender. Wellman and his wife would be the catalysts in the death of D. C. McCanles.

In early March 1861 the Overland Stage Company sent twenty-three-year-old James Butler Hickok to the Rock Creek Station as assistant stock tender. Hickok would live to become the legendary gunfighter "Wild Bill," but at this time he was an inured wagon driver sent to Rock Creek for light duties. There is a persistent rumor that Hickok had been mauled in a fight with a bear the previous autumn, but his injuries were more likely due to a wagon accident or a personal fight. Whatever the reason, Hickok limped around the station with a useless left arm, cleaning harnesses and doing other small jobs. He lived in a small dugout nearby and remained aloof from the other men.

Examples of McCanles' rowdy brand of humor were well-known in Nebraska, and young Hickok did not escape his roughhouse ways. According to Joseph G. Rosa:

Young Jim avoided mixing perhaps because his wound made him feel inferior. At any rate he failed to appreciate some of McCanles' humor. With the use of only one arm he could not do much when McCanles pretended to wrestle with him and threw him on the ground. It may have seemed funny to McCanles, but to Hickok it was exactly the opposite. Gradually, as Jim's wounds healed, McCanles found other outlets for his humor and left him alone.

McCanles added more fuel to the fire with disparaging remarks about Hickok's thin, protruding lips and large, hooked nose. Hanson reported:

> On account of some peculiarity of Hickok's nose and prominent upper lip, not then covered by a moustache, McCanles dubbed him "Duck Bill," which nickname stuck and irritated and exasperated him. This nickname was sometimes perverted to Dutch Bill.

Dawson gives a different reason for the animosity between the two men:

> His [Hickok's] weakness was gambling, and it is alleged that he created suspicion in the minds of several fellow-gamblers by his methods of winning. Words followed, and these big burly men, not caring to take a boy's life, used their fist or open hand in administering rebuke and justice upon the wrong-doer.
> McCanles took Wild Bill to task one day, manhandling him with the departing injunction that he cease his gambling or leave the station.
> Wild Bill never openly resented this treatment. Meekly taking it all, he silently awaited his opportunity to return it all with a vengeance many fold. [33]

For whatever reasons, probably a combination of all of the above, McCanles would pay the ultimate price for this animosity in July.

During the autumn of 1860, James McCanles decided to move to a more populated area, and after an agreeable settlement was reached, D. C. took over the farm on the Little Blue and James moved fifty miles east to Johnson County, Nebraska, where he bought three farms. In February 1861 the Rocky Mountain Dispatch Company ceased using the westside ranch and left owing McCanles money. The company also took four horses and two sets of harnesses belonging to him. In Beatrice McCanles filed an action for attachment against the company for $318.19.

On April 22, 1861, D. C. sold the West Rock Creek Ranch, including 120 acres, to (David) Wolfe & (Fredrick) Hagenstein with payment to be made one year from that date. As security, McCanles kept the title and gave the purchasers a $1,200 bond for deed. At the same time, McCanles sold the East Rock Creek Ranch to the Overland Stage Company for one-third down and the rest in two monthly payments to be made through Horace Wellman. McCanles kept the title as security.

After the sale of both ranches, McCanles moved his family in May to the ranch on the little Blue, where his last child, Jennie, was born. In early May, Wellman and his wife moved into the East Rock Creek Ranch house. Sarah Shull moved to a dugout owned by French Harris, which was located on a hilltop near the Little Blue River south of Rock Creek. However, she kept Mrs. Wellman company and assisted her at the eastside ranch.

Unknown to McCanles, the Overland Stage Company was in deep financial trouble and could not meet its obligations. In June McCanles went to collect his payment from Wellman but was told that superintendent Ben Ficklin had not sent the money. Throughout the month, McCanles was continually put off by Wellman. On July 1, when the second payment came due, McCanles again confronted Wellman and angrily demanded that he go to Brownville and settle the matter: either get the money or an equivalent amount of supplies, or turn the station back over to him. The irate McCanles continued his insistence, and Wellman finally agreed to his demands. McCanles' indignation is understandable, but his attitude and actions caused a wide breach between the two men.

On July 2 Wellman left for Brownville accompanied by McCanles' twelve-year-old son, William Monroe McCanles, who was to pick up supplies for his father. Hickok assumed Wellman's duties until he returned and moved from his dugout to the ranch house.

The more McCanles considered the situation, the angrier and more apprehensive he became, and during Wellman's absence he made several trips to Rock Creek, demanding that Mrs. Wellman turn the ranch over to him. The resolute woman refused, and the situation remained at a standstill until Wellman and young Monroe McCanles returned at four o'clock on the afternoon of July 11. It was also during this period that McCanles allegedly punished Mrs. Welllman's father, Joseph Holmes, as described earlier.

Monroe McCanles reported that he found his father at the ranch of Jack Nye and told him that Wellman was unsuccessful in obtaining the payments or supplies. That was the straw that broke the camel's back. [34]

To fully understand the subsequent events, let us examine all the allegations, starting with Wilstach's interview with Sarah Shull at Shulls Mill in 1925. He admittedly badgered her constantly for months until she reluctantly gave in. What information she did divulge was given solely to stop him from pestering her. The following is what Wilstach reported that Sarah told him, however it is not in accordance with what Sarah later told her close friends in North Carolina:

> Having been located, she [Sarah Shull] consented only with great reluctance to discuss the tragedy. Even after a lapse of more than half a century the incident is an exceedingly painful remembrance to her. Inducing her to talk was much like opening an oyster with a blade of grass. It was a task of months to obtain anything significant from her. Here follow the answers to such questions as Sarah Shull was willing to give.

> "Was money owed by Wellman the cause of the tragedy?"
> "No."
> "Were you at the cabin when McCanles was shot?"
> "No. I was at my home two miles away."
> "In your opinion, and from what you were told at the time, did Hickok kill McCanles in self-defense?"

"Certainly—yes."

"What makes you think this is true?"

"Because on the morning of the tragedy I heard McCanles say he was going to clean up on the people at the Station."

"You say McCanles stole horses?"

"Yes, he stole horses."

"Were those horses for the use of the Confederate cavalry?"

"Yes."[35]

Besides Wilstach's statements, there are other allegations that: (1) McCanles wanted a quick settlement because he wanted supplies for friends who were going to join the Confederate army; (2) McCanles needed the money because he intended to either head west with Sarah Shull and leave his family to fend for themselves or return to North Carolina to join the Confederacy; (3) McCanles was going to attack the station to steal horses for the Confederacy; and (4) McCanles' problems with Hickok were over the affections of Sarah Shull.

In regard to McCanles' affiliation with the Confederacy, it has already been shown that McCanles was a supporter of the Union cause, and there is no evidence that he intended to attack the station to steal horses. In fact, this story first came to light twenty years later in J. W. Buel's 1882 thriller, *Heroes of the Plains*. Rosa undoubtedly made the correct judgment regarding Sarah Shull's answer when he wrote:

> . . . she may well have fobbed Wilstach off with reference to the Confederate cavalry, hoping that he would not dwell too much on her own personal relationship with Dave.

The fact that McCanles sold the West Rock Creek Ranch in April and deferred payment for one year eliminates the assertion that he planned to quickly leave the country with or without Sarah Shull. The only allegation that may have some truth to it is Sarah Shull's involvement with Hickok.

A damning but unsubstantiated account involving McCanles, Sarah Shull, and Hickok was written by William E. Connelley, a former director of the Kansas State Historical Society. He did not mince words, but his allegations are not documented and appear biased. This is not the approach of a professional historian. In essence, he claimed that Sarah Shull enticed Hickok to fall in love with her to spite McCanles because "she demanded supremacy in his [McCanles'] heart." Of Sarah, he wrote:

> And through the heart of such a woman as was Sarah Shull at Rock Springs in the spring and summer of 1861 there surges a burning, stanchless, passionate irrepressible tumult of emotions which may carry her down to the lowest depths or inspire her to sublimity—martyrdom. Such women do not cease to love, but joy runs through their souls as they inflict on the lover once doubted torments such as hell would not employ against the damned. And McCanles suffered these as Sarah Shull fascinated Hickok with the witcheries of her charms and drew him to her side with a power he could not resist. . . . He never loved another woman. To the end of his life there was no room in his heart for any other than Sarah

Shull. . . . He was always looking for her—hoping she would pass by again that he might see her, take her, have her.

There is not one shred of proof to substantiate these disparaging accusations. In fact, as will be subsequently reported, Hickok could have very easily found Sarah Shull and pursued her after McCanles was dead. His actions will show that he did not have that inclination.

For the sake of history, it is fortunate that Sarah Shull did make some definitive statements about Hickok to Jessie Williams. In Sarah's own words, "Hickok had steel-blue eyes that were beautiful and gentle but could change in a second and look dangerous. You had better watch his eyes; he wasn't one to run from a fight. I came close to having an affair with Hickok." So McCanles and Hickok may well have had words over Sarah Shull, but the charge that Sarah Shull became Hickok's mistress is false. Sarah's association with Hickok was likely due to loneliness, and she may have inadvertently referred to this when she told Wilstach that money was not the cause of the tragedy. Also consider Sarah's six-year involvement with McCanles, an important and successful man in both North Carolina and Nebraska. Would she risk losing this to have an affair with an assistant stock tender?[36]

Now for the events of the fateful day, July 12, 1861. The most accurate account of what transpired is the eye-witness report of William Monroe McCanles, the definitive research of Joseph G. Rosa in his book *They Called Him Wild Bill*, and Sarah's statements to Jessie Williams.

Sarah told Wilstach that McCanles told her in the forenoon of July 12 that he was going to clean up on the people at the station. Most reports state that this occurred at the Rock Creek Station. In all likelihood, however, McCanles saw Sarah at her dugout, otherwise the confrontation would likely have taken place at this time. In regard to McCanles' threat to clean up on the people at the station, keep in mind that he had never resorted to the use of weapons and always settled his disputes with his fists.

Late in the afternoon of the twelfth, McCanles returned to the station with his son, William Monroe, his nephew, James Woods, and an employee named James Gordon. Some accounts claim that McCanles was armed with a shotgun, but Monroe McCanles stated that his father, Woods, and Gordon did not have weapons. They dismounted near the barn, and after conferring for a few moments, McCanles and his son walked to the west door of the house, leaving Woods and Gordon leaning on the fence rail. McCanles called out for Wellman and verbally abused the man when he appeared, demanding to know why Wellman did not get his money. Refusing to accept any excuse, McCanles demanded his rights and threatened to take over the station. Wellman knew he had no chance in a physical bout with McCanles and fled back inside the house. Mrs. Wellman then appeared and scathingly told McCanles what she thought of him. Now thoroughly enraged, McCanles told her his business was with men not women and to send Wellman back out. At this point Hickok stepped up to the doorway.

Taken aback, McCanles asked Hickok, "What in hell, Hickok, have you got to do with this? My business is with Wellman, not you, and if you want to take a hand in it, come out here, and we will settle it like men."

Hickok unhurriedly replied, "Perhaps 'tis or 'taint."

McCanles countered, "Well, then, we are friends, ain't we? I want to know. We have been, ain't we, Hickok?"

"I guess so," responded Hickok.

"Then," replied McCanles, "send Wellman out here so I can settle with him, or I will come in and drag him out."

Nodding his head and then shrugging his shoulders, Hickok walked back inside the house. Now confused and somewhat uncertain, McCanles told his son to remain where he was and then proceeded to the south door. He had seen Sarah Shull and Sarah Kelsey, a step-daughter of McCanles' former employee, Joe Baker, who was also helping Mrs. Wellman at the station, standing near the chimney, which served as a kitchen. It has been reported that he anticipated an encounter and wanted to see what was transpiring inside the house. When he reached the south door, he saw Hickok and the overwrought Wellman arguing.

Sighting McCanles, the two men stopped arguing and looked at him. Uncomfortable with the situation, McCanles asked for a drink of water, and Hickok poured him a tin cup from a pitcher, took it to him, and walked backward to a curtain that separated the two rooms. Behind the curtain was a rifle belonging to McCanles and a navy revolver owned by the station. McCanles then called to Hickok to come out and face him. Hickok replied that he was welcome to try, but if he did, "there will be one less _____ when you try that."

Some sources report that McCanles was carrying the shotgun when he confronted Wellman and Hickok. Young Monroe McCanles claimed his father was unarmed. Armed or unarmed, at Hickok's remark McCanles made a movement, and a rifle was fired from inside the house. The shot entered McCanles' heart, the impact throwing him on his back. Monroe McCanles ran to his father as he tried to raise himself from the ground. It was too late. David Colbert McCanles attempted to speak, but his eyes glazed over and he fell back dead.

This incident has been thoroughly researched, and the conclusion is that James Butler Hickok fired the fatal shot. The reported conversation that led to the conflict reveals that the only reason McCanles was there was to collect the money due him or to take control of the Rock Creek Station. There was no quarrel over the favors of Sarah Shull. It is also apparent that McCanles was more than willing to battle it out with Hickok or Wellman with his fists, not guns, and that he was shot and killed because neither man was brave enough to face him. It was a cowardly murder despite McCanles' character.

Since Sarah Shull was inside the station when McCanles was killed, it seems that she could have shed light on who actually fired the fatal shot, however, she never divulged that information to anyone. A plausible reason for this was that Sarah never actually saw who shot McCanles.

The Rock Creek Station house has been accurately reconstructed, and the curtain that separated the kitchen from the room where the shot was fired blocks the view between the two rooms, thus Sarah could not have seen who it was that fired from behind the curtain.

Woods and Gordon ran unarmed to the house when they heard the shot, and both were fired on and severely wounded by Hickok with the navy revolver. Woods staggered to the north side of the house, where he collapsed in a clump of weeds, and Gordon ran toward the creek while Mrs. Wellman screamed from the house, "Kill them! Kill them all!" Hickok was joined by Dock Brink and stage driver George Hulbert, who came up from the stables. Brink was armed with a shotgun, and the three men followed Gordon. About four hundred yards down the creek, they found the wounded man, who was either prostrate from the loss of blood or trying to fight off a bloodhound, and shot him to death with the shotgun.

While Hickok and the others were chasing Gordon, Wellman grabbed a grubbing hoe and took off after Woods. Finding the man lying near the northeast corner of the house, he beat him to death with the hoe, crushing his head. Wellman then ran to where Monroe McCanles was standing and tried to kill him with the hoe, shouting, "Let's kill them all." The terrified boy dodged the blow and, outrunning Wellman, found a hiding place in a ravine south of the station.

In recounting these violent events to Jessie Williams, her mother, and Bina Teague, Sarah Shull not only verified that she was there when the killings took place, but also added a previously unknown detail. The moment the first shot was fired, the women were ordered to take shelter in the root cellar, which was on the north side of the house. Sarah stated that there were others in the cellar, so apparently Jane Wellman and Sarah Kelsey were with her. The top of the cellar was made of split logs, and when Wellman beat Woods to death with the hoe, the blood ran through the cracks onto Sarah Shull's head, completely matting her hair. It was the most horrifying experience she ever had.

Sarah's statement that the women were in the root cellar with her disputes Dawson's claim that a woman (Jane Wellman?) killed Woods with the hoe. As confirmation, eyewitness Monroe McCanles declared that it was Horace Wellman that killed Woods.

When Hickok and the others returned to the house, they encountered Joe Baker. Hickok threatened to kill him, and the man pleaded for his life, pointing out he no longer worked for McCanles. At this point, the women fled from their bloody refuge in the cellar, and Sarah Kelsey threw herself between the two men and begged Hickok not to kill her step-father. Relenting somewhat, Hickok growled, "Well, you got to take that anyway," and clouted Baker across the head with the barrel of his revolver. This was the end of the violence.

Monroe McCanles ran the three miles to his home and broke the tragic news to his mother. She immediately went to the Rock Creek Station and, after viewing the bodies of the murdered men, sent an employee named Tom Finan to the home of James McCanles. Riding throughout the night into the morning hours, McCanles reached Beatrice around one in the afternoon. He swore out a complaint before Justice of the Peace T. M. Coulter, charging Dutch Bill, Dock, and Wellman with murder, not knowing their full names. He then proceeded to Rock Creek Station.

The morning after the killings, Frank Thomas, and Jasper Helvey went to the station and found the three murdered men in the same position in which they died. There were no weapons found on or near the bodies. With Mrs. McCanles and her children in attendance, the Helveys buried the three men on a hill south of the station. In 1885 McCanles' children reinterred the bodies of their father and Woods in the cemetery at Fairbury, Nebraska.

James McCanles took charge of his brother's family and moved everything possible to his home in Johnson County, where he disposed of the stock and other property. Mary McCanles and her children remained at his home until the following spring and then returned to their ranch on the Little Blue River.

There were divided sentiments about the killing, so Hickok borrowed a horse and left on July 13 for Marysville, Kansas, where he asked the firm of Brumbaugh and Bollinger to defend him in the event of a trial. He returned to the station and was arrested with Brink and Wellman on July 15 by Gage County sheriff E. B. Hendee.

On July 15, 16, and 18, a hearing was held in Beatrice before Justice of the Peace Coulter. Jane Wellman, even though the wife of one of the defendants, was allowed to testify "in favor of the Territory." Neither Sarah Shull nor Sarah Kelsey were subpoenaed as witnesses, and Monroe McCanles was not allowed to testify nor to hear any of the testimony by the accused. The hearing was a sham: Coulter found that the charge of murder was not sustained, and the three men were freed. [37]

The reasons for Coulter's decision are given by Hanson:

> There were other circumstances contributing to the decision which the justice seemed to desire to make. It was the first criminal case ever heard in the county. Neither the defendants nor the men they killed were known to the few people who lived in Beatrice, and they had no great interest in the case except that they would have the costs to pay, a most serious matter at that time. There was no jail in the county, and the prisoners, if bound over to the next term of district court, must be guarded day and night, fed and sheltered for more than two years. There was no money in the treasury, and it was difficult to obtain men to act as temporary guards during the trial. The cost for guarding and feeding the prisoners was already $56.60. Sheriff, witness, and justice cost $141.95; and accounts against the county were worth only fifty cents on the dollar. The only direct testimony produced or permitted regarding the shooting was that of the accused men themselves and Mrs. Wellman, who testified that they were attacked and the killing was done in self defense. None of the other witnesses knew anything about the shooting. The defendants were employees of the Overland Stage Company, the most influential corporation west of the Missouri river, and many of its stage drivers were present at the trial. Coulter was a candidate for popular favor and for County Treasurer, and a few months later was elected to that office.

Coulter's true colors were revealed when he was arrested for embezzlement after his term of office expired in 1864 and defaulted in the amount of $548.98. He escaped before he came to trial.[38]

And what of Sarah Shull? All reports state that on the morning after the killing she was put on a west-bound stage by the station crowd — and faded into oblivion.[39]

PART FOUR: The Lost Years

CONTRARY TO ALL THAT HAS BEEN written, Sarah Shull did not head west on the morning of July 13, 1861. There is documentation to show that she remained in Nebraska for at least one month after the Rock Creek killings. If Hickok was so inclined to find the woman he would love forever, he could have easily found Sarah, as he had ample time to do it. Shortly after his exoneration on the charge of murder on July 18, Hickok left for Fort Leavenworth, Kansas, where he enlisted as a civilian scout in the Union army. He took part in the battle of Wilson's Creek in Missouri, a Confederate victory over Union troops on August 10, 1861. He then lived on to become the legendary Wild Bill Hickok, a product of the pulp writers and dime novelists of the day who enhanced his story of the Rock Creek killings to a single-handed rout of nine desperadoes under the leadership of the notorious desperado D. C. McCanles.[40]

There is no record to show where Sarah Shull resided after the killings at Rock Creek, although she stated to Jessie Williams that she did leave the station the next day. It is likely she went with James McCanles and remained at his home in Johnson County, at least for the following month, because on August 12 James paid his brother's debt of $480 to Sarah Shull. On each of the receipts, Sarah wrote:

> For value received I hereby assign the written note to J. L. McCanles, August 12, 1861.
>   Sarah Shull[41]

It was shortly after this that Sarah Shull headed west to the area where McCanles originally planned to seek his fortune, Denver, Colorado.

There are no existing records to show when Sarah Shull arrived in Denver or what she did when she got there, nor did she relate this information to anyone in North Carolina. However, the past and subsequent events in her life indicate that she probably went to work as a domestic, cleaning and cooking for the U.S. Army. The Civil War had begun the previous

April, and the First Regiment of Colorado Infantry was headquartered in Denver. It was here that she met and fell in love with the last man in her life, Philip Theodore DeVald.

According to Sarah's statements to Jessie Williams, DeVald was an extremely handsome, charming man and an accomplished musician who could play several instruments, excelling at the piano. She also stated that he was a dandy who dressed immaculately in the best clothing possible. According to his military records and pension file, DeVald was born in 1835 in Germany, probably in the Alsace-Lorraine area, and was five feet eight and one half inches in height, with blue eyes, brown hair, and a fair complexion.

It is unknown when Philip DeVald migrated to the United States, but his records show he was a miner before his enlistment in the army, so it was likely he came to Colorado during the Pikes Peak gold rush in 1858. He enlisted in Denver on August 8, 1861, as a private in Company A, First Colorado Infantry, which became the First Colorado Cavalry in 1862. On August 17, he was appointed corporal.[42]

The First Colorado was a rough-and-tumble outfit whose members were mainly frontiersmen, miners, and denizens of the Denver saloons, and they were spoiling for a fight. In March 1862 they got their chance. With a victory at Valverde in late February and their occupation of Santa Fe, on March 10, Confederate forces under Brigadier General H. H. Sibley had complete control of New Mexico. The First Colorado, under Colonel John P. Slough, quickly marched south to New Mexico, where they were joined by regular and New Mexican troops. On March 28, at Glorietta Pass, the two forces collided. The Union forces, though outnumbered, cut off the Confederate supply lines, destroyed their supply base, and forced the Confederates to retreat. Although losses were small—the Union lost one hundred men and the Confederates lost thirty-six—this battle prevented the Confederates from taking over the Southwest.[43]

A month later, on April 10, 1862, DeVald was promoted to sergeant, a position he held until he resigned the rank on January 22, 1863. On June 30, 1863, he joined the Brigade Band on detached service at Camp Weld, outside of Denver. At some point during this period, he met and courted Sarah Shull, and the two were married in Denver on July 15, 1863, by the Reverend Joseph Keeler, chaplain of the First Colorado Cavalry.

DeVald's enlistment ran out in January 1864, and he reenlisted in Company A, Veteran Battalion, on January 5. He remained on detached service at Fort Garland, Camp Weld, and Fort Lyon until he was mustered out on October 26, 1865, in Denver.[44]

For the next seven years the history of Philip and Sarah DeVald is sketchy, but they probably remained in Denver a short while and then moved to Minnesota. Although DeVald stated he was in Rawlins, Wyoming, in 1872, there is validation that their residence was in Duluth, Minnesota, until the end of that year. Sarah stated that DeVald taught music wherever they lived and, to her dismay, that he was a confirmed woman chaser who had numerous affairs with his music students. This would plague her until the end of their marraige and possibly was the cause of their frequent moves across the United States.[45]

In the fall of 1872, Philip and Sarah left Minnesota for Harrison County, Iowa. On November 23, they bought 120 acres of land in the northeast portion of Cass Township from F. H. Whitney for six hundred dollars. They bought an additional 120 acres from John S. Hall for six hundred dollars the following April 15. On December 2, 1874, they purchased a half a quarter of land for one hundred dollars from Cyrus Donaldson. It was during this time that Sarah had the only known photograph of her taken at Council Bluffs. The 1880 Harrison County, Iowa, census listed DeVald as a farmer and Sarah as keeping house in Cass Township.[46]

On September 20, 1880, the DeValds sold their land in Cass Township for $2,200. The following March 22, they purchased forty-nine acres in the northeast section of the town of Woodbine for two thousand dollars and ten acres in Lincoln Township for one dollar. Apparently they were speculating in land, because they sold the Woodbine acreage on July 21, 1882, to Sophronia Stephens for three thousand dollars. Stephens defaulted on the payments and an execution for $2,275 was levied against William Stephens et al. on September 10, 1884. The DeValds repurchased this land at public sale for $2,340 on October 13, 1885. Apparently the DeValds remained in Woodbine after their original land purchase, as DeVald had obtained membership in the Eaton Post of the Grand Army of the Republic at Woodbine on June 29, 1882, and the 1885 Harrison County, Iowa, Census recorded them as living there on January 1.[47]

It appears that either Philip and Sarah visited North Carolina before 1880 or Sarah's brother Simon and his wife, Martha, visited them in Iowa. Regardless, Simon Shull apparently thought well of Philip DeVald, for in 1880 he named his newborn son Charles DeVald Shull.

Two years later, on September 29, 1882, Sarah's mother died in Watauga County. Although Sarah's father had died sixteen years before on January 9, 1866, the estate had not settled until the death of her mother. On December 1, 1882, in the county clerk's office in Harrison County, Iowa, Sarah appointed Simon to represent her and to sell her interest in the estate. This was registered in the Watauga County Courthouse on October 8, 1884. It is apparent that Sarah did not attend her mother's funeral, and the fact that she did not want any part of the estate indicates that she likely harbored bitter feelings toward her parents.[48]

By late 1886, the DeValds had decided to leave Iowa. Whether it was because of DeVald's promiscuity or a joint decision to move to a warmer climate is unknown; however, on January 28, 1887, they sold their land in Woodbine to J. D. DeTar for two thousand dollars and moved to Putnam County, Florida.[49]

On March 28, 1887, the DeValds bought a store in Mannville, an outskirt of Palatka, Florida, for $561.60. Their purchase included merchandise, store fixtures, a street lamp, and a stove. Four years later, on May 16, they sold the store for eight hundred dollars.

One month previously, on April 13, the DeValds bought fifteen acres of land in Putnam County for two dollars. On the following June 6, they bought an additional ten acres for three hundred dollars. This land included orange groves, and both Sarah and her husband saw a bargain. It was here that Sarah lived in a house that gave her the greatest pleasure in her life, and she mentioned this numerous times to Jessie Williams. She described it as a lovely, long two-story house with two full-length verandas, affording a beautiful view of twenty-six small lakes. Sarah's contentment would be shattered in less than three years.[50]

In Jessie Williams' interview, she stated that Sarah said that her marriage broke up because Philip DeVald ran off with a sixteen-year-old music student. During the time the DeValds were in Florida, Philip taught music, mainly the piano, to students in his home. At some point in the early 1890s, he began teaching piano to a young girl named Hertha Berkelman.

Hertha was born on December 22, 1877, in Duluth, Minnesota, the daughter of George and Mina Berkelman. In 1885 the Berkelmans moved to Interlachen, Florida, very close to where the DeValds settled in 1891. Both the Berkelmans and the DeValds were German, and it is probable that they knew each other in Minnesota. By early 1894, Sarah found out that the barely sixteen-year-old girl and her fifty-eight-year-old husband were involved in a love affair.

There was so much friction and trouble over Philip DeVald's infidelity that the DeValds moved to Johnson City, Tennessee. However, the arguments continued, Sarah claiming that one time Philip beat her until she was black and blue and threatened her life on several occasions. Philip accused Sarah of cruel treatment because of her ungovernable temper. The conflict reached its peak on December 11, 1894. Both Philip and Sarah claimed that in an argument over the affair, each one beat and choked the other and threatened to take the other's life. Nevertheless, Philip DeVald left Johnson City that day and headed back to Florida and Hertha Berkelman. He claimed that he gave Sarah $2,150, half of his net worth, before he left; Sarah said he left with the intention of finding a home for them in Georgia.

In 1895 Philip DeVald filed divorce papers at Mount Vernon, Montgomery County, Georgia, charging Sarah with cruelty. The divorce was granted on April 30, 1896, and DeVald brought Hertha Berkelman to Cordele, Georgia, where he married her on May 7. They settled at Mount Vernon, and Philip continued to teach band and music. When this news reached Sarah in Johnson City, it shattered her pride, and in bitter resentment, she immediately contested the divorce on the grounds that DeVald had not been a resident of Georgia for one year. The court agreed, and the divorce was set aside at Mount Vernon on April 29, 1898.

Philip and his young bride found themselves in an awkward situation. Hertha immediately found lodging with a family named Thompson in Mount Vernon, and Philip refiled for divorce. The divorce proceedings were again tried in Montgomery County Superior Court during the November 1899 term. DeVald's second divorce was granted on November 15, and he and Hertha were remarried in Mount Vernon the same day.

This was not the only conflict that occurred between the DeValds and Sarah. On July 16, 1890, Philip had applied for a Civil War pension. It was approved on April 22, 1891, at a monthly rate of eight dollars, retroactive to the application date. On July 22, 1899, through attorney J. D. Morrell in Johnson City, Sarah applied for part of the pension, declaring she was a deserted wife with no financial support. The claim was denied on March 28, 1900, on the grounds that Philip and Sarah were legally divorced. Sarah would try again.

Philip and Hertha DeVald remained in Mount Vernon until June 1900, moving to 401 West Central Avenue, Fitzgerald, Ben Hill County, Georgia. DeVald was suffering from an enlarged prostrate and stomach cancer and was bedridden most of the time. Hertha DeVald, as well as nursing her husband, began teaching music to support their needs. Philip DeVald died at age sixty-five on February 23, 1901, and was buried in the Evergreen Cemetery in Fitzgerald. Hertha DeVald undoubtedly loved her husband very much, and contrary to what one would think a young woman of twenty-three would do, she never remarried or became involved with another man. Hertha continued to teach music and rent rooms in her house for support and later played piano in the Grand Theatre in Fitzgerald.

In late 1899 or early 1900, Sarah returned to Shulls Mill, North Carolina, after an absence of forty years. She was now sixty-six years old. It is evident that she had little money and was taken into the home of her brother Joseph. However, even after all that time, the old residents had not forgotten or forgiven her past mistakes and still shunned her and treated her with disdain.

When Sarah received the news that Philip DeVald had died, she filed another application, on April 2, 1901, this time for a widow's pension through attorney John Huff of Fitzgerald, Georgia. On August 2 her application was again denied because of the divorce. Sarah refused to give up and filed for the third time, on February 3, 1902, through Washington, D.C., attorney R. S. Lacey; and for the third time her claim was denied, on April 25.

Sarah Shull DeVald was a very determined woman, and after thirty years of heartaches in her marriage, she firmly believed she was entitled to the pension, divorce or not. In 1910 she contacted Congressman Charles H. Cowles in Washington, D.C., about her rights to the pension. In a letter dated March 23, the commissioner of the Bureau of Pensions wrote Congressman Cowles that the claim had been denied. Two years later she tried again, contacting Congressman C. L. Bartlett, and on January 13, 1912, she got the same results. Sarah finally gave up.

In Fitzgerald, Georgia, Hertha DeVald had better luck with the pension. On June 5, 1914, she filed for a widow's pension, but because of the previous controversy regarding the claims, she had to obtain personal affidavits, divorce decrees, and a marriage license. She was finally awarded the pension on September 28, 1916, which had now been raised to twelve dollars a month. She remained in the same house she and Philip DeVald had lived in until her death at age sixty-eight on October 19, 1946. [51]

By 1910 Sarah was living in a one-room cabin on the side of a mountain about a half a mile west of Shulls Mill. The small cabin had been
provided for her by her relatives and contained all of her belongings, a
beautifully carved wardrobe, a flat-topped stove with two burners, a bed,
a couple of chairs, and a wooden trunk with metal bands containing all
of her memorabilia from her life. The 1910 Watauga County census shows
she worked for herself at odd jobs, was renting the house, and had been
out of work thirty weeks the previous year.

During this decade, the Boone Fork Lumber Company provided a
booming economy at Shulls Mill. Sarah likely worked at odd jobs for
her niece, Luna Robbins, and her husband, George, who owned the Robbins Hotel, which was commonly known as the Blue Goose. Luna Robbins, born August 24, 1873, was the daughter of Sarah's deceased brother
William Shull. At age eighty-seven, Sarah DeVald was still going strong
when Jessie Williams moved to Shulls Mill in 1920.

Jessie Williams was born Jessie Ida Garland in Shady Valley, near
Mountain City, Tennessee, on October 1, 1904. In November 1920 Jessie's
parents, Caleb and Nannie Elizabeth Garland, left Tennessee and moved
to Shulls Mill, where Mr. Garland ran the commissary for W. S. Whiting.
During the last week of September 1921, Sarah DeVald went to shop at
the commissary, where she engaged in conversation with Mr. Garland.
In Jessie Williams' words, this is what transpired:

> Aunt Sarah came to the store and was talking to my father, and she
> said, "Next week I'll have a birthday," and Papa just says, "My daughter
> has a birthday next week," and Aunt Sarah says "We'll have to get together.
> I'd like to meet your daughter." Papa said, "I'll tell my wife, and she can
> get in touch with you," and he came home and told Mama, and Mama
> says, "Oh, why not let's us just have her a birthday party." And so Mama
> got in touch with her, and she said, "Why, I'll be glad to come to a birth-
> day party," and I walked down and got her. Our houses were not so
> far apart then, and I walked down and walked back with Aunt Sarah.
> . . . She said, "This is the first birthday party I've ever had," and I said,
> "Well, we'll go on record; this is the first birthday party that I've had
> in North Carolina." Then we moved up to what they call Lassiter's Creek.
> But after that, every October, why, Aunt Sarah came to our house for
> a birthday party. . . . I'd walk halfway home with her. . . and one time
> Papa brought her home in the buggy, and mother would always give
> her some butter, country butter she called it, and eggs and things, you
> know, to eat on. . . . Her secrets were closed, but I imagine she told
> my mother more than she did anyone else.

Sarah Shull and the Garland family became very close, and from the
contents of the interviews with Jessie Williams, there is no doubt that Sarah
revealed more to her and her mother than to anyone else. When Sarah
told Mrs. Garland about Philip DeVald running off with a sixteen-year-
old girl, she remarked that no one else knew this. The kindness of these
gracious people fulfilled Sarah's need for happiness during these last years
of her life. [52]

Mrs. Bina Teague of Boone, North Carolina, also knew Sarah during her last years, having worked at the Robbins Hotel for a period of time. Mrs. Teague tells a rather humorous story that Sarah and her brother Simon's widow, Louisa Shull, had a habit of going to different houses in the neighborhood, making sure they arrived around dinnertime. The two women got free meals at Mrs. Teague's home several times. Mrs. Teague also recalled a presistent rumor that Sarah brought back to Shulls Mill a large amount of money, allegedly part of the stolen Watauga County tax funds, and buried it in iron kettles near her one-room house. As Sarah got older, her mind dimmed and she forgot where she buried it. Mrs. Teague said that Sarah's niece, Luna Robbins, was a firm believer that there was buried money near Sarah's house. This, like many treasure tales, seems highly unlikely, since Sarah had to live on the charity of her family after her return to North Carolina.[53]

Sarah continued to live in her one-room cabin until early 1932, when she became too feeble to care for herself. Luna Robbins brought Sarah back down the mountain and gave her a small house to live in behind the hotel, where she was provided for. Jessie Williams visited her in the spring and found Sarah still lucid. By early May, however, Sarah could no longer function and became so helpless that on May 10, she was placed in the Watauga County Home, west of Boone.

This was undoubtedly the worst indignity Sarah ever endured. Although she was under the care of Dr. H. B. Perry, the County Home was a disgrace, a filthy place that offered very poor service to the aged and infirm who were placed there. Pearl Luttrel, Luna Robbins' daughter, visited Sarah on the evening of May 31, bringing her two children under the care of Bina Teague. Mrs. Teague vividly remembers the scene. May nights in the Blue Ridge Mountains can be extremely cool, and this night was no exception. Mrs. Teague found Sarah shaking uncontrollably, lying on a filthy straw tick with nothing but a dirty gray sheet to cover her. She never recognized anyone who visited her that night. Mercifully, Sarah died at seven o'clock the next morning of mitral lesion of the heart. She lived for ninety-eight years, seven months, and twenty-eight days, her last twenty-one days spent in utter hell.

Luna Robbins brought Sarah's body back to the hotel that day and placed her remains in the large sitting room. Many people, including Bina Teague, came to "sit up" with Sarah that night; however, Mrs. Robbins would not let anyone in, telling them, "Sarah is dead, and nobody can do anything for her." Her funeral was held the next day, June 2, at the Shulls Mill Baptist Church, the service conducted by the Reverends Sebastian and McKaughn. Sarah was laid to rest next to her daughter in the Shull Cemetery on the high hill overlooking the place of her birth.

In closing, these words of Jessie Williams' mother are most appropriate, "Aunt Sarah was a lot more gracious and a nicer woman at that time than the others who looked down on her when she came back here."[54]

Only known photograph of Sarah Shull, taken in Council Bluffs, Iowa, around 1873.
AUTHOR'S COLLECTION

Above: Original log cabin built by Phillip Shull at Shulls Mill in 1820–1821. The cabin is still standing as of 1990.
AUTHOR'S COLLECTION

Right: Phillip Shull's tombstone in the Shull Cemetery at Shulls Mill, North Carolina.
AUTHOR'S COLLECTION

Frame house later constructed by Philip Shull in the 1830s. Dwelling is still standing as of 1990. AUTHOR'S COLLECTION

Original Shulls Mill store, which is still in use, built by Philip Shull in 1850.
AUTHOR'S COLLECTION

David Colbert McCanles, circa 1859. AUTHOR'S COLLECTION

John Horton (circa 1880s), who was defeated by D. C. McCanles for the office of Sheriff of Watauga County Sheriff in 1852 and 1856.

COURTESY: WATAUGA COUNTY SHERIFF'S DEPARTMENT, BOONE, NORTH CAROLINA

State of North Carolina
Watauga county

Know all men by these presents That the undersigned, Sheriff of the county of Watauga and State above written, by virtue of Execution issued from the Superior Court of said county in the case following to wit Sanders stiled J.M. Keith vs H. Burns N.C. as of record doth appear. Upon levying said Execution on the land and tenements of the said H. McCanlis hereinafter described on the 1st day of June 1859; and having made advertisement according to law, and sold said lands and tenements at public sale for cash, on this 15th day of June 1859 at the Court House door in said county, where and when R.C. Miller assinee of W.F.Shull of the county of Watauga and State of North Carolina became last and highest bidder, at the sum of one hundred and eighty Dollars which said sum has been paid to the undersigned in accordance with the terms of said sale.

In consideration of the premises, and in further consideration of the purchase money paid as aforesaid by the said R.C. Miller assinee of W.F.Shull the receipt whereof is hereby acknowledged, hath bargained and sold and by these presents doth bargain and sell unto the said R.C. Miller assinee of W.F.Shull and his heirs all the right title and interest of the said H. McCanlis as aforesaid, in and to the following tract or parcels of land leved on as aforesaid situate in Watauga and bounded as follows to wit. First Tract Beginning on a black sum on the bank of the River thence North 23° West Seventy Six poles to a poplar then West 45° Seventy four poles to a Cucumber. thence South 40° West Sixty two poles to a chestnut. thence East thirty two poles to a double chestnut. thence South 12° twenty two poles to a large white oak. thence West 80 poles to a Hickory. thence North 112 poles to a Spruce pine thence North 25° East fourty four poles to a buck eye near the bank of the River. thence up the River to the beginning containing one hundred acres more or less. 2nd Tract Beginning on a white Oak on the bank of the River thence North ___ Eighty poles to a white oak thence West to a Stake in Joseph Shulls line thence South with said line to the River; thence with the River to the beginning containing sixty acres more or less.

To have and to hold said land and premises

with its improvements and appurtenances to the said R. C.
Miller exp. W. F. Shull heirs and assigns in as full and ample
a manner as the undersigned is empowered by virtue of his office
to convey and assure the same. And the undersigned Sheriff
as aforesaid doth covenant promise and agree to and with
the said R. C. Miller exp, W. F. Shull heirs and assigns, that he
and they shall and may at all times hereafter have, hold
occupy, use and possess said lands and premises free
and clear of and from all incumberances, had made or
done by the undersigned or by his order, means or procure
=ment, and that the undersigned will for ever warrant
and defend said lands and premises to the said R. C. Miller
assinee of W. F. Shull heirs and assigns so far as the said
office of Sheriff no ~~aforesaid~~ will authorize and enable
him to do and no further
In testimony whereof, the undersigned Sheriff as aforesaid
hath hereunto set his hand and seal this fourth day of
April A.D. 1876

           S. Deal Sheriff (Seal)

State of North Carolina } In the Probate Court
Watauga County
       The Execution of the foregoing
and within Sheriff's Deed from S. Deal Ex Sheriff of Watauga
county to W. F. Shull dated 4th day of April A.D. 1876 was on the
4th day of April A.D. 1876 duly proven in open Probate Court
by the acknowledgments of the said Deal Ex Sheriff the
person therein named for the purpose therein contained
Therefore let the foregoing and within deed with their certificate
be registered in the Register's office of our said county.
           J. H. Hardin
            Probate J. &c.

State of North Carolina, (No. 572)
Know ye, that we, for and in consideration of the sum of five
cents for every acre hereby granted, and paid into our Treasury
by Jacob M. Councill have given and granted and by these
presents do give and grant unto the said Jacob M. Councill
a tract of land containing thirty two acres, lying and being
in the county of Watauga in the waters of Elk Creek
Beginning on a white oak Jacob Greer's corner Running with
with the line of his seventy one acre tract fifty eight poles to
a Stake, thence West with the same twenty three poles to
a chestnut oak, thence North four poles to a Stake

Watauga County Deed showing execution against the land of D. C. McCanles in favor of J. M. Weith of Ashboro, North Carolina. Watauga County Deed Book G, pp. 56 and 57.
WATAUGA COUNTY COURTHOUSE, BOONE, NORTH CAROLINA

Watauga **County :---In the Superior Court.**

The State of North Carolina,

To the Sheriff of *Watauga* County—GREETING :

Whereas, Judgment was rendered on the 16 *day of* March 1874, *in the Superior Court of* Yadkin *County, in an action between* J & C J Cowles

_____ *Plaintiff s, and* W C McCaules, John Horton et al

_____ *Defendant s, in favor of the said* J & C J Cowles *against the said* D C McCaules, John Horton et al *for the sum of* Two hundred,

Dollars, as appears to us by the Judgment-roll filed in the office of the Clerk of said County. And whereas, the said judgment was docketed in this County, on the 11th *day of* Sept , 1874, *and the sum of* Two hundred _____ *Dollars is due thereon, with interest on* Two hundred, _____ *Dollars from the* 16th *day of* March 1874. *And the further sum of* Eighty one & 21/100

Dollars for cost and disbursements in said suit expended, whereof the said D C McCaules, John Horton et al are *liable.*

You are therefore Commanded, *To satisfy the said judgment out of the personal property of the Defendant s within your County ; or, if sufficient personal property can not be found, then out of the real property in your County, belonging to such Defendant s on the day when the said judgment was so docketed in your County, or at any time thereafter, in whose hands soever the same may be ; and have you this execution, together with the money, before our said Court at the Court House in* Boone *on the* 6th *Monday after the* 3 *Monday in* February *next, 1876 then and there to render the same to the said Plaintiff .*

Issued the 25 *day of* Oct , 1875.

J H Gurdin

Clerk Superior Court of *Watauga* **County.**

r W H Presnell D C

Execution against property of D. C. McCanles and Judgment in favor of J. and C. J. Cowles; Superior Court of Yadkin County, North Carolina.
CLERK OF THE SUPERIOR COURT, WATAUGA COUNTY COURTHOUSE, BOONE, NORTH CAROLINA

Transcript of Judgment from the Judgment Docket of _Yadkin_ Superior Court.

Yadkin County---In the Superior Court.

Josiah C. J. Cowles
        Plaintiff's

Against

S. C. McCanlas
  And Others
        Defendant's

Transcript of Judgment.

At a Superior Court held for the County of _Yadkin_, at the Court House in _Yadkinville_ the _16th_ day of _March_, 1874, before his Honor Judge _____ Judgment was rendered in favor of _Josiah Cowles And C. J. Cowles_

the above named Plaintiff's against _S. C. McCanless, J. C. Council, John Sterlin, John McGuire, L. McCanles, David Lewis, James Ragan, J. W. Council, James Swift, Duncan Hodges, J. P. Matthison_, the Defendant's, for the sum of _Two hundred_ Dollars, with interest on _Two hundred_ Dollars from the _16th_ day of _March_, 1874, till paid, and cost of suit $ _97.38_.

Yadkin **County---ss.**

I, _J. C. Wilson_ _____ Clerk of the Superior Court of said County, do hereby certify that the foregoing is a true and perfect Transcript from the Judgment Docket in my office.

In **Testimony Whereof,** I have hereunto set my hand, and affixed the seal of said Court at office in _Yadkinville_, the _6th_ day of _Nov._, 1875.

J. C. Wilson
        Clerk Superior **Court.**

By E. F. Green, D. C.

Rock Creek Station, 1860–1861. Figure at right is claimed to be D. C. McCanles.
COURTESY WAYNE BRANDT, NEBRASKA GAME AND PARKS COMMISSION, FAIRBURY, NEBRASKA.
Inset: Rock Creek Station as it looks today. AUTHOR'S COLLECTION

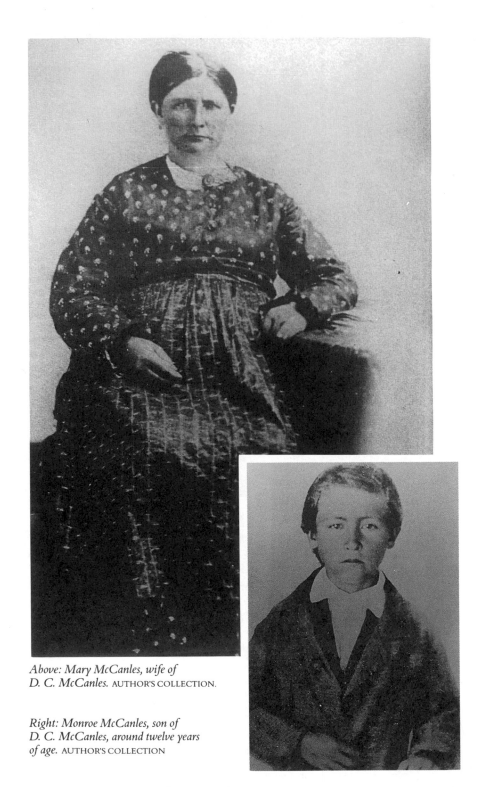

*Above: Mary McCanles, wife of
D. C. McCanles.* AUTHOR'S COLLECTION.

*Right: Monroe McCanles, son of
D. C. McCanles, around twelve years
of age.* AUTHOR'S COLLECTION

James Butler "Wild Bill" Hickok in 1863.
FROM THE ETHEL HICKOK COLLECTION, KANSAS STATE HISTORICAL SOCIETY

Gravestone of D. C. McCanles and James Woods in the Fairbury, Nebraska, Cemetery.
AUTHOR'S COLLECTION

73 ★ NORTH CAROLINA *[Sarah Shull]*

LAW DIVISION.

3—254.

SPSK, Ex'r.

#1622

Certificate No. *56 3752*
Pensioner *Philip T. De Vald*
Service *A. T. Colo. Cav.*

Department of the Interior,

BUREAU OF PENSIONS,

Washington, D. C., *Oct. 14/99*, 1____

SIR:

Relative to your above cited claim, you are hereby notified

that *Sarah De Vald* ____, whose post-office address

is *Johnson City* ____, county of ____

State of *Tenn* ____, did, on *Aug. 18/99*, 1____, file

an application to have one-half of your pension paid *to her*

____

under the provisions of the act of March 3, 1899, on the ground that you

have deserted her for a period of six months or more,

____

Thirty days will be allowed you to file such evidence in the premises as you

may deem necessary. All evidence must be under oath.

This letter should be attached to and filed with your reply.

Very respectfully,

Philip T. De Vald
Mount Vernon
Montgomery Co.
Ga.

NOV 10 99

Acting Commissioner.

9756b10m3-99

0-2

Notification to Philip DeVald that Sarah had filed for one half of his Civil War pension. War of the Rebellion Pension File, XC-02 692 569, Philip T. DeVald.
VETERANS ADMINISTRATION OFFICE, WASHINGTON, D.C.

The Shull Cemetery at Shulls Mill, North Carolina. Sarah's grave is at the far right.
AUTHOR'S COLLECTION

Grave of Sarah's mother, Phoebe Shull, in the Shull Cemetery. AUTHOR'S COLLECTION

Remains of the foundation of Sarah Shull's one-room cabin. The spring can be seen at the far center right. AUTHOR'S COLLECTION

Shulls Mill around 1920. The little cabin behind the Robbins Hotel at far center right is where Sarah spent the last few months of her life in 1932.
APPLACHIAN COLLECTION, APPLACHIAN STATE UNIVERSITY, BOONE, NORTH CAROLINA

Graves of Sarah and her daughter in the Shull Cemetery at Shulls Mill, North Carolina.
AUTHOR'S COLLECTION

III. OKLAHOMA

ED SHORT

"He Feared Neither Man nor the Devil"

*T*HESE WORDS WERE USED TO describe U.S. Marshal Ed Short by a fellow law officer one day following Short's mortal gunfight with "Black-Faced Charley" Bryant, a notorious member of the Dalton Gang. Anyone who avidly reads western American history is familiar with the results: the death-dealing shoot-out at the railroad depot in Waukomis, Oklahoma. Outside of this famous shoot-out, Short remains no more than a footnote in history. [1]

There are no detailed descriptions or in-depth characterizations of Ed Short. *The State Journal* in Topeka, Kansas, described Short as "about 32 years old [actually 26], of medium height and good-looking." *The Oklahoma Daily Times Journal* wrote, "Small in stature, quiet in manner, dudish in dress, he was not a man to inspire fear." [2]

As to Short's character, what does exist is contradictory. According to former Oklahoma governor Thomson B. Ferguson in an interview in 1920:

> A martyr to law enforcement! He gave his life to a commonwealth in an effort to protect society, and organized government. Among the many tragedies of the border, when brave men were risking their lives, and giving their all in defense of the law, there is none sadder than the one connected with the passing on of Ed Short. He was one man who died too soon. He was a man the people could not afford to lose. Brave, cool and ever ready to take the lead in time of danger but never following in the rear.

While on the marshal's force in Oklahoma, if bad men were to be hunted, he was among the first to volunteer for the task.

A dead shot, quick as a flash with a gun, yet he was not a man killer by choice. His plan was to capture without shooting when it could be done, yet there was not a "bad man" on the border that he was afraid to go up against under any kind of circumstances, favorable or unfavorable. [3]

The other side of the coin was reported in *The Oklahoma Daily Times Journal.*

The west has produced many such characters such as Ed Short. His class was a shade higher than that of a desperado, yet he was a bad man. He was a bad man in the sense that he was a dangerous man. There was little of the bravado about him. He was totally unlike the dime novel hero, yet he reveled in deeds of blood and more than one man in Oklahoma will breathe easier now that he is dead. [4]

Although there are two schools of thought as to the character of Ed Short, there can be no controversy over his stormy early life and the reason why he came west.

Charles Edwin Short was born at his grandfather Short's home in New Marion, Indiana, on October 27, 1864. His father, Charles Cassel Short, born June 16, 1834, in Switzerland County, Indiana, and mother, Lucinda Mink Short, born on October 7, 1844, in Ohio, were married in Osgood, Ripley County, Indiana on January 27, 1864. Charles Edwin was the only son and the oldest of the four children. He was called Ed to distinguish him from his father. Ed's three sisters were Mary Frances, born November 12, 1866; Ida Dorothy "Dode," born December 19, 1868; and Martha "Mattie," born December 19, 1870. [5]

The Shorts were one of the first pioneer families to settle in Indiana Territory. Ed Short's grandfather Joseph Short was born on February 21, 1804, and according to the *Versailles Republican*:

At the age of six years, Mr. Short crossed the Ohio River with his Father, March 25, 1810, and proceeded to carve out a home in the wilderness of the Indiana Territory, with only Indians for neighbors. A cabin was constructed on the farm just inside the Ripley County line near Barbersville, Ind. and the farm is still in the possession of the family. In 1812, during the second war with Britain, there were several families in the vicinity and the Indians becoming hostile, a fort or blockade house was erected on Mr. Short's farm for mutual protection and saved the community on several occasions from being massacred by the noble red man, and the sentries never relaxed their vigilance during the continuance of the struggle. Mr. Short has been a resident of the state almost 72 years. [6]

Ed Short grew up in the little town of Osgood, in southeast Indiana, about twenty-five miles west of where Ohio, Kentucky, and Indiana converge along the Ohio River. His childhood was typical of small-town, rural nineteenth-century America; he had close ties to both his family and his community. In June 1878 he reportedly appeared in a music recital at the Osgood Methodist Church and went on to graduate from Osgood School in 1883. However, young Short was also exposed to open lawlessness at an early age, for Osgood, since the end of the Civil War, had been the headquarters for a widespread gang of criminals and horse-thieves. This may have had a great impact on Short, influencing him to take up a career as a lawman.

Ed's father had served in Company A of the Thirty-seventh Indiana Volunteers during the Civil War and rose to the rank of captain. Because of ill health, he resigned from service in early 1864. He was then appointed assistant assessor for the Fourth Internal Revenue District and moved to Osgood. The Shorts purchased a house in Osgood on October 15, 1867. Charles was later appointed deputy collector for the Fourth District by Governor Cumback, a position he held until he was forced to resign on May 1, 1881, again because of ill health.

On September 21, 1881, Charles C. Short died at his home in Osgood. For several months he had been bedridden, and on September 6 he dictated his last will and testament. He left all his real estate and personal property, which included three pension drafts valued at one thousand dollars each, to his wife, Lucinda, with instructions to make a loan of their proceeds on mortgage securities and real estate for a term of ten years only. In essence, Charles Short left his family substantially well provided for.[7]

Seventeen-year-old Ed was now the head of the family, and in March 1882 he joined several other young boys to work in a stone quarry in Westport, Indiana. Within a month, his mother became ill and Ed returned to Osgood, where he went to work as a clerk in the Glasgow Store. In Osgood he was considered quite a ladies' man, enlisting this comment in 1884 in an article titled "Bouquet of Bachelors," "Ed Short—Changes his love like his winter clothes & chooses a new mate every Valentine's Day."[8]

Most young boys during their adolescence suffer intimidation and harassment at the hands of a local bully. Ed Short was no exception. His nemesis was Frederick Wagner, a boy who was stronger and more aggressive than Short, even though they were basically the same age. The enmity between the two began when both were children, and several confrontations occurred until they reached early manhood, with Wagner always the victor. In most cases, these childhood difficulties diminish with time and maturity; however, in this instance it ended violently.

The fatal day was May 12, 1883, and Ed Short was eighteen years old. That morning Frederick Wagner was in an agitated state of mind and, as the day wore on, became intoxicated and had confrontations with several people. In the afternoon Wagner fell in with a young man named Col Harlan, who further agitated Wagner by repeatedly calling him a coward and goading him on, telling him that when he undertook to do something, to make "sure work of it."

At six that afternoon, Ed Short and his friend Newt Smith were walking west on the Osgood depot platform, when they were hailed by Wagner, who approached Short and asked him if he wanted to "thump" him. Short told him no. Wagner was not to be put off and stated, "If you want to whip me, I am here now and now is the time to do it." Short replied that he did not want to whip him. Persistently, Wagner repeated, "If you want to whip me, I am here now." Defensively, Short began backing up and asked Wagner to go away and leave him alone. Taking a stone from his pocket, Wagner threateningly advanced on Short, who quickly drew a pistol.

Wagner continued to pursue Short as he walked rapidly backward. Friends of the assailant tried to persuade him to leave, but Wagner was spoiling for a fight and paid them no attention. After retreating about a hundred feet, Short stopped and told Wagner to stop or he would shoot. Paying no heed to the warning, Wagner kept advancing and asked Short why he did not fire. In his frustration, Short held his fire, retreated another forty feet and made another stand, warning Wagner that he didn't want to shoot him, but if Wagner came another step, he would.

Wagner foolishly continued his pursuit. Short backed up again and, when Wagner was in the act of hurling the stone at him, fired two quick shots at his antagonist at a distance of fifteen or twenty feet. Wagner turned away and walked a step or two before staggering and falling to the ground. In a daze, Short walked away. Forty-seven hours later, Wagner was dead. [9]

Ed Short was immediately arrested and jailed by Constable Richard Watts. The next day, May 13, Short was released on two thousand dollars' bond, furnished by his mother and six citizens of Osgood on condition "that the said Charles E. Short shall personally appear before the judge of the Ripley County Circuit Court on the first day of next term." [10]

Ed Short came very close to never coming to trial. On June 10, 1883, a devastating cyclone struck Osgood. When the tempest hit, Ed was standing outside his home and was literally picked up and hurled to the ground, severely spraining his shoulder. Two other men were killed during the storm. [11]

On September 6, 1883, in the courtroom at Versailles, the grand jury under foreman Joseph Newman indicted Charles E. Short for murder in the second degree and for carrying a concealed weapon. Ed was held in the Ripley County jail from September 11 through 14. The case was highly emotional as well as controversial, generating these remarks from the *Republican*:

> The indictment was for murder, in the second degree, and no criminal case for many years at this place was more ably prosecuted and defended, and no case in the history of the county elected so much interest. This maybe accounted from the fact that the dead Frederick Wagner and Charles E. Short, the defendant, both belonged among the best families in the community. [12]

It took a year and a half after the killing before Ed Short came to trial, on November 20, 1884. The State was represented by prosecuting attorney William G. Holland, and the defense was handled by Jud Berkshire, who entered a plea of self-defense for his client. Selection of a jury took up the first two days, and the next several days were spent presenting the evidence. Two more days were required for summation and arguments from both sides. At nine o'clock in the morning on November 30, the jury began its deliberation.

After eight hours of weighing the evidence, the jury returned to the courtroom at 5:30 p.m. with the verdict: not guilty. It had been a harrowing ordeal for the whole Short family and apparently took its toll on young Ed Short.

Besides covering the case in great detail, *The Ripley County Journal* stated that reporter Kent Stiles from *The Cincinnati Commercial Gazette*, who covered the Short trial, misled the public as to the aftermath. According to *The Journal*:

> That a mob was organized, either of German Catholics or any other nationality or religious denomination, to do violence to Ed Short is a bare and bold falsehood. Such a thing was never thought of, and had it been Peter Wagner, the father of the victim, would have been the first and fiercest in denouncing it. Opinion differed at the time of the tragedy, does now, and will hereafter, so long as the merits and memory of the case exist as to whether Short was warranted in doing what he did. The law justified it, and everybody acquiesces in the verdict.

Stiles also referred to Wagner as a drunkard and hinted that both the prosecution and defense were on opposite sides of the political fence and that the trial was no more than a battleground for political adversaries. *The Journal* also debunked these accusations, remarking:

> Mr. Stiles should practice reporting dog fights and mule races until his puerility and prejudice had become trained in the laws of sincerity, system and syntax before writing upon a subject involving a disputed principle, diversified elements and distinct phases. [13]

Even though the jury agreed that Short was justified in shooting Wagner, the whole affair was shrouded in controversy that would stain Short's reputation for as long as he remained in Osgood. Whether or not he feared mob violence, in May 1884 Ed Short bid his family good-bye and headed west, reportedly for Emporia, Kansas. [14]

Short's stay in Emporia was apparently brief, and there is evidence that he also spent time in Caldwell, Kansas, during the town's waning period as a booming cattle town. The most authoritative book on the Kansas cowtowns, *Why the West Was Wild*, gives this description of Caldwell:

> Sharing the spotlight [with Dodge City] from 1880 through 1885 was Caldwell, the self-styled "Border Queen." Like Wichita, Caldwell had been on the Chisholm trail since the town was established in 1871, but lack of railroad facilities prevented her from achieving status as a trail-end resort. Finally, in 1880, this deficiency was eliminated by the coming of the Cowley, Sumner & Fort Smith railroad (operated by the Santa Fe) and for the next six years Caldwell challenged Dodge City for the cattle trade. [15]

If Short did spend some time in Caldwell, his stay there was also brief:

> Short lived in Topeka [Kansas] several years and was known about town as a quiet man who never sought a quarrel and never backed out of one. He drove a laundry wagon for McMillan for some time. From here he went to Dodge City. . . . [16]

It was apparently during the year 1886 that Ed Short went to Dodge City, where he made the acquaintance of Samuel Newitt Wood, a man who would have great influence on the young man's future. Wood, born in Mount Gilead, Ohio, on December 30, 1825, became a prominent figure in Kansas, arriving there in its infant days in July 1854. Settling on a claim near the hotbed abolitionist town of Lawrence, he became a leader in the free-state party. In 1859 Wood left for Chase County and represented the county in the territorial legislature in 1860–1861. He was a member of the state senate in 1861 and served an additional four terms in the state legislature. Wood also founded the first newspapers in Cottonwood Falls and Council Grove, and later an additional two in Woodsdale. [17]

In 1885 Sam Wood became interested in an area soon to become Stevens County, located in the southwest corner of Kansas and bordered by the neutral strip, the panhandle of Oklahoma known as No Man's Land. Through Wood, Short would soon be embroiled in the bitter and bloody county-seat war in Stevens County.

A contingent of men from McPherson, Kansas, formed the first settlement in the area in 1885, naming it Hugoton. Plans were quickly made to organize Stevens County and to establish Hugoton as the county seat. It is evident that widespread fraud was practiced and would have gone unchecked if not for Sam Wood.

On July 3, 1886, from Mead Center, Kansas, Wood sent his partner, I. C. Price, to the area to locate land for a rival town. Price, who was unknown to the residents of Hugoton, located a section of government land on the north side of the sand hills about eight miles east of Hugoton. While in Hugoton, Price discovered that a fraudulent census was being taken to ensure formation of the county.

Wood soon arrived at the new town site and offered free lots to anyone who would settle in the new town named Woodsdale. People flocked to Woodsdale, including many residents of Hugoton, and wood shanties sprang up everywhere.

Around the first of August, Wood and Price held a ratification meeting regarding the fraudulent census, which had been procured from Topeka and showed a population of 2,662 inhabitants, including two hundred pairs of twins and at least 1,200 fictitious names. Kansas law required all organized counties to have a minimum population of 2,500 residents. The town employed Wood to take legal steps to halt further proceedings in the organization of Stevens County, and he immediately left to present these findings to the governor.

The residents of Hugoton were fully aware of Wood's intention and issued a bogus warrant charging him with libel. They captured him at a dugout near the Cimarron River and returned him to Hugoton, where a mock trial was held and bail was refused. Wood was placed under guards, who proceeded to take him across the state line into the neutral strip until the organization of Stevens County was ratified. To cover his absence, a story was circulated that Wood had been paid off to abandon the fight and had gone into the territory to hunt buffalo.

None of Wood's friends believed the story, and a group of twenty-four Woodsdale men under Captain S. O. Aubrey trailed the Hugoton kidnappers to the headwaters of the Beaver River, where they rescued Wood and captured the Hugoton party. Aubrey took the prisoners to Garden City, Kansas, where civil and criminal charges were brought against them. All their goods were sold to pay the court costs, and Wood bought them at a public auction. The charges were later dismissed without trial. Nevertheless, the Hugoton group got what they wanted, because on August 3, 1886, Governor John A. Martin issued a proclamation for the organization of Stevens County, and in 1887 the legislature passed an act legalizing the preceding actions.

On September 9, 1886, an election was held that fanned the oncoming flames of violence. Hugoton was chosen as the county seat, but Wood made a bitter enemy of Sam Robinson when he chose John Cross over Robinson as candidate for sheriff. Although the election was contested by the Hugoton residents, Cross was declared the winner, which further angered Robinson.

Forty-year-old Robinson was a native of Kentucky and considered a dangerous man who had killed at least two men. He was town marshal of Woodsdale and owned the local hotel, but when Wood bypassed him for Cross, Robinson immediately left for Hugoton and became town marshal and constable. This left the town marshal's job in Woodsdale open, and Wood sent for Ed Short to fill the vacancy.

For a year and a half the situation remained tense but quiet until Wood sponsored a railroad bond issue that would bring the railroad to Woodsdale and Voorhees and bypass Hugoton. Naturally, the Hugoton residents opposed the measure, and a meeting between the opposing forces was held in the neutral town of Voorhees in May 1888. An altercation took place, and Sam Robinson struck Deputy Sheriff James Gerund on the head with his revolver, knocking him to the floor.

Within a few days, a warrant charging Robinson with assault and battery was given to Ed Short to execute. With two Woodsdale men accompanying him in a buckboard, Short rode to Hugoton. The most comprehensive account is this report in *The Oklahoma Daily Times Journal*:

> Robinson was standing in the door of his office on the west side of Main Street, keeping close watch on Short, when the latter rode quickly up to him and thrusting his revolver towards him, fired, at the same time crying, "I have a warrant for you." He missed his mark and Robinson jumped inside the door and pushing the barrel of his gun through a broken window pane returned the compliment paid him by the Woodsdale officer. Short rode away to the north firing as he ran. Half a block down

the street was J. B. Chamberlain, chairman of the board of county commissioners, standing in front of his grocery store. As Short rode by he sent two balls crashing through the front of the store, but neither took effect on Chamberlain, at who they were aimed.

The poor marksman and his race horse kept right on down the street and across the prairie to Woodsdale. His companions in the buckboard didn't linger in Hugoton a minute after Short began his flight and they, too, struck out across the prairie. Pursuit was given by Robinson and others. Short had a good lead as did the men in the buckboard, but the latter paying little attention to the road ran into a plowed field and found their progress retarded. Seeing that they were likely to be captured they cut the traces and mounting the horses rode into Woodsdale with short tugs.

In the meantime, the railroad bond election had been held, and a dispute arose as to the regularity of the returns. Armed conflict seemed imminent. Sheriff Cross wired Governor Martin and requested that the militia immediately be sent. Two companies of militia under the command of Brigadier General Murray Myers arrived and set up camp on June 19. Finding both towns fortified and willing to fight it out, General Myers remained in the area until satisfied that no action would be taken by either side. The militia broke camp on June 24, and General Myers wrote Sam Wood of the imprudence of placing the arrest warrant for Robinson in Short's hands.

The situation quietly simmered until July 22. At Voorhees, Short learned that Robinson and his companions, who were accompanied by their families, were on a pleasure trip across the state line in the neutral strip. Short returned to Woodsdale, rounded up a posse of seven men, and started in pursuit. They found their quarry preparing dinner at a ranch owned by a man named Patterson. Surrounding the ranch, Short sent a courier to Woodsdale for reinforcements and then ordered Robinson to surrender within ten minutes or he would fire on the house. Fearing the worst from Short and his men, and not wanting to endanger the women and children, Robinson waited for a chance to escape. When the guard on the south side of the house left his post to confer with Short, Robinson rushed from the house, mounted his race horse, and dashed off to the south. Short and four men quickly gave chase, firing at the fleeing horseman. They doggedly followed Robinson the entire day, but the fugitive was better mounted and finally outdistanced the posse. Upon their return to the Patterson ranch, they found that Robinson's companions had also escaped.

Receiving Short's request for assistance, Sheriff Cross and four men, Theodocius Eaton, Rolla Wilcox, Bob Hubbard, and Herbert Tonney, headed for the neutral strip, where they searched for Short. Failing to find the marshal, they stopped for the night at a haymaker's camp near Wild Horse Lake on the evening of July 25.

Learning of Robinson's plight, several of his Hugoton friends organized a rescue party and headed for the neutral strip. They reportedly overtook Short and his men and chased them twenty-five miles until they reached safety at Springfield in Seward County.

Somewhere along the way, Robinson joined up with the Hugoton rescuers and within a short time reached the camp where Sheriff Cross and his posse were sleeping. What occurred became known as the Haymeadow Massacre, one of the most atrocious acts of violence on the western frontier.

Riding into the camp, Robinson called out for everyone to surrender. Cross, Tonney, and Hubbard immediately stood up and raised their hands. After telling Cross, who was unarmed, to give up his weapons, Robinson deliberately shot and killed the sheriff with a Winchester. He then turned and shot down Hubbard. Tonney was then gunned down by J. B. Chamberlain, the chairman of the Stevens County board of commissioners. Tonney lived to tell the tale by feigning death. The other two members of the posse, Wilcox and Eaton, had been asleep in a wagon and at the sound of gunfire had tried to escape. Eaton was killed by Robinson when he attempted to run for his horse, and Wilcox was caught, brought back into camp, and executed by Robinson. Thus ended the Haymeadow Massacre and, for all practical purposes, the Stevens County War.

The militia were again called out, and the area was virtually placed under martial law. Arrests were made, but no court had jurisdiction, since the act took place in No Man's Land, a territory where no federal administration of justice had been established. Only the diligence of Sam Wood settled the jurisdiction problem, and six of the guilty parties, except ringleader Sam Robinson, who escaped to Colorado, were indicted and tried in July 1890 in federal court at Paris, Texas. All were convicted and sentenced to hang.

In December an appeal was made and argued before the Supreme Court. On January 26, 1891, Justice Harlan gave the decision that No Man's Land was not attached to the Eastern District of Texas and the court had no jurisdiction, so the convictions were reversed and a new trial was ordered. Efforts to discontinue prosecution were successful, and the men were never tried again. In the fall of 1889, Sam Robinson was convicted in El Paso County, Colorado, for robbery of a U.S. post office and sentenced to fourteen years at the Colorado State Penitentiary at Canon City. He was released on January 30, 1898, and disappeared.

Ed Short's mentor, Sam Wood, was to meet a tragic end three years later. According to George Rainey's *No Man's Land*:

> Sam Wood won a great victory at the memorable trial at Paris, but his troubles were not ended. A district judge, Theodosis Bodkin [Theodocious Botkin], had been impeached by the Kansas house of representatives, but the senate failed to convict him. He laid the cause of this impeachment at the door of Sam Wood who was a resident of his district. A complaint was later filed in Judge Bodkin's court charging him with bribery. On June 23, 1891, he went to Hugoton to face the charge. A few minutes before Mr. Wood arrived Judge Bodkin adjourned court and walked across the street. The colonel [Wood] was about to enter the court room (a small church building in which court was held) when a Hugoton man, James Brennen, approached and shot him in the back. The

Colonel ran when Brennen again shot twice, both balls taking effect, the last being through the brain causing instant death. Colonel Wood fell at the feet of his wife who, pointing an accusing finger at Judge Bodkin, exclaimed as did Nathan of old, "Thou art the man."

Judge Botkin was disqualified from trying the case, the prosecution was barred from making an application for a change of venue, and the court was faced with the fact that it would be impossible to hold an impartial trial in Stevens County. Consequently, Brennen was never tried for Wood's murder. This was the last act in the Stevens County War. [18]

Shortly after the end of the Stevens County conflict, Ed Short headed south to a new frontier, the territory called Oklahoma. By 1889 he had settled on the western edge of Oklahoma in the newly created town of Hennessey. Short's reputation as a lawman during the Kansas troubles preceded him, and he was made city marshal. [19]

On April 22, 1889, Oklahoma was opened for homesteading, and thousands upon thousands of determined settlers flooded the area to stake their claims. Following in their wake came the unsavory element: claim jumpers, renegades, crooks, outlaws, and all-around desperadoes who swarmed to the border area between Oklahoma and the Indian territories. It soon became known as Hell's Fringe. [20]

This influx of criminals prompted the hiring of more U.S. deputy marshals, including Ed Short. He was sworn in and appointed to the area around Hennessey and Kingfisher on December 19, 1889, by R. L. Walker, U.S. marshal for the District of Kansas. With a force of twenty deputies to patrol the district, Walker made this statement regarding the conditions they had to face:

> That there was a vast multitude of people crowded into said Territory on April 22, 1889, and thereafter, from all sections, from all classes and kinds of men and women; that gamblers, robbers, prostitutes and villains generally congregated in said Territory in great numbers, men and women dangerous and desperate, with whom it was unsafe to come in contact, and realizing that they were governed by no law, and fearing none, his deputies had a trying time indeed; and yet they discharged their duty with such judgment, consideration, and fidelity that there was less murder and robbery during their administration of affairs in Oklahoma Territory, not withstanding its chaotic condition and peculiar combination of peoples, than could be found probably anywhere else in the United States among the same number of people. In the discharge of these duties these deputies were necessarily alert always, night and day, and neither weather nor opposition deterred them in such discharge of duty. [21]

Undoubtedly the most notorious and well-known gang of desperadoes in the area were the Daltons. Gang leader Robert Dalton and his brother Gratton were former U.S. deputy marshals who, tiring of the toil of a lawman's life for so little remuneration, turned to a life of crime. Their younger brother Emmett, a cowboy on the Bar X Bar Ranch and part-time posseman for his brothers, easily fell in with Bob Dalton's schemes.

Starting out as horse thieves in July 1890, they soon upgraded their criminal activities into the fine art of train robbery. Forming a loose-knit band of six followers, the gang held up the Texas Express on May 9, 1891, at Wharton, a small way station on the Santa Fe railroad around sixty miles south of the Kansas border. The take was nearly eighteen hundred dollars.

Immediately after the robbery the station agent at Wharton wired the news, and a large force of U.S. deputy marshals was sent in pursuit. A special train was dispatched to Wharton from Oklahoma City and Guthrie with fresh horses and additional deputy marshals, one of whom was Ed Short. For forty days the lawmen unsuccessfully combed the area. It was the greatest manhunt in the area's history.[22]

If the frustration of not finding the Daltons was not enough, the news of Sam Wood's death in late June totally enraged Ed Short, and *The Oklahoma Times Journal* reported that the young marshal threatened to kill Theodocious Botkin if he presided over the trial of Wood's killer. When Botkin heard the news, he supposedly fled to Topeka, Kansas. *The State Journal* stated that U.S. Marshal Walker and his deputies declared that they did not believe Short ever made the threat. Deputy Leon DeBost said:

> Short was not that kind of man. If he had shot Botkin I should not have been surprised but he never told what he was going to do until it was done. He feared neither man nor the devil.

Botkin was later disqualified, but this would not matter to Short, who would also fall to a killer's gun two months to the day after his friend's death.[23]

For two days following the Wharton robbery, the Dalton Gang furiously rode westward until they reached a safe haven at the ranch of Jim Riley in the Cheyenne-Arapahoe country. By mid-summer the manhunt had subsided, and the gang headed north and east toward Wagoner and another train holdup. After three days of traveling, one of the gang, Charley Bryant, came down with one of his frequent bouts of malaria and was left at a cowboy camp at Buffalo Springs near Hennessey.[24]

There are two versions of what followed. George Rainey in his book *The Cherokee Strip* stated:

> Saturday, August 2, 1891 [actually August 2 fell on a Sunday], Marshal Short received a tip that the outlaw was at a deserted cow camp a few miles over the Strip line and slightly ill. He sent George Baldwin, a mere youth, to induce him to come to Hennessey. Aided by his youth, young Baldwin succeeded in disarming the bandit of suspicion and accompanied him to Hennessey where he engaged a room at the Rock Island Hotel then managed by a Mr. Thorne. No sooner was he assigned to a room than young Baldwin sought the marshal and informed him of the outlaw's location.[25]

According to Glenn Shirley:

Bryant remained at the cow camp two weeks, and his condition grew worse. Finally, he became so dangerously ill that the cowboys persuaded him to let them take him to Hennessey for medical treatment. A doctor examined the outlaw and ordered him to bed. He was placed in an upstairs room at the Rock Island Hotel with his rifle and six-shooter beside him.

Short saw Bryant when the cowboys brought him in. While the pain-racked outlaw tossed on his bed, too sick to sleep yet too groggy to remain fully awake or cautious, the marshal thumbed through warrants and reward posters and read the description of Black-Faced Charley. [26]

Not much is known of Charley Bryant. Author Harold Preece called him moody, sardonic, and ready to shoot at a drop of a tin cup. Shirley stated he was a "rail thin, sinister looking, trigger-happy fellow with shining black eyes" who once told Emmett Dalton, "Me, I want to get killed—in one hell-firin' minute of smoking action." Charley Bryant would get his wish. [27]

Contemporary accounts by people who knew him show a different side of "Black-Faced Charley" Bryant. Former Oklahoma governor Tom Ferguson claimed he knew Bryant when they were small boys on the Neosho River near Emporia, Kansas, where they went to district school together. *The Oklahoma Daily Times Journal* stated that the outlaw was a native of Decatur, Wise County, Texas, where his parents and relatives still resided and were regarded as highly respected and wealthy people. He came to the Cherokee Strip around 1881 and earned his nickname after a saloon shoot-out that left the left side of his face powder-burned.

In 1920 Ferguson also reported that while traveling in a covered wagon with his wife and two children in 1890, they stopped at the Turkey Creek ranch on the south side of the Cimarron trail for directions. Although Ferguson did not immediately recognize Bryant as the one who gave him the directions to the Cimarron Crossing, he later stated, "He was one of the most courteous, accommodating fellows that one ever met. No one would have dreamed that he was even then a member of an outlaw gang . . . ." [28]

Mr. C. P. Wickmiller, an early resident of Oklahoma, also knew Bryant, and during an interview in 1937 he made these comments about the outlaw:

> Charlie Bryant was an old-timer in Oklahoma and stayed in the Cherokee Strip in a camp. He was a very good shot and practiced pulling his six-shooter to see how quick he was with his gun; he was considered one of the best shots in camp but also one of these slow, easy-going fellows with no bad habits. Sometimes he would leave camp for a month or so but when he returned there was very little he would say concerning his absence. The last trip he made was when the Santa Fe was held up at Red Rock [Wharton robbery] although no one thought of his being connected with the robbery. [29]

Regardless how Ed Short recognized Bryant, he was determined to arrest the outlaw and made this prophetic remark: "He will kill rather than be killed and I know it, but there have been such men taken." [30]

The marshal visited with the hotel manager, Ben Thorne, and his sister, Jean Thorne, who worked at the hotel and took Bryant his meals and medicine. On August 22, unaware of Short's purpose, the Thornes inadvertently informed him that the outlaw was well enough to be moved.

After Short produced a "Wanted" poster for Bryant, Thorne advised the marshal to arrest the outlaw when his sister took him his evening meal but also insisted he go along to protect her. The only way to reach Bryant's room was an outside stairway, and the two men hid themselves in the hallway corner. Jean Thorne ascended the stairway, knocked at the door, spoke to the bandit, and opened the door. Rushing past the woman, the two men entered the room and leveled their revolvers at the startled outlaw. "Hands up! You are under arrest," ordered Short, and Bryant, taken completely by surprise, was handcuffed before he had time to reach his weapons.

Even with the outlaw secured, Short faced a dilemma. There was no jail at Hennessey, and the possibility of Bryant's rescue from the nearest jail at Guthrie by his outlaw cronies had to be considered. Short decided to take him to the federal jail at Wichita, Kansas. Since the next train to Wichita was not due until 5 p.m. the next day, Short sat up all night of August 22, guarding his prisoner. By the next morning, Short badly needed rest, and he turned Bryant over to the Rock Island agent, R. C. Overton, for safekeeping. Overton was a very cautious man and handcuffed the complaining bandit's hands behind him.

That afternoon, Bryant claimed he needed exercise because of his illness and asked Overton to escort him through town. Overton obliged, and as it was Sunday, when many people were strolling around town, the outlaw became the center of attention. Upon entering J. H. Cryder's general store, Overton noticed three suspicious men loitering about. Keeping an eye on the trio, he spotted one of them slipping a revolver into a pile of blankets. When the agent quickly retrieved the weapon, the three men fled from the store.

Just prior to the train's departure, Short, carrying Bryant's weapons plus his own revolver, took possession of his prisoner. To thwart any rescue attempt, Short received permission to keep his prisoner in the mail-and-baggage car. Upon boarding the train, Bryant painfully pleaded with the marshal to handcuff his hands in front, and the marshal complied. Short would pay for this act of compassion.

When the train was under way, Bryant, seemingly in high spirits, proclaimed his innocence, boasting that the first judge he faced would set him free. As the train reached Waukomis, the first station stop to the north, Bryant suddenly quit talking. Spotting several riders on the prairie, Short suspected a rescue attempt and pulled a Colt six-shooter from his waistband, handed it to the baggage man, and told him to keep an eye on the prisoner. Grabbing Bryant's Winchester rifle, Short stepped to the platform between the baggage car and the smoker to keep his eye on the oncoming horsemen.

The baggage man apparently did not comprehend the seriousness of the situation and carelessly thrust the revolver into a pigeonhole used for sorting mail. Leaping from his seat, Bryant grabbed the revolver at the same time conductor Jim Collins entered the car. The outlaw pointed the revolver at both men, then quietly opened the vestibule door and saw Short on the platform beginning to turn in his direction.

Having satisfied himself that the riders were only cowboys, Short turned to enter the car and saw the danger he was in. As he swiftly raised the rifle, Bryant's first slug slammed into his left shoulder and exited through his back under the right arm. Automatically firing from the hip, the mortally wounded marshal managed to send a bullet into the outlaw's chest.

The furious gun duel that continued was nothing short of phenomenal. Short kept levering shells into the rifle and firing as fast as he could, putting every shot into Bryant's body. The bandit grimly held on, firing a slug through Short's right arm and sending a wild shot through the wall of the smoker, wounding Caldwell implement dealer John Dobson in the forearm. Bryant was still shooting wildly as he fell headlong on the platform.

Short was dying on his feet, but his adrenalin kept him going, as he grabbed Bryant by the leg and called to Collins to help pull the nearly dead outlaw into the baggage car. Before collapsing, Ed Short groaned, "The damn bastard got me, but I got him. I wish I could see Mother." By the time the train halted, both men were dead.

When the train reached Enid, Oklahoma, a telegram was sent to railroad officials with orders to ship the bodies to Caldwell, Kansas. Both bodies were prepared for burial by the Schaeffer Undertaking Parlor. Bryant's body was shipped to Arkansas City, Kansas, where relatives from Decatur, Texas, claimed the outlaw's remains. [31]

U.S. Marshal William C. Grimes, Ed Short's superior, paid for all the undertaking bills, purchased an elegant $150 casket, and shipped Short's body to his mother's home in Osgood, Indiana.

The train bearing Ed Short's remains arrived in Osgood on the evening of August 26 and was met by his mother and three sisters. The next afternoon funeral services were conducted in the Short home by the Reverend Guthrie, a Methodist minister. Ed Short was buried next to his father in the Glendale Cemetery in Osgood, and the local newspapers sang his praises. [32]

On September 3, 1891, a letter of appreciation for Ed Short's actions was written to U.S. Marshal Grimes by G. M. Foulk, general claims agent for the Santa Fe Railroad. A portion of this letter reads:

> I beg leave to advise you that I have today made voucher in favor of Mrs. L. M. Short of Osgood, Ind., for $500, the amount of the reward offered by this company for the arrest and conviction of each and every one engaged in the robbery of our train No. 403 near Wharton, O.T. May 9.
>
> While the conditions under which the reward was to be paid were for the arrest and conviction, yet the company concluded not to stand on any technical point in the case, having sufficient proof to lead them to believe that Bryant was one of the men engaged in the robbery, and for the further fact that C. E. Short lost his life in the efforts to bring Bryant to justice, the Co. concluded to pay this amount to the mother, Mrs. Short, regardless of any legal rights they may have in the matter. [33]

So the young man who left his home in Indiana under a cloud of darkness got the wish of all such young men; he came home a hero. The tragedy was that Ed Short never knew it.

This photograph of Ed Short, taken around 1885 or 1886 in Topeka, Kansas, is the only known photo of him. It was furnished to the author by Mary Manship, director of the Ripley County, Indiana, Historical Society. Mary wrote of the photograph, "It was found in an old desk in back of a drawer. The desk was bought at an auction. It was in an album belonging to the Thum family, distant relatives of Ed Short's uncle by marriage. The inscription under the picture read: Ed Short 'Shorty' who went west."

State of Indiana
County of Ripley } SS.

We Charles E. Short, John O. Cravens,
Wm H. Smith, Jacob E. Willson, Chas. W. Adams,
Lucinda M. Short, E. H. Row, W L S Jones.
owe the State of Indiana two thousand (3000) dollars to be levied
of our property.

The condition of the above
is, that if the said Charles E. Short
_____ shall personally
appear before the Judge of the Ripley
Circuit Court State of Indiana
on the first day of the next term
thereof to answer to a charge
of Assault and Battery, on one
Fred Wagner with intent to
kill the said Wagner, and
abide the order of the court and
not depart thence without
leave, then this recognizance
shall be void; else to remain
in full force,

Witness our hands and seals this 13th
day of May A.D. 1883,

Ewing H. Row   [seal] Charles. E. Short,   [seal]
L. M. Short   [seal] Jno. O. Cravens,   [seal]
Wm. Claypool,   [seal] Wm H. Smith   [seal]
W. L. S. Jones   [seal] Thomas E. Willson   [seal]
                            Chas. W. Adams   [seal]

Ed Short's bond for the killing of Frederick Wagner in 1883. Ripley County Circuit Court Case No. 1231, State of Indiana vs. Charles E. Short.

CLERK OF THE RIPLEY COUNTY CIRCUIT COURT, VERSAILLES, INDIANA.

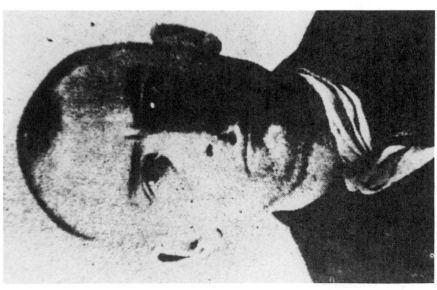

Left: Sam Robinson, Ed Short's adversary in the Stevens County War. COLORADO DEPARTMENT OF CORRECTIONS, CANON CITY, COLORADO

Right: Samuel Newitt Wood, close friend and mentor of Ed Short in Kansas. KANSAS STATE HISTORICAL SOCIETY, TOPEKA

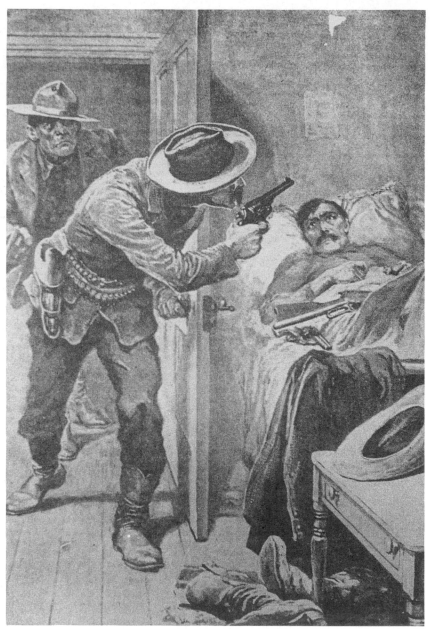

Artist's sketch of the arrest of "Black-Faced Charley" Bryant by Ed Short and Ben Thorne. From Wide World Magazine, *July 1918.*

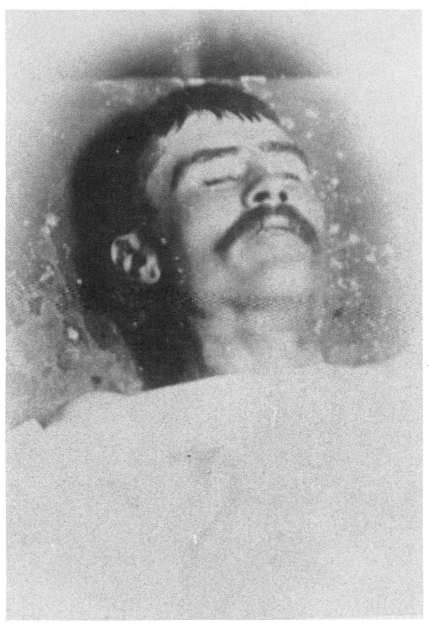

Charles "Black-Faced Charley" Bryant in death at the Schaeffer Undertaking Parlor in Caldwell, Kansas. Photo taken from the Wells Fargo Mug Book.

COURTESY GREG MARTIN, SAN FRANCISCO, CALIFORNIA.

*Ed Short's tombstone in the Glendale Cemetery, Osgood, Indiana. The inscription reads,
"Charles E. Short Son Of C. & L. Short Died Aug. 23, 1891 Aged 26 yrs. 9 mos. 26
days."* AUTHOR'S COLLECTION

Main Street, looking north, Waukomis, Oklahoma, 1910. OKLAHOMA HISTORICAL SOCIETY,
OKLAHOMA CITY.

IV. NEW MEXICO

PUNCH COLLINS

Gone Glimmering

A BRIGHT MOON WAS SHINING down on the small village of Escondida, New Mexico, a little before seven o'clock on the evening of October 30, 1884. It was six days before the election of Grover Cleveland as the country's twenty-second president. But politics was not on the minds of the five men who rode to the railroad tracks, some distance from the village, and dismounted. Four of these men were of average height and weight, but the fifth was a hulking, powerfully built man of over six feet and weighing nearly two hundred pounds. Most of the native New Mexican residents were just finishing their dinner or doing evening chores when these men attempted, with a monkey wrench, to unscrew a splice plate that held the rails in place. If anyone had seen them, there would be no doubt of their intentions — to derail a train and rob it.

Failing to remove the plate, they pulled up their crude handkerchief masks with eyeholes and frantically piled rocks on the tracks before the approaching train arrived. Their plan was for two of their number to rifle the express, two others to prevent the trainmen and passengers from leaving the train, and the big man to hold up the engineer and fireman.

Engineer James Skuce, driving Atchison, Topeka & Santa Fe Railroad's train No. 102, spotted the bandits and the moonlit pile of rocks on the tracks at the same time. Skuce was not a fainthearted man, and as the robbers shouted for him to halt, he squatted down in the engine with fireman George Scott, slammed the throttle wide open, and plowed his way through the rocks.

The frustrated bandits fired about twenty shots at the train as it roared past them. *The Albuquerque Evening Democrat* reported:

The robbers: for such they undoubtedly were, fired about a hundred [sic] shots into the train, one ball at Conductor [J. D.] Hedrick, who was standing on the platform of a coach, one passing through the cab of the engine, one lodging in the mail car and two in the sleeper. In the latter car a lady named Mrs. Amparo de la Guardia, from the City of Mexico, narrowly escaped death. The bullet came whizzing through the window of the Pullman, passing through the bed on which she was preparing to repose, and after having spent its force on the opposite side of the car, falling into the lap of her sister, who was also preparing to retire for the night. After running a short distance at a high rate of speed, the train was slowed up. One of the boldest of the robbers then galloped up to the engineer and engaged him in conversation.

In the confusion, the larger man took control of the robbery and rode up to the engine, ordering Skuce, "Hold up now, for I have got you." The engineer quickly replied, "Don't shoot, and I will get down." The brakes were off when the train slowed down, and Skuce again put on the steam and sped out of danger with a trainload of excited passengers, leaving the dumbfounded bandits in his wake. The passengers were so impressed with the heroic actions of engineer Skuce that they raised a purse of money and presented it to him. [1]

Completely outwitted, the five would-be train robbers rode to the village of Escondida and poured out their wrath on the town. They fired several shots into the house of Vivian Baca and alarmed the other residents of the settlement before riding to an *acequia* (irrigating canal) outside of town. One of the residents quickly mounted his horse and rode rapidly toward Socorro, three miles to the south, to inform the authorities. As he passed the *acequia*, two shots were fired at him by the bandits, but he put the spurs to his horse and reached Socorro in record time. The five bandits knew that it would not be long before a posse would take their trail, and they quickly headed southwest before splitting up. [2]

The attempted train robbery was in no way remarkable, but it was unique in one respect. The large man who attempted to take control of the robbery was black. Most people in the United States have always been fascinated with the Old West, which is proven by the host of movies, TV productions and popular dime novels depicting this colorful era. We tend to relate to tarnished heroes in our own ethnic groups. For instance, the whites have Jesse James, the Hispanics have Joaquin Murietta, and the Indians have Henry Starr. While researching New Mexican history, I ran across a reference to the train robbery attempt near Socorro, New Mexico, in which the spokesman was black. His name was Punch Collins, and here is his story.

Punch S. Collins, whose true family name was reported as Brockman, was born in Caldwell County, Texas, in 1858. In every document and newspaper article, he reported that his first name was Punch. This is probably correct because Collins was born in slavery and the name was likely given to him by the family who owned him. Around 1867, Punch's family went to work for James D. Reed of Goliad County, Texas. [3]

Born in Alabama in 1830, Reed came to Goliad County at age fifteen. He served in the Confederate army during the Civil War and was wounded and taken prisoner at Arkansas Post in 1863. This wound caused him to lose an arm, which earned him the nickname "One-Armed Reed." In 1867 Reed began buying cattle for other cattlemen and was one of the first to take the cattle trails to Louisiana and then Kansas after the war. In 1877 Reed bought a ranch near Fort Worth and continued to run it until 1883, when he sold it. With his partner, Wes Bruton, he started another ranch in Socorro County, New Mexico. [4]

At age fifteen, Punch Collins was out on his own but continued working for Reed. The bond between the white rancher and the black cowboy was strong, which is proven on Collins' New Mexico Penitentiary record where he listed J. D. Reed of Fort Worth, Texas, in the column titled "Nearest Relative or Friend." Collins was considered a good worker and, according to *The Las Vegas Daily Optic*, "enjoyed the good opinion of his employers."

Around the latter part of 1883, Collins went to work for Reed's partner, Wes Bruton, on their ranch, fifty miles west of Socorro, New Mexico. Reed and Bruton had bought the ranch from Joel Fowler for $52,000 in early October. Fowler immediately went to Socorro, banked his money, and went on a drunken binge. He caused such a disturbance that a group of citizens surrounded him and were attempting to take him to jail when he pulled a knife and stabbed Vermont native James Cale to death. In the early hours of January 22, 1884, a mob took him from the jail and hanged him on a nearby cottonwood tree. The lynching of Fowler would have a profound effect on Collins and his four cohorts. [5]

Around May 1884, Bruton hired a cowboy named Edwin White. He was described as a light-haired, light-complexioned average-sized man with light blue eyes who was not overly bright. A year younger than Collins, he had come to New Mexico from Johnson County, Texas, in 1882 and had worked on the Tom Slaughter ranch in Socorro County before Bruton hired him. Another cowboy who apparently worked for Bruton was twenty-six-year-old Jefferson Kirkindall from Goliad County, Texas. Collins and these two, plus two other cowboys—J. W. Pointer, twenty-six, from Jefferson County, Texas, and Bill Allen, thirty, from Llano County, Texas—struck a friendship that would subsequently lead to the botched train robbery.

Bruton discharged Collins for some reason around September 1884, and he headed for his own small ranch on the Hilosa River above Bruton's ranch. Shortly after this some horses were stolen from Bruton, supposedly by Collins, but this was never proven. It was during September that the five cowboys, tired of working for grubstake wages, planned the train robbery.

In late October, White quit his job on the Bruton ranch and moved nearby to a cabin owned by a man named Scott on Short Horn Cattle Company land. A few days before the robbery, the would-be bandits were seen in Socorro by a prominent citizen who described them as hard cases wearing broad-brimmed sombreros and cowboy-style clothing. On October 30, the five men headed for a canyon northeast of Socorro, remained there until dusk, and rode to the railroad tracks near Escondida, where they executed their fiasco.[6]

The courier from Escondida reached Socorro a little after 8 p.m. and hailed Sheriff Pete Simpson on Mananares Avenue. Simpson hastily gathered a posse of a few men, including his deputy, T. J. Terry, and headed for the little village at a dead run. A body of twenty citizens under F. A. Thompson soon followed by rail in an engine and caboose secured from H. Moorehouse.

Reaching the robbery scene, the two posses found the pile of rocks scattered around the rails, horse tracks, some footprints, and the discarded monkey wrench, which was discovered beside the railroad tracks by Deputy Sheriff Hunter. The unmounted citizens posse traveled by rail to Alamillo, where they escorted a waiting southbound train to Socorro. Deputy Terry returned to Socorro on October 31 and reported that Simpson and his posse had trailed the fugitives westward to the Snake Ranch. On November 9 the outlaws were reported as heading west with a herd of stolen horses. On the tenth, *The Albuquerque Evening Democrat* left is readers with a sardonic remarks, "The Socorro train robbers have gone glimmering, as it were."[7]

As soon as A. T. & S. F. railroad division superintendent P. F. Barr in San Marcial received news of the robbery attempt, he offered a reward of five hundred dollars each for the bandits. By November 12 the reward had been raised to $2,200 for each man. Barr also assigned Harry Franklin to investigate the case. Franklin, a former city marshal at Las Vegas and now depot watchman for the A. T. & S. F. at Demming, was a shrewd lawman and discovered that the monkey wrench had been stolen from the Bruton ranch. A size-ten footprint found at the robbery site was apparently identified by Bruton as belonging to Punch Collins. Franklin shadowed both Collins and his pal Ed White, collecting evidence, while the sheriff and his posse continued chasing phantoms.

On November 10, Deputy Sheriff Rose went to Scott's cabin and captured White after ordering him to throw up his hands. The bandit offered no resistance. On the same day, Franklin and Wes Bruton converged on Collins' house, where Bruton bravely walked up to the burly bandit and pulled Collins' six-shooter from its holster while remarking, "I'm sorry, Punch, but I'll have to arrest you." Franklin then stepped out from the side of the house and took charge of the big man. Both prisoners were taken to the Windsor Hotel in Socorro and held under guard. Franklin would never share in the reward due to his employment with the railroad.

That evening, the two prisoners were questioned, prompting this report in the November 12 edition of *The Las Vegas Daily Optic*:

> White is also a cowboy, not over bright, and was finally induced to squeal on the gang. He has given the names of the three other members of the gang, and it is expected that they will be in the clutches of the law before another day rolls by. For obvious reasons their names are withheld for the present.

Punch Collins was questioned by F. A. Thompson, and when confronted with the evidence of his large footprints being found at the crime scene, he remarked rather humorously, "Well, boss, I guess those big feet gave me away. They been always gettin' me into trouble."[8]

The officials were worried that their prisoners would shortly become victims of mob violence and decided to send them to Santa Fe for safekeeping. Harry Franklin, with Collins and White heavily ironed, boarded the first train out at three o'clock the next morning. Following their incarceration at Santa Fe, both bandits expressed relief at getting out of Socorro alive. Collins said he was glad to shake the dust of Socorro from his feet because he was afraid they would repeat the Fowler act on him. With their fears lessened in Santa Fe, both prisoners now proclaimed their innocence, saying they were arrested to shield the real criminals.[9]

The New Mexico newspapers had conflicting views of the bandits and their capture. *The Albuquerque Evening Democrat* purported, "This is fortunate for the territory, as it would have been quite a drawback to our development if a regular James gang had been able to obtain a permanent foothold among us." *The Santa Fe New Mexican Review* gave its readers a more rational view when it described the would-be bandits as "greenies."[10]

Law officers across the territory were anxious to put the remaining members of the gang behind bars and were somewhat overzealous when they captured a cowboy named Richard A. "Lon" Bass in Arizona. Bass was in charge of a herd of cattle and was delivering them in Arizona when he was arrested near Duncan around November 11 by Deputy Sheriff Stocking, Charley Allen, and Dick Reynolds. Bass was taken to Socorro on November 13 by Deputy Sheriff J. E. Boss and turned over to Sheriff Simpson. Bass had associated with the five bandits but stated he had a dozen men who would swear he was with them in Socorro on the night of the robbery. He was cleared of the charges on the nineteenth.[11]

No more than two days after the arrest of Bass, the officers had better luck. Deputy Sheriff Stocking of Deming, who had helped capture Bass, arrested J. W. Pointer and took him to Albuquerque, where he was transferred to Santa Fe. Jeff Kirkindall's arrest on November 13 was vividly described in the November 21 issue of *The Las Vegas Daily Optic*:

> On last Sunday Charley Russell and Wes Bruton brought in Jeff Kirkindall, one of the supposed would-be train robbers, and sent him to Santa Fe. They found him at Horse ranch, about 110 miles west, on last Thursday night, and although they expected to find him there they came upon him unexpectedly, and throwing their weapons down on him commanded him to throw up his arms, when he put his right hand to his hip pocket to draw his gun, but recognizing Mr. Bruton, said: "Is that you, Wes?" and when Mr. Bruton answered in the affirmative he said: "Well, then I give up, but if it had been one of those d--m detectives I would have sold out." The prisoner frequently remarked afterward that he regretted that he gave up so easily.

F. L. McLean, of Socorro, took Kirkindall to Santa Fe on November 18 for safekeeping.[12]

On Wednesday, November 19, the four prisoners were returned to Socorro and arraigned in Territorial District Court on charges of assault with intent to kill and obstructing railroad tracks. Collins, Kirkindall, and Pointer were scheduled to be tried the next day.

The trial was held under Judge Bell and was prosecuted by District Attorney Charles McComas. At first the defendants pleaded not guilty to all charges. Then the court dropped the assault charges, which were stricken from the record on March 30, 1885, and the three defendants pleaded guilty to obstructing railroad tracks. On the twenty-first they were sentenced to seven years imprisonment in the Kansas State Penitentiary at Lansing, as the New Mexico Penitentiary was still under construction. The next day they were taken by train to the Kansas penitentiary by Special Deputy Sheriff A. M. Case of Socorro.

Because of Ed White's confession and testimony, his trial was delayed until December 1, and he received a reduced sentence of five years in the Kansas penitentiary. In the custody of Harry Franklin, White was hustled aboard the train for Kansas that afternoon. [13]

Collins, Kirkindall, and Pointer entered the Kansas State Penitentiary on November 24. White's turn came on December 4. *The Las Vegas Daily Optic* of December 8 quoted this article from *The Topeka Commonwealth*:

> An officer from New Mexico, named Franklin, arrived in the city yesterday [December 4] morning from Socorro, New Mexico, with another of the train robbers, captured in that country. This man [White] claims to be the son of a Methodist minister and gave the gang away. He was sentenced for five years; the three others were sentenced to seven years. The fifth man is still at large. Franklin took his man to the penitentiary yesterday.

A later edition of *The Las Vegas Daily Optic* stated that White's real name was Norwood and that he was wanted for murder at Tascosa, Texas. [14]

By late March 1885, Bill Allen, whose actual name was Frank Nichols, was finally captured. Detectives had trailed him throughout Arizona, but reportedly he returned to Socorro, where he was identified and arrested. He was brought before Judge Bell on March 30, pleaded guilty to obstructing railroad tracks, and was sentenced to seven years imprisonment in the Kansas penitentiary. Placed in the custody of Harry Franklin, Allen was taken to Lansing the same day and entered the penitentiary on April 2. [15]

On February 28, 1886, the five convicted Socorro bandits were transferred to the newly constructed New Mexico Penitentiary near Santa Fe to complete their sentences. On March 14, 1884, the New Mexico legislature had authorized the construction of a penitentiary two miles from the Plaza de Santa Fe at a cost of $150,000. By August 17, 1885, the penitentiary was ready to receive the first batch of prisoners. [16]

When Punch Collins and his four cohorts entered the new penitentiary on March 2, it housed only 106 other convicts. On November 29, 1886, Ed White unsuccessfully attempted to escape, yet he was the first of five luckless bandits to leave the penitentiary. He went out feet first, having died of consumption on March 12, 1887. Jeff Kirkindall, who was the son of a prominent family in Goliad County, Texas, was pardoned by Governor Rose on January 20, 1889. Collins, Pointer, and Allen were all released with good time in 1889, the first two on August 21 and Allen on December 30.

All of the New Mexican newspapers that covered the story of the five would-be bandits named at different times White, Kirkindall, and Allen as the leader of the gang. Not once did they refer to Collins as the chief, yet it was the burly black man who was the spokesman during the attempted robbery, and it was his presence of mind and quick thinking that stopped the train. The robbery would undoubtedly have been successful if engineer James Skuse had not been as quick-thinking as Collins. The man was black, and that unquestionably was the reason the others got the credit for leadership.

It had been the first imprisonment for all of the Socorro bandits, and as far as it was known, for four of them it was their last. Following their release from the New Mexico Penitentiary, they apparently fulfilled the prophecy of *The Albuquerque Evening Democrat*: "The Socorro train robbers have gone glimmering. . . ."[17]

This photograph was taken in Socorro County in 1884 by freelance photographer J. E. Smith, who was working as a cowboy at the time. Since black cowboys were almost non-existent in this area and the fact that this photo was taken at the time Punch Collins was in Socorro County, it is probable that this is a photo of Collins. COURTESY J. E. COLLECTIBLES, SOCORRO, NEW MEXICO.

Socorro, New Mexico, circa late 1880s. NEW MEXICO INSTITUTE OF MINING AND
TECHNOLOGY, SOCORRO.

*Windsor Hotel, Socorro, New Mexico, where Punch Collins was held after his capture in
November, 1884. The hotel was destroyed by fire in 1905.*
COURTESY J. E. SMITH COLLECTIBLES, SOCORRO, NEW MEXICO

Socorro; Obstructing &c,
R.R,

No. 686

TERRITORY OF NEW MEXICO

versus

J. W. Sowter, Punch Collins,
Edwin White, Jefferson Kirkendoll
and Bill Allen

A TRUE BILL

Antonio Abeytay M,

Foreman of Grand Jury,

Filed in my office this *19th* day of
Nov, 188 *4*

Edmund H. Smith
Clerk

WITNESSES

James Skuer
J. D. Hedrick
F. M. Atchison
George D. Scott
W. G. McGee
Thomas Scott

C. H. Moonhouse
R. B. Featherston
M. McLeish
J. W. Hunter
Vivian Baca

Nov. 20, 1884 — J. W. Sowter
arraigned & pleads guilty,
Punch Collins arraigned &
pleads guilty.
Jefferson Kirkendoll arraigned
& pleads guilty.
Edmund H. Smith clk

Dec. 1, 1884 — Deft. Edwin
White arraigned &
pleads guilty — Sentence
5 years —

Edmund H. Smith
Clerk,

Deft Bill Allen ar-
raigned, pleads guilty,
& sentence 7 years,
Mch. 30, 1885,
Edmund H. Smith clk

Above and pages 109 & 110: Bill of indictments and charges against Punch Collins and his gang for the attempted train robbery near Socorro, New Mexico, in 1884. Socorro County District Court Records, Criminal Case No. 686.

STATE OF NEW MEXICO RECORDS CENTER AND ARCHIVES, SANTE FE

TERRITORY OF NEW MEXICO | ss.   IN THE DISTRICT COURT:
COUNTY OF _Socorro_   AT THE _November_ TERM, A. D. 188_4_

THE Grand Jurors for the Territory of New Mexico,
taken from the good and lawful men of the County of _Socorro_ of the Territory of
New Mexico aforesaid, duly elected, empaneled, sworn and charged at the term aforesaid, to enquire in and for the
County of _Socorro_ aforesaid, upon their oaths do present that _J. W. Pointer,
Punch Collins, Edwin White, Jefferson Kirkendale and Bill Allen
whose full names are to the Jurors aforesaid unknown_,
late of the County of _Socorro_, Territory of New Mexico on the _Thirtieth_
day of _October_ in the year of our Lord One Thousand Eight Hundred and Eighty
Four at and in the County _of Socorro_ aforesaid: _With force and arms
wilfully, maliciously and feloniously did put place, cast
and throw in and upon the railroad track of the New
Mexico and Southern Pacific Railroad Company, then and
there being a corporation formed under the laws of the Territory of New Mexico aforesaid, divers stones and other obstructions with intent thereby then and there to throw from and
off the said track certain locomotives cars and trains then and
there being, contrary to the form of the statute in such case made
and provided, and against the peace and dignity of the Territory of New Mexico._

-- _Second Count._ --

_And the Grand Jurors
aforesaid, upon their oaths aforesaid do further present that
J. W. Pointer, Punch Collins, Edwin White, Jefferson Kirkendale
and Bill Allen, whose full names are to the Grand Jurors aforesaid unknown, late of the County of Socorro aforesaid, on the thirtieth day of October, one thousand Eight hundred and Eighty four, at the County of Socorro aforesaid
with force and arms, wantonly, wilfully, maliciously and
feloniously did put, place, throw, cast and pile upon and
across the railroad track of the New Mexico and Southern
Pacific Railroad Company then and there being a corporation formed under the laws of the Territory of New Mexico,
divers obstructions and stones, said acts being then and there
calculated to endanger the safety of the locomotives cars and
trains then and there running upon said track, contrary to
the form of the statute in such case, made and provided and
against the peace and dignity of the Territory of New Mexico._

Third Count.—

And the grand jurors aforesaid, upon their oaths aforesaid do further present that J. W. Pointer, Punch Collins, Edwin White, Jefferson Kirkendale and Bill Allen whose full names are to the Grand Jurors aforesaid unknown, late of the County of Socorro, on the thirtieth day of October one thousand Eight hundred and eighty four, at the County of Socorro aforesaid, with force and arms, wilfully, maliciously and feloniously did put, place, cast, throw and pile in, upon and across a certain rail road track of the New Mexico and Southern Pacific Rail road Company then and there being a corporation formed under the laws of the Territory of New Mexico, divers stones and other obstructions with intent thereby, then and there, feloniously to cause a Collision between certain locomotives, cars and trains upon said track, then and there being, and the said stones and other obstructions and obstacles so as aforesaid in,upon and across the said rail road track, put, placed cast, thrown and piled Contrary to the form of the statute in such case made and provided, and against the peace and dignity of the Territory of New Mexico.

contrary to the form of the statute in such case made and provided, and against the peace and dignity of the Territory of New Mexico.

Charles C. McComas

District Attorney for Second District of New Mexico.

Socorro County Courthouse, built in 1884, where Punch Collins and his Confederates were tried in November of that year. COURTESY J. E. SMITH COLLECTIBLES, SOCORRO, NEW MEXICO

V. ARKANSAS

PETE LOGGINS

Doctor, Lawyer, Ladies' Man, Thief

PETE LOGGINS WAS POSSIBLY the most extraordinary character to emerge upon the American western frontier during the nineteenth century. During his lifetime he was a licensed attorney, a physician, a pharmacist, an elected public official, and a newspaper editor and writer. Looking at Loggins' dark side, he was also a murderer, a forger, a thief, a jailbreaker, a bigamist, and a convict. This may be difficult for the reader to believe, but documentation substantiates these assertions. For example, consider these words from Loggins' court records in the Texas Court of Criminal Appeals: "It was shown that defendant was at various times in his life lawyer, doctor, and newspaper editor." [1]

Pete Loggins was a charismatic man with a keen mind and a quick tongue. His persuasive powers allowed him to exert his will over others, and he was hell on wheels with women. He was either a genius or very close to being one, and that was the crux of his problem; he believed he could outsmart and outfox everyone and was bold enough to try to prove it. In Loggins' own words, taken from his letter to Texas governor Joseph D. Sayers in 1901 requesting a pardon, he related what he considered the core of his trouble:

> But the hardest fight of my life has been to overcome an impetuous, unbending and obdurate temper. And as I now look back retrospectively over the blackened and charred field of my life I can very clearly see that most of my trouble is alone attributable to hard-headed obstinacy . . . . I was never "fussy"; but I was quick to form prejudices and slow, very slow, to either forgive or forget. [2]

His life was like a rubber ball, continually bouncing up and down. He bulldozed his way across East Texas with abandon and taunted lawmen with his audacity, daring them to catch him, which they never did. It took the State of Arkansas to bring about Loggins' downfall; hence, the reason for crediting this story to that state.

Pete's grandparents, Samuel and Susannah Loggins, were from Maury County, Tennessee, in the exact center of the state. In the late 1830s or early 1840s, they migrated with their ten children to San Augustine County, in what was then the Republic of Texas. Pete's father, William Henry Loggins, at twenty-seven married fourteen-year-old Harriet Sanders in the town of San Augustine on February 23, 1851. Pete, whose rightful name was Louis Lynn Loggins, was the firstborn, entering the world in San Augustine on February 6, 1854. The Loggins had three other children, Mary E. in 1856, Susannah in 1859, and another son, N.C., in 1865.

In the early 1870s, Pete went to Jasper, Texas, where he studied law under a local attorney or law firm. There he met and courted Mary Elizabeth Gilbreath, a Louisiana native who was two months his junior. The two were married under a magnolia tree on February 19, 1873, by a justice of the peace in Jasper. Pete didn't waste any time, and in two years he had fathered two children: John Edgar on November 23, 1873, and Maud Elizabeth on August 27, 1875. [3]

Obviously Loggins' reputation as a rising young lawyer grew, for in 1876 he ran for county attorney of Jasper County. He was elected for a two-year term on February 15, 1876, qualified for the office on April 18, and was commissioned on June 14. Pete's mother died during that year, but at least she had the pleasure of seeing him elected to public office. [4]

At the end of his term in November 1878, Loggins moved his family to the southern part of San Augustine County, ten miles west of Brookeland and the Sabine County line. He then purchased, edited, and published one of the most famous early Texas newspapers, *The Redlander*. During this period, Pete fathered two more children, Louis Lynn Junior in 1877 and Anna in March 1880.

There is a family story that Loggins vividly described and glorified the exploits of the James Gang to some of the local boys who hung out at the newspaper office. His graphic commentary was so infectious that he actually persuaded them to head for Missouri, where they robbed a bank and were caught. [5]

Pete published his newspaper for nearly three years before devising his first crooked scheme, in the fall of 1881. The George English survey of 1,107 acres lying in Sabine County was unclaimed in 1881, and Loggins concocted a plan to illegally obtain title to this land. Using his knowledge of law, he did not find it hard to forge a deed; however, he needed outside help. Through persuasive eloquence and a promise to share in the spoils, he prevailed upon Abraham Smith, a forty-six-year-old mill owner in Brookeland, Texas, to sign his name as a witness on the forged deed.

On October 13, 1881, Loggins drew up the fraudulent deed, noting that he had purchased the land from William Gibson of Calcasieu Parish, Louisiana, and then forged Gibson's name. Smith signed the deed and the next day took it to the county clerk's office in Leesville, Vernon Parish, Louisiana, where he took an oath that he had witnessed the transaction. On October 17, Loggins filed the bogus deed at the Sabine County clerk's office in Hemphill, Texas.[6]

Within a few months Loggins had sold part of this land, and soon a bitter conflict developed over the division of the money, Smith claiming that Loggins had not paid him his share. The disgruntled mill owner threatened to disclose the fraud to the authorities if Loggins did not come across with the money. Loggins warned Smith he would kill him if he talked. The matter was not resolved, and the hostility continued until late summer.

In early September 1882, Smith blew the whistle on Loggins to the authorities in Sabine County and agreed to be a state's witness. Loggins was indicted and arrested for forgery on September 9. Before reaching the Sabine County jail in Hemphill that night, Pete escaped but was recaptured within minutes. Upon reaching Hemphill, he was taken into court, where bail was set at $1,500. Loggins was unable to raise this amount and was remanded to jail. Following his capture and incarceration, Pete let it be known that he would kill Smith when he got out. The officers did not realize what a calculating prisoner they had locked up, and after eight weeks behind bars, Loggins broke jail.[7]

Pete was determined to carry out his threat against Abe Smith, and instead of leaving the country, he fled to his parents' home in San Augustine, where his wife and family were residing. He concealed himself in the woods near his parents' house and had his wife bring him provisions. He carefully laid his plans for revenge, waiting until early July before making his move. Assuming that Smith had relaxed his vigilance, Pete scouted an area between Smith's house and the mill at Brookeland and found a perfect spot for concealment in a thicket near the road. With his .38-calibre Winchester, a sack containing boiled guinea-hen eggs, a tin of soot to blacken his features, and a quart whiskey flask filled with coffee and cream, Pete Loggins began his vigil.

At dusk on the inauspicious day of Friday the thirteenth in July 1883, Pete got his revenge. Abe Smith was returning to his house from the mill and had no idea of the fate that awaited him. As Smith passed the thicket where Loggins hid, two rifle shots were fired into his back, dropping him to the ground. To make absolutely sure that Smith was dead, the gunman ran to his fallen victim, placed the muzzle of his Winchester on the back of the dying man's head, and fired, powder-burning his hair.

In the excitement of the moment, Loggins immediately fled back to San Augustine County, leaving all of his belongings at the scene of the murder. When Loggins applied for a pardon in 1901, he vehemently denied having murdered Smith. All the articles found at the murder site, however, were traced to him, and it was noted that the only .38-calibre Winchester in the area belonged to Pete Loggins. The Sabine County officials took six months to investigate the killing, and on February 2, 1884, Loggins was indicted for the murder. A second indictment was issued on February 11, 1885.[8]

Meanwhile, the ups and downs in the life of Pete Loggins took an upward swing, and he began the study of medicine. Pete had left the San Augustine area soon after the killing, but let him tell it in his own way:

> Prior to my indictment for murder I was fired upon from ambush on two different occasions, presumably by the relatives of Smith. . . . To satisfy my alarmed wife I went away; and having noted the advantages a medical education would give a lawyer, and having received one course of lectures, I entered a medical college fully intending to make medicine an adjunct or auxiliary to law.

The only medical college that was operating in Texas at this time was the Texas Medical College at Galveston, and it was here that Loggins must have studied. Since he was wanted for forgery and murder, his name and description had undoubtedly been sent to law officers throughout East Texas. For this reason, Loggins likely entered medical school under an alias.[9]

A little more than a year and a half later, Pete was back in San Augustine County, and his life now took a downward plunge. He decided to set right an injustice, and in the process, he committed another crime. Loggins masterminded the jailbreak of the Conner clan, who were locked up in the Sabine County jail for murder. The complete story of the Conners and the so-called Sabine County War is recorded in the author's forthcoming book *Judge Not*. Here is a brief summary of their troubles.

The Conners, father and six sons, were an illiterate clannish ranching-and-farming family living in the south of Sabine County. In late 1883, four of them were involved in a shoot-out over hog range, and two men were killed. Five of the Conners gave up peaceably and were bound over for trial after a preliminary hearing. A year later, two of the Conners were convicted in a trial in which the evidence was blatantly concocted and witnesses perjured themselves to ensure conviction. One of the Conners, who was nowhere near the scene of the killings, was sentenced to twenty-five years imprisonment. The other, Fed Conner, was granted another trial on an appeal but was again convicted and sentenced to life; however, he was still in the Sabine County jail when the jailbreak occurred. The other three Conners had been held in jail a year and three months without coming to trial.

Jim Sanders, a cousin of Pete Loggins, was a neighbor of the Conners, and it was likely through him that a meeting was set up in early February 1885 between two of the Conner clan and Pete Loggins to discuss the jailbreak. Loggins became the leader, taking charge of the planning and organization. Through his influence and persuasive clout, Pete united fifteen men into the scheme. These men realized the injustice that had been done, and it took little to persuade them to set the Conners free.

One of the jailbreakers, Sterling Eddings, said Loggins became involved because the Conners had helped him escape jail in 1882. This is completely false, however, and Loggins likely told the story to keep the conspirators united. Pete Loggins' third cousin, G. Clyde Lewis of San Augustine, told the author in 1982 that Loggins was paid a fee by the Conner family to organize and carry out the jailbreak, which is probably the truth of the whole matter. [10]

The jailbreak was scheduled for the night of March 15, but because of personal problems in the Conner family, the plan was aborted. On the night of March 25, the liberation of the Conners was carried out. That evening the men gathered on a little knoll near Geneva, Texas, and rode to the outskirts of Hemphill, where they left Wade Noble in charge of the horses, including three for the jailed Conners. The rest of the men proceeded to the jail, posted guards, and broke down the jail door. The three Conners and their rescuers quickly made their way back to the horses and fled to their respective homes.

It was that simple and would have remained so if Wade Noble had not told the whole story to a woman who held a grudge against one of the jailbreakers. She told the story to the authorities in Sabine County. On September 10, 11, and 12, 1885, most of the jailbreakers were indicted. Although Loggins' name is absent in the indictments, he was included in the case of *The State of Texas vs. W. E. T. Ogeltree et al.* Under the column "Orders Present Term" was this entry, "Cont [Continued] on app [application] of State for testimony of Lisk Conn and Lewis Loggins (sick)." This was only a ruse, because Pete had no intention of giving testimony with a forgery and murder indictment hanging over his head. By the fall of 1887, nine of these men had been convicted and served prison terms for their participation, but not Loggins. He would pay later. [11]

All hell broke loose in East Texas following the jailbreak. To counteract the accusation of complicity in the jailbreak and failure to capture the fugitives, Sabine County sheriff William Smith fired off a letter full of exaggerated fears to Governor John Ireland on May 20. Here is an excerpt:

> I would respectfully represent to you that the said Loggins is at large and owing to the sparcely settled portions of this [Sabine], San Augustine and Angelina Counties and the number of persons in said portions of said counties are favorable to him, the said Loggins. And as Loggins is now the leader of band composed of the escaped prisoners 'To wit' Willis, Fed, William and John Conner and they with said Loggins having a number of relatives and friends to watch aid and assist them my work has been of no avail and unless I can prevail on you to offer a good reward for Loggins and also Willis, William, and John Conner so that I can put detectives on their track it does seem to me to be impossible to capture them. . . . L. L. Loggins is a man of good sense and unless captured I fear he will organize a band that will be a terror to civilization.

Governor Ireland responded to the sheriff's letter on May 25 by issuing a reward proclamation of three hundred dollars and extradition papers for Pete Loggins for the murder of Abe Smith.

This "terror to civilization" theory was ludicrous, to say the least. The Conners went right back to southern Sabine County and, with caution, continued their lives as if nothing had happened. Loggins returned to San Augustine County. Albeit the jailbreak was a criminal offense, Pete Loggins saw himself as a fighter of injustice and had the audacity to send word to district court judge James I. Perkins that he would personally see to it that the Conner trouble would end if it could be handled in court in a civilized manner. Perkins indignantly retorted that he would make no compromise with a violator of the law. [12]

In early February 1886, Judge Perkins sent a letter to Governor Ireland requesting aid in running down the Conners and Loggins. Like Sheriff Smith, Perkins gave this exaggerated view of the situation:

> Ex Senator Weatherred informs me he will visit Austin the latter part of this week for the purpose of endeavoring to obtain from you such State aid as will be calculated to effect the arrest of the outlaws Loggins and Conners who are still at large and not only terrorizing this and San Augustine Counties but it is believed by me and those best informed as to their character and intuitions imperiling the lives of many good citizens of this section.

At the time Perkins wrote this letter, Pete Loggins was long gone from San Augustine County. Nevertheless, Perkins got his way, and on March 18 a detachment of Texas Rangers arrived in Sabine County. [13]

Now that Loggins' career as a lawyer, newspaper editor, doctor, elected public official, murderer, forger, thief, and jailbreaker has been established, it is time for a look at Pete Loggins, ladies' man. In 1982 Pete's third cousin, G. Clyde Lewis, told the author that Loggins always carried a little black book with more than four hundred women's names in it. Although there is no record of Loggins' infidelity up to this point, no doubt Lewis was stating facts, to which Pete's subsequent track record will attest. What he told his long-suffering wife before leaving San Augustine County is not known, but her heartaches were just beginning. If she had been born in the next generation, she very well could have related to Al Jolson's famous line, "You ain't seen nothin' yet."

Loggins probably left San Augustine County during the spring or summer of 1885, but he was definitely back home in January 1886. During that month his wife became pregnant with their fifth and last child, Myrtie Willie Loggins, who was born on October 17. Pete had fled to Sherman, Grayson County, Texas, where using the alias of R. P. Wright, he set up a medical practice. Here he met and courted a local woman named Mattie N. George. The pair were married by Grayson County justice of the peace J. M. Adams on March 31, 1886. Pete must have had a very difficult time handling this delicate situation, sharing his time between his two wives. [14]

In late March 1887 the Rangers came back to East Texas in force, culminating in a devastating shoot-out with the Conners. The manhunt for the Conners and Loggins intensified. By mid-1887, fearing capture and unable to deal with the pressures of his dual matrimonial situation, Pete fled to Little Rock, Arkansas. Here he set up a new medical practice but foolishly continued using the alias of R. P. Wright. It would be his undoing.

While in Little Rock Pete found another woman, twenty-four-year-old Alice White. On September 23, 1887, R. P. Wright bigamously married for the second time, wedding Alice White at Searcy in White County, Arkansas.

Mattie George Wright was made of much sterner stuff than her predecessor, Mary Elizabeth Loggins, and that proved disastrous for Pete Loggins. In late 1887 or early January 1888, Mattie tracked Loggins to Arkansas, where she discovered him living serenely with his third wife. She immediately filed a charge of bigamy against Loggins a.k.a. Wright in White County Circuit Court at Searcy, and on January 25 he was indicted by the grand jury. Pete came to trial on July 20, pleaded guilty, and was sentenced to five years at hard labor at the Arkansas State Prison in Little Rock. He entered the penitentiary on July 24, 1888.[15]

Pete Loggins' roller-coaster life now took its deepest plunge. Before Pete's trial and imprisonment, another Governor's Proclamation offering a reward of three hundred dollars was issued in Texas on October 10, 1887. By early 1888 the authorities in Sabine County received word that Loggins had fled to Arkansas, and extradition papers on the charge of forgery were sent to the governor of Arkansas on April 2, 1888. On June 26, 1889, a third Governor's Proclamation for three hundred dollars reward was issued from Austin.[16]

Pete had his physical problems too. While in the Arkansas penitentiary, he became blind in his left eye. Contrary to rumors that he deliberately put out his own eye, the actual cause was neuralgia that progressed until he lost his sight. He would eventually obtain an artificial eye. This, however, was just the beginning of Loggins' problems.[17]

Around the spring of 1892, a resident of Shelby County, Texas, was visiting the Arkansas penitentiary and recognized the convict R. P. Wright as Pete Loggins. Upon his return to Texas, he passed this information to Shelby County district attorney James T. Polley, who immediately began extradition proceedings. On July 11, 1892, Polley made an application for extradition on the charges of murder and forgery to Governor James Stephen Hogg in Austin, recommending B. F. Sims as agent to bring Loggins back to Texas. A portion of this document reads:

> Penitentiary convict of Arkansas by name of Dr. R. P. Wright has been identified by a man living near here as L. L. Loggins alias Pete Loggins and communication with the Arkansas Penitentiary officials informs me that he is still confined there.

On July 14, 1892, the requisition was approved by the governor's office.[18]

The next step was the release of Loggins, which is somewhat unclear. The old convict records of the Arkansas State Penitentiary generally do not give the date of discharge if the prisoner served his full sentence and records the date only if he is released early or due to extenuating circumstances. If Loggins had been released on the extradition request, the records would have recorded this. The Texas Court of Appeals stated that Loggins served his full five-year sentence, so apparently he was discharged on July

20, 1893. The authorities in Texas had been made aware of this, and the extradition agent took Loggins into custody and brought him back for trial.

As a lawyer, Pete knew just what to do and immediately filed a writ of habeas corpus, and a hearing was held before Judge Hampton Ford in Beaumont, Texas. As a result, Loggins was admitted to bail in the amount of one thousand dollars, which he paid. Pete now did the unexpected: he did not jump bail. With his knowledge of the law, he no doubt thought that he would never be convicted.[19]

In August 1893 Pete Loggins was brought to trial in Sabine County District Court on two charges, breaking jail to rescue prisoners and the murder of Abe Smith. Pete was never tried on the forgery charge as he had killed the only witness against him. Two special judges were brought in for the trials. On August 14, before Special Judge S. W. Blount, Loggins pleaded not guilty and was tried on the jailbreaking charge. On the sixteenth, the jury found him guilty.

The court wasted no time, and Pete's trial for murder began the next day, August 17, under Special Judge Rufus Price. Loggins again pleaded not guilty and was represented by attorney Hugh B. Short. The prosecution brought out that the motive for the murder was a disagreement over money from the sale of the fraudulently deeded land and proved that the articles found at the murder site belonged to Loggins. Pete's defense was extremely weak, according to this report from the Court of Appeals records:

> The defense was alibi, but the testimony supporting it was principally that of his immediate family, and was uncertain in many particulars, indefinite and inconclusive.
> Defendant testified in his own behalf; denied the killing, but told of his escape from jail; his lying in the brush —"on the scout," as he termed it—near his residence; his being furnished with provisions by his wife, and his owning a .38 calibre Winchester.

That did it for Loggins, and the jury found him guilty on the twenty-fourth. On August 25 the court sentenced him to two years for jailbreaking and life imprisonment for murder.

Pete immediately appealed both convictions through his attorney and was brought before the Texas Court of Appeals in Tyler the following October 21. Loggins lost again. Judgment in both convictions was affirmed, and a motion for a rehearing in the murder conviction was dismissed by Judge E. J. Simkins. Regarding Loggins' conviction for murder, Judge Simkins made this statement in the court records:

> The evidence is voluminous, and the inculpatory facts, though mostly circumstantial, are so positive and overwhelming as to leave no question of appellant's guilt, and he stands justly convicted of one of the most deliberate and cowardly assassinations to be found in criminal records.

Pete Loggins entered the Rusk Penitentiary at Rusk, Texas, as convict No. 10057 on December 7, 1893. He was thirty-nine years old, but for some reason he gave his age as forty-five. His stats and physical description read: Height, 5'9"; Weight, 150#; Complexion, Dark; Eyes, Hazel; Style of whiskers, Moustache; Occupation, Physician; Use of Tobacco, Yes; Habits of life, Temperate; Education, Good; Wears #6 Shoe; Bald in front; Left eye artificial; Scar on left breast from shoulder to nipple 1/8 inch wide; Scar underneath left nipple 5 inches long, 3/4 inches wide. The strangest entry on his record is under "Number of years at school," where Loggins listed "three years"; however, he did state in his request for pardon, "I had struggled hard to educate myself and became a lawyer."

Upon entering Rusk Penitentiary, Pete was put to work as a druggist in the prison hospital. Three months later he was transferred to the Texas State Penitentiary at Huntsville and was assigned the job of steward in the prison hospital. For the next eight years, Loggins' record was exemplary, and he built himself an excellent reputation as a medical man. Governor Joseph D. Sayers visited the prison sometime in 1901 and had this to say about Pete:

> When I was down in Huntsville I met Dr. Loggins in the hospital there. He seemed intent on securing the release of two unfortunate boys who were assisting him in the drug department. He brought them before me and discoursed eloquently as to the merits of his young friends. He did not appear to think of himself, and he thereby impressed me most favorably.

No doubt Loggins knew how the governor felt and immediately began his quest for a pardon.

Pete Loggins hustled as he never had before, enlisting the support of many leading citizens of Jasper and Montgomery counties and other important personages throughout Texas. He also had the backing of the officers of the prison, including Superintendent Rice, who recommended the pardon in these words:

> Conduct exceptionally good, and he has rendered most valuable service in the prison hospital and for the further fact that the officers of this prison have strongly recommended executive clemency, I consider the case deserving of especial consideration.

In conjunction with all this support, Loggins wrote a forty-one-page letter to the governor, dated August 20, 1901. It is beyond a doubt one of the most remarkable pardon requests ever written. He argued his case like a lawyer, cited the Bible and Blackstone, discussed social problems, and played heavily on the sympathy of the governor regarding the impoverished condition of his family. He even supplied humor, surely unintentional, when he stated that the reason he was convicted was because the jury consisted of eleven Populists and one Democrat. Governor Sayers was even more impressed, and Pete got his pardon: a Christmas pardon. It was signed on December 13, and Loggins was to be released on December 22. As that day fell on Sunday, Pete Loggins walked out of prison at 2 p.m., Saturday, December 21, 1901.[20]

Unbelievable as it may seem, Pete's first wife, Mary Elizabeth, in spite of all the years of humiliation and suffering, was still waiting for him. Prior to Pete's release, his family and his father had moved to Willis, Montgomery County, Texas. William Henry Loggins, however, never saw his son as a free man, having passed away the same year Pete was pardoned. Upon his release, Pete came to Willis and began practicing medicine. But this trouble-prone man was not to live happily ever after.

Around 1903 Pete Loggins was summoned by Constable D. A. Hooks to examine his young son, who was suffering with a badly infected leg. Pete recommended amputation, and another physician was consulted. Deciding to follow the advice of Loggins, Hooks allowed the operation, and as a result, the boy died. This caused bad blood between the two men. Their bitterness and animosity continued to intensify until it reached its zenith on April 1, 1905. The headlines in *The Galveston Daily News* screamed:

DR. LOGGINS KILLED—TROUBLE OF A PERSONAL NATURE RESULTS IN A TRAGEDY—Willis, Montgomery County, Tex., April 2—The long monotony of peace and quiet, which Willis had enjoyed for many years, was rudely broken up yesterday evening between 5 and 6 o'clock. Some trouble had been pending of a personal nature between Dr. L. L. Loggins, a practicing physician at this place for several years past, and Mr. D. A. Hooks, a long resident here and former deputy Sheriff and Constable of this precinct, but for several months past in night charge of the planning mill and lumber yard of the Carson Morris Company, located at this place. These troubles culminated at the time above mentioned at the Crescent Drug Building in the mortal wounding and subsequent death from these wounds of Dr. Loggins by Mr. Hooks. It seems that Mr. Hooks was inside the building and Loggins was in the act of entering the same armed with a double barreled shotgun, when Hooks met him at the door entrance and opened fire on him with a revolver. Apparently the first shot took effect in the breast of Loggins and so paralyzed him that he was unable to handle his gun and made no shot. Several other shots were fired by Mr. Hooks but missed. Loggins beat a retreat toward his office, but fell before reaching it, and was picked up and carried to his office, where he was attended to by Drs. Leslie and Powell, but their efforts were futile. He expired from internal hemorrhage in about a half an hour.

Mr. Hooks gave himself up to Constable Davis. An examining trial, conducted by District Attorney S. A. McCall was held which resulted in placing the prisoner under $500 bond for his appearance before the next grand jury.

The deceased Loggins leaves a wife and several grown sons and daughters. The funeral occurred at this place this evening.

Hooks was never brought to trial for the killing, likely because of the nature of the feud. [21]

Pete Loggins died as he had lived. No matter what one might think of the man, he had one exceptional characteristic: whatever he did, lawful or unlawful, he did it to the best of his ability.

Sabine County Courthouse in the 1880s. COURTESY THELMA MURRAY, HEMPHILL, TEXAS

Back view of Sabine County Courthouse, which housed jury members. COURTESY THELMA MURRAY, HEMPHILL, TEXAS

Sabine County Courthouse today. The log jail from which Loggins escaped stood where the two cedar trees are growing. AUTHOR'S COLLECTION

*Louis Lynn "Pete" Loggins,
circa 1880.* COURTESY LINDA
PANSANO, OF BRIDGE CITY,
TEXAS, GREAT GRANDDAUGHTER
OF PETE LOGGINS

PROCLAMATION

BY THE GOVERNOR OF THE STATE OF TEXAS.

$ _300 oo_ REWARD.

To all to Whom these Presents shall Come:

WHEREAS, It has been made known to me that on the _____ day of _____ 188_5_ in the County of _Sabine_ _Pete Loggins_ did _Commit Murder_ and that said _Pete Loggins_ (s) now at large and _a_ fugitive from justice:

Now, therefore, I, _L S Ross_ Governor of Texas, do, by virtue of the authority vested in me by the Constitution and Laws of this State, hereby offer a Reward of _Three hundred_ Dollars, for the arrest and delivery of the said _Pete Loggins_ to the Sheriff of _Sabine_ County, inside the jail door of said County. This _within 6 months from this 1st date or conviction thereafter_ Reward is payable only on condition of the arrest and return of said fugitive ~~by virtue of a requisition this day made on the~~ ~~Governor of~~ _____

_____ Agent.

In Testimony Whereof I have hereto signed my name and caused the Seal of State to be affixed, at the CITY OF AUSTIN, this _10_ day of _October_ A. D. 188_7_

(L S)

L S Ross
Governor of Texas.

BY THE GOVERNOR:

Jno M Moore
Secretary of State.

PROCLAMATION

BY THE GOVERNOR OF THE STATE OF TEXAS.

$ 300⁰⁰   REWARD.

To all to Whom these Presents shall Come:

WHEREAS, It has been made known to me that on the _16_ day of _June_ _____ 188_3_ in the County of _Sabine_ _L L Loggins_ did _Commit Murder_ and that said _L L Loggins_ now at large and _a_ fugitive from justice:

Now, therefore, I, _Jno Ireland_ _____ Governor of Texas, do, by virtue of the authority vested in me by the Constitution and Laws of this State, hereby offer a Reward of _Three Hundred_ _____ Dollars for the arrest and delivery of the said _L L Loggins_ _____ to the Sheriff of _Sabine_ County, inside the jail door of said County. This Reward is payable only on condition of the arrest and return of said fugitive by virtue of a requisition this day made on the Governor of _____ _____ Agent .

In Testimony Whereof I have hereto signed my name and caused the Seal of State to be affixed, at the CITY OF AUSTIN, this _25_ day of _May_ _____ A. D. 188_5_.

(Signed) _Jno Ireland_
Governor of Texas.

BY THE GOVERNOR:

(Signed) _J W Baines_
Secretary of State.

PROCLAMATION

BY THE

GOVERNOR OF THE STATE OF TEXAS

$ 300.00 _____ Reward

To all to Whom these Presents shall Come:

Whereas, It has been made known to me that on the ____ day of _____ 1889 in the County of _Sabine_ _Pete Loggins_ did Commit Murder and that said _Pete Loggins_ is now at large and a fugitive from justice:

Now, Therefore, I, _L. S. Ross_ Governor of Texas, do, by virtue of the authority vested in me by the Constitution and Laws of this State, hereby offer a Reward of _Three Hundred_ Dollars ____ for the arrest and delivery of the said _____ _Pete Loggins_ to the Sheriff of _Sabine_ County, inside the jail door of said County. Reward is payable only on condition of the arrest and return of said fugitive within six months from this day and conviction thereafter, by virtue of a Requisition this day made on the Governor of _____

_____ Agent

In Testimony Whereof, I have hereto signed my name and caused the Seal of State to be affixed, at the City of Austin, this _26th_ day of _June_ A. D. 1889

(Signed) L. S. Ross
Governor.

By the Governor:
(Signed) J. M. Moore
Secretary of State.

[L. S.]

Received the foregoing reward at the ____ Secretary of State's office ____ this day of Act ____ 1889

PROCLAMATION
BY THE
GOVERNOR OF THE STATE OF TEXAS.

No. 6529

TO ALL TO WHOM THESE PRESENTS SHALL COME:

Whereas, At the _August_ Term, A. D. 1893,

in the _District_ Court of _Sabine_ County, State of Texas,

L. L. Loggins

was convicted of the offence of _murder 1st degree_ and sentenced to the penitentiary

for the term of his natural life; and,

Whereas, defendant, who is a physician, has rendered faithful and constant

service in the drug and hospital department at the Huntsville penitentiary for the past eight years; and,

Whereas his record is good, and Supt. Rice recommends his pardon in the following language: "Conduct exceptionally good, and he has rendered most valuable service in the prison hospital and for the further fact that the officers of this prison have strongly recommended executive clemency, I consider the case deserving of special consideration", and,

Whereas his pardon is also recommended by many of the leading citizens and county officials of Jasper and Montgomery counties, by the prison physician, the chaplain and other prison officials at Huntsville; and,

Whereas, he has a wife and one small child who need his care and attention, and his pardon is also recommended by Hon. A. H. Norris, Searcy Baker, Hon. Jos. Lee Jameson and other citizens throughout the state,

Now, Therefore, I, _Joseph D. Sayers_, Governor of Texas, do, by virtue of the authority vested in me by the Constitution and Laws of this State, hereby, for the reasons specified, now on file in the office of Secretary of State,

grant the above named convict a full pardon and restore him to full citizenship and the right of suffrage,

effective December 22, 1901—

In Testimony Whereof, I have hereto signed my name and caused the Seal of State to be hereon impressed, at the City of Austin, this 13th day of _December_ A. D. 1901.

By the Governor:
John G. Tod
Secretary of State.

Joseph D. Sayers,
Governor of Texas.

Governor's Proclamation pardoning Pete Loggins. TEXAS STATE ARCHIVES, AUSTIN

1 2 6 ★ ARKANSAS [Pete Loggins]

VI. WASHINGTON

JAKE TERRY

A Desperado's Desperado

PART ONE: He Earned a Hard Name

*T*O HIS FACE, THEY CALLED HIM "Cowboy Jake"; behind his back, they called him "Terrible Terry," among other things. Terry earned his nicknames—on one occasion, he terrorized and held an entire town at bay for a week—yet he remains relatively unknown. Nonetheless, Terry was unequivocally a desperado's desperado.

Jake Terry's major contribution to the world of crime was engineering "Old Bill" Miner's most famous train robberies without gaining the tarnished laurels for himself. The combination of these two outlaws proved to be successful, in a criminal sense. Their personalities, however, were completely opposite. Bill Miner, an old-time stage robber and one of the most notorious outlaws in California, was congenial and pleasant, a nonviolent man who preferred anonymity; Jake Terry was outspoken, reckless, cocky, and at times extremely ruthless. Yet the careers of these two aging criminals were never successful until they joined forces. And when their association ended, their success ended with it.

"Cowboy Jake" Terry, whose actual name was John E. Terry, was born in Missouri in 1853.[1] He arrived in the territory of Washington in the early 1870s and committed his first known criminal act on July 19, 1873, in Seattle. *The Olympia Washington Standard* reported:

> A man named J. H. Terry shot Delbert Wright in the Fashion Saloon, at Seattle, last Saturday evening, inflicting a wound that will probably prove

fatal. It appears that Terry refused to pay for drinks, and Wright remonstrated, when Terry left the saloon, and soon afterwards returned with a pistol and deliberately shot Wright, the ball entering the left side near the breast. Terry was arrested and lodged in jail.[2]

Terry was arrested by Sheriff H. A. Adkins on July 21 and lodged in the King County jail. Evidently, Delbert Wright survived, because Terry was charged with assault with intent to murder and was tried before Justice D. S. Smith during the August term of the Third District Court at Seattle. On August 5, the jury under foreman E. K. Hill brought in a verdict of guilty. Terry's attorneys, W. H. White and J. P. Judson, appealed to arrest judgment and to set aside the verdict on the grounds that the facts stated in the indictment did not constitute the crime of assault with intent to murder. The appeal was overruled, and on August 7 Terry was sentenced to serve five years in the Territorial Penitentiary. For some reason, he was referred to as J. H. Terry and Joseph Terry as well as John Terry throughout the trial.[3]

On August 16 Terry was removed from the county jail and transported by ship, the *Zephyr*, to the Territorial Penitentiary at Steilacoom. Before 1874, the territory of Washington did not have a penitentiary. The Walla Walla County jail was used to house prisoners from the eastern side of the Cascades, and the United States Army stockade at Steilacoom was used west of the Cascades. In 1874 the territorial legislature passed a bill authorizing the building of a penitentiary and the use of convicts for labor in exchange for their food, housing, and clothing. During that year, a penitentiary was built at Seatco, now Bucoda, in Thurston County and was used until a new penitentiary was built at Walla Walla in 1888. Whether Terry was transferred to Seatco or served out his term at Fort Steilacoom is unknown as no records exist for either institution.[4]

Given that Terry served his full five-year term, he would have been released in August 1878. He apparently left Washington, headed east, and according to Roy Franklin Jones in his book *Boundary Town*, became a railroad engineer in Montana and North Dakota. In North Dakota, Terry engineered a run that crossed the United States–Canadian border. According to the State Historical Society of North Dakota, the railroad line that Terry worked for was the St. Paul, Minneapolis, and Manitoba Railroad. This line, which operated from 1878 until 1887, crossed the U.S. border into the state of Minnesota.

It was here that Terry began his career as a smuggler by carrying illegal Chinese aliens in the train's water tank and dropping them off on a curving grade just before the freight train arrived in Minot. Jones reported that Terry was caught and served three terms in the penitentiary; however, this is incorrect. There is no record of a John E. Terry or a Jake Terry in the general register of the North Dakota Penitentiary at Bismarck from 1885 through 1906. Persons convicted in North Dakota prior to 1885 were sent to the South Dakota State Penitentiary at Sioux Falls, and the names "John E. Terry" or "Jake Terry" do not appear in the South Dakota Penitentiary records from 1878 through 1890. Roy Franklin Jones apparently confused these three prison terms with three terms Terry served later in Washington. However, during Terry's smuggling runs, several shooting incidents reportedly did occur, and after Terry's fellow railroaders and law officers became aware of his illegal operations, he fled the area and headed west.[5]

From North Dakota, Terry went to Montana, where he married a woman named Annie, whose maiden name is unknown, and who was originally from Wisconsin. Leaving Montana, Terry and his wife settled in Island County, Washington, by late 1883 or 1884. They were listed on the 1885 Washington territorial census as Jacob Terry, aged 33, with his wife, aged 24. They remained here until 1889, when they separated. While living in Island County, Terry most likely worked as a railroad engineer and continued smuggling, although he was never caught.[6]

From Island county, Terry came to Seattle. According to *The Seattle Post-Intelligencer*:

> Jake Terry came to Seattle in 1889, soon after the great fire, and from his general appearance and habits of life soon earned the appellation of "Cowboy Jake." He hung around the streets and resorts and became a well known figure as stage driver on the conveyance that was used between Cherry street and Ravenna park, driving four horses and making a trip every hour.
>
> Later Terry was appointed pound master of the city and in the course of time was given a position as a patrol man on the city police force. He became dissolute in his habits and consorted with men known to the police to be crooks, and he was discharged from the police force. He seemed to have a tendency to dabble in counterfeit money, and was in trouble a number of times for passing bogus currency.

Terry realized he was tempting fate by passing counterfeit money and left Seattle around 1891. He soon obtained a job taking charge of the Kellytown township near Seattle. However, this did not prevent him from returning to smuggling, which was much more profitable.[7]

From the late 1880s through the early 1900s, smuggling illegal Chinese aliens and opium across the Canadian border into Washington was a lucrative enterprise. Beginning in 1862, the United States passed a series of Exclusion Acts limiting the entry of Chinese into the country. Because of the heavy influx of Chinese immigrants who had entered the United States to work at extremely low wages, U.S. citizens, nationally as well as in Washington, were up in arms over the situation. Residents in Washington claimed that the Chinese were stopping the demand for white labor and spreading disease and vice.

Because of the pressure, the United States Congress took further action by passing the Exclusion Act of May 5, 1882. In essence this act halted any future Chinese laborers from entering the U.S. and specified that only those Chinese who had entered the United States before November 17, 1880, would be allowed to remain. These legal aliens were issued certificates as proof of residence. After this act was passed, the smuggling of illegal Chinese became extremely profitable and caused serious problems for the United States Customs Service. This was especially true in Washington, as smuggling could be accomplished by water as well as by land. For each Chinese smuggled into the United States in 1890, the going rate was anywhere from twenty-three dollars to sixty dollars.

The other moneymaking smuggling commodity was opium. Although opium was not illegal in the United States, there were heavy duties placed on it, thus the smuggling of opium became a profitable business. The Tariff Act of 1897 placed a duty as high as six dollars per pound of smoking opium. In 1890 it was estimated that 172 illegal Chinese aliens and 1,400 pounds of opium were being smuggled into Washington every month. [8]

During this turbulent period, Jake Terry became one of the most active smugglers along the border, and from 1891 his activities can be accounted for. Terry became notoriously well-known throughout northern Washington, where he earned the nickname of "Terrible Terry." He had some redeeming qualities, and *The Bellingham Herald* showed this other side of the notorious desperado:

> There was nothing he would not do and he feared nothing that walked the earth in the shape of man or beast.
> With all he was generous to a fault. His money belonged to anyone who needed it. He was to a certain extent, a man of his word. If he promised a man anything he would carry out his agreement if he had to go through fire and water to do it. The police and peace officials he despised and regarded them as mere nuisances. He might keep his word to one of them as far as the officer personally concerned, but his promises to be good were as naught. He did what he pleased in the way that suited his fancy. [9]

What suited Terry's fancy was the smuggling game, and to him it was a game. During his residence in Seattle, Terry consorted with the unsavory element around the city and made contact with certain customs inspectors who were in on the smuggling racket, one of whom was Zachery Taylor Holden. What plan Terry and Holden concocted has never been clearly established. Whether they intended to turn the illegal aliens in for a reward or smuggle them into Seattle or somewhere else is unknown, for the whole incident was shrouded in mystery. Nevertheless, the following evidence shows that the two men were in cahoots.

On July 24, 1891, Terry brought five Chinese aliens across the border at Sumas from British Columbia. Cowboy Jake reached Sedro the next day and sent this telegram on the twenty-sixth to Inspector Holden in Seattle: "Come on first train. Answer." [10]

Holden then enlisted the aid of U.S. Deputy Marshal George W. Poor, who was also a deputy sheriff of King County, and the two arrived in Sedro by train on the evening of July 26. Poor had obtained a leave of absence from King County sheriff Woolery without giving a reason, and Holden had left the customs office without authority.

On July 25, Customs Inspector J. C. Baird at Woolley discovered Terry's contraband Chinese and immediately sent to Blaine for Inspector

James Buchanan to assist him in the capture. Arriving in Sedro on the evening of the twenty-sixth, Baird and Buchanan happened to meet Holden and Poor at 10 p.m. Informing Baird and Buchanan that they were after Chinese aliens, Holden went to the hotel at Sedro while Poor headed up the tracks of the Seattle, Lake Shore, and Eastern Railroad. Baird and Buchanan discreetly followed Poor for some distance until the latter entered the woods, only to quickly reappear with Jake Terry and the contraband Chinese.

Baird commanded Poor and Terry to halt. Displaying his badge, Poor replied that he was a U.S. Deputy Marshal and was taking the Chinese to Seattle as prisoners. Baird, thinking the whole thing a sham, ordered Poor to throw up his hands. Both men suddenly drew their guns and fired. Baird's shot struck Poor in the heart, immediately killing him. Buchanan and Terry then entered the fight. Terry's shot grazed Baird's scalp, but Cowboy Jake received a bullet in his groin, causing a very serious wound. During the melee, the Chinese aliens scattered into the woods but were later captured. Poor's body and the wounded Terry were immediately taken to Woolley. Poor had been wearing a false beard, and a pair of colored glasses was found in his pocket.

On examination, a doctor reported that Terry would not survive his wound, and the smuggler made a supposed death-bed statement that he had located the illegal Chinese and had wired Holden for assistance. After capturing the Chinese, Terry claimed that he and Deputy Poor were fired on without warning while they were taking their prisoners to Woolley to be transferred to Seattle. Being told of Cowboy Jake's expected death, his estranged wife, Annie, was reported to have smiled at the news because of the ill treatment she had suffered while they were married.

Since the whole affair was so confusing, everyone involved was eventually arrested. On July 27 a coroner's jury returned a verdict of manslaughter against Baird and Buchanan, and they were arrested. Holden was taken into custody that morning. Contrary to Terry's version, Baird stated that Cowboy Jake was a known smuggler and was in partnership with Holden. Baird declared that he had positive proof to back up his claims.

On July 29 Buchanan and Baird were tried before Justice J. Y. Terry in Woolley. The evidence presented supported Baird's claims, and both men were discharged amid shouts and applause from the spectators in the crowded courtroom. Within twenty-four hours of the trial, Inspector Holden was discharged from the customs service. The consensus of the people in Sedro and Woolley was that Holden and Terry were both guilty and that Poor was no more than a dupe in the whole scheme. As for Jake Terry, if he lived he was to be held for trial. [11]

PART TWO: And Soon the Law Came

ON JULY 29, 1891, JOHN E. "Jake" Terry was indicted in United States District Court at Seattle on the charge of aiding and abetting Chinese laborers to enter the United States illegally. Contrary to the doctor's predictions, Cowboy Jake not only survived his wound but appeared before U.S. Commissioner C. D. Emory at his preliminary hearing in U.S. Circuit court in Seattle on August 3. According to the court record, "Whereupon prisoner waives further hearing. After due consideration, charge sustained and in default of $1500 bail, prisoner ordered committed and mittimus issued." Terry's trial was set for the December term of court, and he was remanded to jail. [12]

Pending trial, Cowboy Jake was transferred to the U.S. penitentiary at McNeil's Island, Washington. On October 11 he escaped with four other prisoners, but his freedom was short-lived as he was recaptured the next day. [13]

On December 12, 1891, Terry was arraigned on two charges: for unlawfully, knowingly, willfully, and feloniously bringing into the United States from a foreign country five Chinese persons not lawfully entitled to enter the United States, and for aiding and abetting Chinese laborers to enter the United States contrary to law. Terry pleaded not guilty to the indictments, and trial was set for December 15.

Judge Cornelius H. Hanford, who would meet Terry several more times under the same circumstances, presided over Cowboy Jake's trial. The prosecution was handled by U.S. attorneys P. H. Winston and P. C. Sullivan, and Terry was represented by F. H. Jones. The jury was impaneled with C. W. P. Osgood as foreman. After all witnesses were examined and evidence presented, the case was continued until 10 a.m. the next day, when the jury brought in a verdict of not guilty of the first charge but guilty on the second charge.

On December 21 Judge Hanford sentenced Terry to ten months imprisonment in the United States penitentiary at McNeil's Island and to pay all costs of the prosecution. He was turned over to United States Marshal Thomas R. Brown for execution of sentence. Court costs were $550.60, and because Terry was indigent, the court ordered all goods and chattels of John E. Terry be seized on January 24, 1892. Marshal Brown reported, "After diligent search nothing found," and thirty days were added to Terry's sentence to pay court costs. [14]

On December 23 Cowboy Jake was delivered to McNeil's Island and registered as Convict No. 29. The following statistics were reported: Age, 35; Weight, 160 lbs; Height, 5'9¾"; Hair, Brown; Occupation, Laborer;

Religion, Methodist; First Offense; Intemporate Habits; No Property or Residence. Sometime between 1889 and 1891, Terry's wife obtained a divorce, for the penitentiary register reported, "Divorced wife resides Seattle, Wash." During his imprisonment, Terry gave the prison officials no trouble, and he was released with good time on September 30, 1892. [15]

Terry immediately resumed his smuggling operations around the border town of Sumas, Washington, after his release from prison. Roy Franklin Jones, a native of Sumas who obtained firsthand knowledge regarding Terry's character and exploits, wrote:

> Jake Terry had come to Sumas to operate only in the nineties. For about fifteen years he was to pester Customs men, during the times he was in and out of jail. He was quite a slicker and always believed he could outsmart any man he could not intimidate or buy off. He was a great teller of stories and made himself right at home in any company.
>
> Terry had been using an old logging road, back on Barker Hill to get his stuff across the line. Sometimes he used trails east of town or the Telegraph Road. Once across, he carried opium in suitcases or a blanketroll or had a confederate do it for him. Then he could board the train as a passenger at Clearbrook or Nooksack and thus outwit the Customs men. [16]

It was not long before the customs agents caught on to Cowboy Jake's escapades. On May 13, 1893, Special Agent Todd, at Vancouver, British Columbia, sent in a report that included these comments regarding Terry:

> Cow Boy Terry has been around here for the past two weeks. I think he is trying to get hold of some Chinamen to run over the boundary.

Terry successfully smuggled these Chinese aliens over the border, and on May 30, Inspector J. A. Van Bokkelen made this report from Vancouver, British Columbia:

> The notorious smuggler "Cow Boy Terry" is in these parts, and is at his old business. Yesterday he left here on the Whatcom train with three China men, punching the tickets for them himself. It is hard to tell when he leaves the train between here and Sumas. Some person is working within on the other side and they are doing a big business. I am informed that this has been going on for some time and that the Chinamen get on the train anywhere between here and Mission or Sumas.

On August 18, Inspector Van Bokkelen sent another report from Vancouver:

> "Cowboy Terry" is doing a rushing business along the border. He has been taking Chinamen out of this City for two different Chinese firms. Traveling by night and sleeping in the day time is the principal way he takes them through. About seventy-five pounds of opium goes from here every week to a Chinese camp at Abbotsford, a small place in B.C. about three miles from Sumas. There is an organized gang in the business, with Terry as the chief to do the dirty work.

By October the customs officers were finally able to identify Terry's partner. The man was a Chinese named Leong Youk Tong, who kept a brothel on Adler Street in Portland, Oregon. Tong had devised a unique system for bringing illegal Chinese over from Canada. Phony certificates were produced in Portland and sent to a house in Vancouver, British Columbia, where fifty or sixty alien Chinese at a time were being housed. The aliens were then schooled in how to give correct answers to questions asked by the customs officers when they reached the United States. In his report of October 3 from Vancouver regarding this smuggling ring, Inspector Van Bokkelen reported:

> All the Chinese that cannot be schooled very well, by the ring, are being smuggled across the boundary via Westminster and Blaine. Cow Boy Terry doing the work.

Terry's reputation as a dangerous man is confirmed in this October 8 report from Customs Inspector John T. Plum at Sedro, Washington:

> The conductor on train #2 of the Seattle, Lake Shore, and Eastern told me yesterday that he saw Jake (cowboy) Terry in Sumas last Monday. That Terry wanted to borrow $2.00 from him to pay his fare to Vancouver and that he would pay it back the last of this week as he would be on this side of the line about Thursday or Friday. He told the conductor that he run in 14 Chinamen the last week in September and was, when he was talking to him, on his way to collect $400.00 that he had earned by the venture. I would like to capture Terry but I am not satisfied with the revolver that I have with me to perform such a hazardous task. [17]

Although Terry was a brazen and dangerous man, he definitely had a humorous side. In January 1894 Deputy Marshal Rugar in Seattle suggested to Customs Inspector Samuel C. Walker that he might be able to capture some Chinese aliens or retrieve opium through information obtained from Cowboy Jake. This information was relayed to Terry in Sedro, and on January 31 he sent the following telegram to Walker, "Come on first train. Answer." Walker made a few inquiries about Terry, and on February 2 with reservations he decided to meet him in Sedro. Upon arrival, Walker found that Terry had quartered himself at the Sedro Hotel at Walker's expense. That night the two had a brief meeting, which enlisted this report from the chagrined Walker on February 10:

> I found that Terry had taken me in. I paid his hotel bill rather than have my name associated with that of a marauding bandit and left the next morning the 3rd inst. taking particular pains to inform the proprietor of the Hotel Sedro that I would not be responsible for any future hotel bills contracted by Terry and that he was not authorized to act for me in any way. I returned to Seattle with no profits arising from my trip save something in the line of experience. [18]

Shortly after this, Terry pulled another of his so-called jokes on Customs Inspector Lawrence J. Flanigan, who was stationed at Sumas.

Flanigan had received confidential information that a shipment of opium was aboard a train to Wikersham. He ordered the conductor to hold the train while he checked the undercarriages. Spotting a box, Flanigan removed it and immediately took it into the freight station. Remarking to the station agent, "Well, I got the dope," Flanigan hurriedly tore off the wrapping. Inside was a shoe box, and Flanigan ripped off the lid. The duped customs man found that his efforts produced only a box full of horse manure.

A short time later, this joke of Terry's was to backfire on him. He had become increasingly bold in his operations, and on the night of March 4, 1894, he appeared at the customs house at Sumas to study the situation. After hanging around the office for a period of time, Cowboy Jake confided to Flanigan that since the trails were dry he would take the back route so it would not embarrass Flanigan. Terry then brashly told Flanigan, "I'll be coming through after midnight, and nobody will know the difference, Larry. You might as well get a good sleep. You could sure use a little sleep better than a slug of lead in your guts, couldn't you?" Flanigan quickly retorted, "Sometimes lead flies both ways." Terry's actions and words made Flanigan more determined than ever to arrest him, and he enlisted the aid of A. Schumaker, arranging a meeting at one o'clock that morning near the railroad tracks. Flanigan told Schumaker to bring a revolver with him. Flanigan would bring his shotgun.

Meanwhile, Terry had picked up his two Chinese aliens, Ah Sing and Loui Son, on the Canadian side of the border. Using a handcar, Terry started down the railroad tracks for Sumas with his two contraband Chinese.

Flanigan thought Terry's statement of using the back trails a ruse. Anticipating the smuggler's plans, he borrowed a hand-propelled two-seated, three-wheeled velocipede known as a speedster from the roundhouse and placed it as a barrier on the tracks a short distance from Sumas. Periodically, Flanigan would go to the tracks and place his ear on the steel rail. Around 2 a.m. he heard a faint rumble and, with Schumaker, hid beside the tracks. As soon as Terry's handcar was near enough to see the obstruction, the alien Chinese began to shout with alarm. Terry's voice could be heard above the din, ordering them to shut up.

The two officers quickly jumped up and began running beside the handcar, training their shotgun and pistol on Terry. Flanigan then shouted at Terry, "Hands up, you all! Federal officers! Jake Terry, you're under arrest. As soon as the car stops I want you to step out in front. Keep your hands up."

It was all over for Cowboy Jake, and the brazen desperado meekly surrendered and was handcuffed as soon as the handcar stopped. The Chinese aliens took their fate cheerfully, pumping the handcar and its passengers back to Sumas. Terry and the two Chinese were locked up in the city jail. [19]

On the day of his arrest, Terry came before U.S. Commissioner Phil A. Lawrence in U.S. Circuit Court at Sumas, and a complaint was officially filed. Examination trial on the charge of bringing illegal aliens into the United States was set for March 9, and Terry's bail was set at two thousand dollars. Unable to post bond, he was remanded to jail.

On March 9, Terry waived examination in U.S. Circuit Court at Sumas and was committed for trial in U.S. District Court at Seattle during the June term. Bail was set at one thousand dollars, which he could not raise, and Cowboy Jake was placed in custody of U.S. Deputy Marshal Emery McGuinis, who returned him to jail.

On June 5, 1894, John E. "Jake" Terry was tried by jury on the charge of bringing into the United States Chinese aliens not lawfully entitled to enter. Terry pleaded guilty to the charges. On June 23, Cowboy Jake again faced Judge Hanford and was sentenced to serve one year imprisonment at McNeil's Island and ordered to pay a fine of one thousand dollars. He was placed in custody of United States Marshal James C. Drake for deliverance to the penitentiary. [20]

Terry was delivered to McNeil's Island the same day he was convicted. The prison register showed his age as 42, his occupation as engineer, and his residence as Seattle. He also reported to the officials that he had sisters living in Denver, Colorado. Again, Terry served his term without any misconduct and was released on good time on May 24, 1895. [21]

Leaving the penitentiary, the undaunted Jake Terry returned to Sumas and immediately resumed his smuggling activities. Inspector Flanigan noted Terry's return and wryly remarked in his report of June 7, 1895:

> In connection herewith I have to inform you that our friend "Cow Boy Terry" returned to Sumas on May 30th and seems to be inclined to engage in his former occupation. [22]

Terry quickly realized that his actions were being too closely observed by the Customs Service and, by September, changed his line of work to his other easy-money scheme of counterfeiting.

During the month of September 1895, on Camano Island, Terry and his partner, Dave Dixon, counterfeited approximately one hundred silver ten-cent pieces. On September 25, Cowboy Jake fraudulently passed thirty bogus coins to Lillie Weiner on Camano Island. Counterfeit charges and a U.S. warrant were issued against Terry the same day. He was promptly arrested on Camano Island by U.S. Deputy Marshal James M. Quilter, who delivered him to Everett, Washington.

On September 26, Terry's preliminary hearing was held in U.S. Commissioners Court, and he was bound over for trial in the December term of U.S. District Court at Seattle. Bail was set at $2,500, which Cowboy again was unable to raise, and he was confined in King County jail until court convened.

On December 5, he appeared this time as Jake Terry, for the third time before Judge Hanford and pleaded guilty. *The Seattle Post-Intelligencer* clearly indicated that Judge Hanford had seen enough of Jake Terry:

> "I sentence you as an incorrigible," said Judge Hanford yesterday as he began pronouncing sentence upon Jake Terry the counterfeiter. "It

is the judgment of this court that you shall be committed to the United States penitentiary on McNeil's Island for a period of ten years at hard labor. This is the third time you have appeared before this court."

As the words of the court fell upon the ears of the prisoner, his face did not display a tremor, but his feet seemed to weaken beneath him. Terry showed that he is used to such performances as being sentenced, the length of term being the only thing new to him.

Dave Dixon, Terry's partner, was sentenced to one year at McNeil's Island. [23]

This time, however, Jake Terry was not destined to go to McNeil's Island. On November 30, 1895, U.S. Marshal James C. Drake in Seattle wrote the attorney general in Washington, D.C., requesting permission to remove certain prisoners from McNeil's Island for transfer to "some suitable prison that you may designate." Marshal Drake wrote:

> My reason for wishing to remove these men from U.S. Penitentiary at McNeil's Island is, that I consider them desperate criminals and the penitentiary being insecure, I fear I will be unable to hold them until the expiration of their sentence.

Attorney General Gene Harman telegraphed this request to the California State Prison at San Quentin on December 9 and received this reply the next day: "Yes we will receive all U.S. prisoners you may wish to send. W.E. Hale, Warden."

Also on December 9, Marshal Drake sent the following telegram to Attorney General Harman:

> Reference my letter Nov thirtieth authority is also requested for removal Jake Terry sentenced Dec sixth ninety five to ten years at hard labor for counterfeiting.

On December 10, the attorney general wrote to both Marshal Drake and Warden Hale, authorizing the removal of Jake Terry to San Quentin. [24]

On December 26, 1895, Marshal Drake delivered Terry and five other U.S. prisoners to San Quentin. He was registered as Jake Terry, Inmate No. 16612, with the following data: Nativity, Missouri; Occupation, engineer; 5'8" tall; medium complexion; Hair, brown; Age, 46. The register incorrectly reported the color of his eyes as blue. Terry committed no acts of misconduct and as a result was released from San Quentin on June 2, 1902, after serving a total of six years and five months of his ten-year sentence. [25]

While in San Quentin, Terry was a cell mate of Old Bill Miner, and the two became good friends despite opposite temperaments and dispositions. Miner, one of the most notorious west-coast outlaws, had been in San Quentin for nearly twenty years when he was released in June 1901. Because of their association, Bill Miner headed for the bay area of Washington State. After Terry's discharge a year later, the two men resumed their alliance. The affiliation of these two dedicated criminals for the next five years would bring about the crowning point of both their careers. [26]

PART THREE: But He Never Attained Fame

*F*OLLOWING A BOTCHED TRAIN robbery attempt near Portland, Oregon, in September 1903 Bill Miner was aided by Jake Terry in his escape to Canada. Miner settled near Princeton, British Columbia, and during his frequent absences from the area, he joined "Cowboy Jake" in his smuggling operations along the border. According to *The Bellingham Herald*:

> Miner has not only been a train robber, but with Terry he was engaged in the smuggling business for a number of years. He operated on the Canadian side while Terry was the man who did the work on this side of the line. [27]

In 1904 Miner and Terry put their heads together and drew up a plan to rob a train on the Canadian side of the border. Cowboy Jake definitely had the expertise to organize and plan the operation. As a railroad engineer, he had knowledge of train routes, shipment schedules, and timetables, and his smuggling operations had carried him over every hidden trail that crossed the border. By the summer of 1904, after Miner recruited a character from the Princeton area named William "Shorty" Dunn into the scheme, the three men set their plans in motion. [28]

During the summer of 1904, Miner drove a small herd of cattle across the Hope Trail to Chilliwack. From there, he went down the Hope Trail to Vancouver to scout the territory for an escape route after the train robbery.

In September 1904 Miner and Dunn left the Princeton area, supposedly on another hunting trip or cattle drive. Instead, they headed south toward Vancouver to rob a Canadian Pacific Railroad train. The two bandits rendez-voused with Jake Terry somewhere near the international border. [29]

At 9:30 p.m., September 10, 1904, the three train robbers boarded the Canadian Pacific Railway's Transcontinental Express Number 1 at Mission Junction (now Mission City), forty miles east of Vancouver. The three outlaws were not detected when they climbed aboard at the water tower because of the dense fog. They hid in the blind baggage until the train picked up speed. Engineer Nathaniel J. Scott was startled by a hand placed on his shoulder and a command of "Hands up!" Two of the masked bandits were armed with revolvers while the third held a rifle on engineer Scott and fireman Harry Freeman. Miner ordered Scott to halt the train at Silverdale, five miles west of Mission Junction, and nothing more was said until the train stopped. [30]

It was probably Cowboy Jake who tapped the telegraph wires and obtained information that a consignment of gold dust for the United States Assay Office in Seattle would be in the express safe. Terry also knew that it was railroad policy to keep the express safe locked between the stations, and on the day of the robbery, he tapped the wires again. By implying that the message came from headquarters, Terry telegraphed the agent at Mission Junction that the combination to the safe was lost and to leave the safe unlocked. As a result, the express safe was easy prey for the three bandits. [31]

At Silverdale, fireman Freeman was ordered by Miner to go with him back to the express car. Brakeman Bill Abbott stuck his head out of the car the minute the train stopped and came face to face with Miner. Abbott was told to get back inside or get his head blown off. Abbott jerked his head back, but shortly afterward made a break and rushed back to Mission Junction, reporting the holdup to the agent, who foolishly refused to believe him.

Express messenger Herb Mitchell opened the top portion of the car door just as Miner and Freeman reached the express car. Upon spotting the fireman through the fog, Mitchell thought the fruit cars were being sidetracked and closed the door, unaware of the impending robbery. Miner ordered the fireman to uncouple the express car from the rest of the train, and then he returned to the engine. The engineer was ordered to proceed to the Whonock mile post and stop in front of the church. Terry was left to guard the fireman while Miner and Dunn took Scott back to the express car.

In 1944 express messenger Herb Mitchell vividly recalled the details of the robbery:

> Then a rock came at the door; hit the outside. I looked out of the window and saw Nat Scott, the engineer, with a torch in his hand. I asked him what he wanted. He said, "Open up the door or the car will be blown up." I said, "Who's going to blow it up?" He says, "Those fellows here." I opened up the door and one of the fellows poked a rifle under my nose. He ordered me to put up my hands and come down As I lit on the ground one of the fellows grabbed me around the waist, and took my gun from me. Then he ordered me back in the car. Bill Miner was holding my own gun at the back of my ear, and Shorty Dunn was standing about ten feet with a rifle, hammer cocked, lined on the point of my nose. Bill Miner said to me when I was in the car that all I had to do was do as I was told, and "I won't hurt a hair of your head," and it is not your money I want."

Inside the express car were two safes, a large combination safe that had been left unlocked and a smaller safe bound for Vancouver. Mitchell was ordered to open the large safe first, which was found to be empty. Miner then told Mitchell to open the smaller safe, which contained four thousand dollars in gold dust consigned to the United States Assay Office in Seattle, two thousand dollars in gold dust for the Bank of British North America in Vancouver, and around one thousand dollars in cash.

After cleaning out the safe, Miner went through the express car gathering up the registered mail and putting it into satchels. Miner stuffed $50,000 in United States bonds and an estimated $250,000 in Australian securities into the satchels, which would later prove to have a great impact on Miner's and Terry's future. As their final act, the bandits threw out the fireman's coal shovel, which delayed both the train and news of the robbery. The holdup took no longer than thirty minutes.

Engineer Scott remarked "Happy journey" to the bandits as they left the train. "Be careful when you are backing up that you don't meet with some accident," Miner politely replied, as he and his two companions slipped into the fog. Whether the bandits realized it or not, they had executed Canada's first train robbery. [32]

The British Columbia Provincial Police and the Canadian Pacific Railroad Police interrogated the train crew upon their arrival in Vancouver. They stated that the three robbers were professionals and had American accents. The British Columbia police had never before dealt with train robbery, so they called in the Pinkerton Detective Agency from Seattle. The Pinkertons quickly dispatched agents to the area around the United States–Canadian border. An immoderate reward of $11,500 was offered for the train robbers by the government of British Columbia and the Canadian Pacific Railroad.

Tracks of three men were found after the discovery of an abandoned boat near Whonock, but the trail was lost near Sumas, Washington. Several arrests were made that proved false, one of which was a man named B. R. Davies, who was arrested by Pinkerton superintendent James Dye near Sumas. Davies later proved to be a detective working on another case in the area. Running out of leads, the British Columbia police and the Pinkertons returned exhausted to their respective posts. After a thorough search of his records, superintendent Dye was convinced that the train robbery had been committed by Bill Miner.

Tracks of three men that led into the mountains over the Hope Pass were discovered by an experienced trailer. The trail was finally lost after a considerable distance. When this information reached the British Columbia police, they completely discredited it, believing the robbers had fled to the United States. [33]

The $50,000 in United States bonds and $250,000 worth of Australian securities stolen during the train robbery by Bill Miner, would, in the near future, become a bargaining power for Miner and Terry. These bonds and securities were apparently negotiable, but if Miner attempted to cash them, he could be easily traced. He likely convinced Terry and Dunn that the bonds and securities were worthless and then hid them in a spot where even his partners couldn't find them. Thus, Miner robbed his comrades as well as the railroad.

The Canadian Pacific Railway was not only embarrassed but also responsible for the return of the bonds and securities, so it attempted to suppress news of the loss. Nonetheless, rumors of the loss soon followed. The face value of three hundred thousand dollars was an enormous sum in those days, equal to more than $6 million in today's money, so the return of these bonds and securities became a chief concern.

Bill Miner and Jake Terry soon learned that Miner was the prime suspect in the train robbery, and they also heard the rumors about the missing bonds and securities. Since Miner could not openly negotiate with the railroad, he contacted Jake Terry and struck a deal with him to act as his agent. Miner likely agreed to split whatever was gained through negotiations or a finder's fee with Terry in return for Miner's immunity from prosecution.

Following the robbery, Terry adopted the alias of Brown and returned to his old haunts around Sumas and Bellingham, Washington. Terry's forte was smuggling, and he was not a suspect in the train robbery. After being contacted by Miner, the nervy outlaw dropped the alias of Brown and, with brazen confidence, publicly declared that he was to be Miner's emissary in any negotiations with the Canadian Pacific Railway. Cowboy Jake, realizing that he and Miner could only gain from these negotiations, openly admitted his close friendship with Miner and stated that the old bandit was guilty. Terry added that the C.P.R. would have to negotiate through him if it wanted the entire amount of stolen bonds and securities returned. However, the railroad was not yet ready to yield to such blatant blackmail. [34]

Flushed by their success at Mission Junction, Miner and Terry planned another train robbery. Around the last of September 1905, Miner and Shorty Dunn headed for the coastal area of British Columbia. [35]

On October 1, Jake Terry supposedly left Bellingham for Portland, Oregon. [36] The eastbound Great Northern Overland passenger train was robbed just outside of Seattle the next evening at 9 p.m. The robbery took place near Ballard and Ravenna Park, an area well-known to Terry, who had been a stage driver there in 1889. [37]

Although Miner and Terry were never officially charged with the Seattle robbery, newspaper reports and statements of witnesses give conclusive evidence that they committed the robbery. How the bandits arrived and escaped has never been fully explained. *The Seattle Post-Intelligencer* covered every aspect of the robbery, and through the reports the story can be pieced together.

Miner and Dunn probably rendezvoused with Terry in the vicinity of Bellingham and headed south to Seattle. Here they picked up a one-horse spring wagon that had been stolen from Issac Calhoun of Kent, Washington, by James "Lem" Short, a small-time Seattle crook who had probably been hired by Terry. Short drove the stolen wagon north, where it was turned over to the three bandits. After cutting the telephone wires between Kirkland and Medina, they frantically drove the wagon around Lake Washington to a point five miles north of Ballard. Terry and Dunn got out of the wagon, and Miner drove it south to Interbay and abandoned it.

Miner climbed into the blind baggage of the train at Interbay, where he encountered two transients, Alfred Frankie and Roland Gibbs. Miner, who was masked, ordered them to lie flat on the tender and keep out of sight. Miner climbed over the tender to the engine, drew two revolvers, and forced engineer Caulder and fireman Julette to keep going until they sighted a campfire beside the railroad tracks. Once they reached the signal fire, Miner ordered them to halt, and Cowboy Jake boarded the engine.[38]

The Seattle Post-Intelligencer gave fireman Julette's version of the robbery:

> There were only two of them and they were old hands at the business. They were as cool as ice and what they didn't know about handling the train crew was not worth knowing. They called each other "Bill" and "Tom." One of them, the larger, had a pronounced stoop to his shoulders. He did all the work. The other was a small man and did the directing. The tall man with the stoop shoulders was "Bill." The short fellow was "Tom."
>
> After they got into the car they opened the way safe first and found nothing in it. "Damn the luck," said Bill, "this is bad as _____" and he mentioned the name of another railroad which I did not catch. Then they went at the through safe and that's where they made use of me. They made me tie a blue handkerchief across my face and they did the same with engineer Caulder.[39]

The bandits made use of Julette by forcing him to place dynamite on the safe and light the fuse. Everyone jumped off the express car, but the blast failed to blow the safe open. Again, Julette was forced to dynamite the safe. Upon reentering the car, they found the safe still undamaged. In frustration, Terry set the third detonation, which shattered the safe, and Julette was ordered to remove the contents.

Miner took charge of the outside, periodically leaving the car and walking from one side to the other, shooting down the sides of the train to keep the passengers inside. Terry looted the contents of the safe, and the two bandits then fled north along the tracks. The dynamite completely destroyed the interior of the express car and all the express matter.

The train robbery ended rather comically. The two tramps, Frankie and Gibbs, climbed out of the blind baggage and went through the train, taking collections from the passengers and claiming they had been robbed and needed money to get to Spokane. Many of the unnerved passengers believed they were members of the gang and gave them their money. Once the train reached Everett, the two tramps were arrested and fined one hundred dollars in police court for vagrancy and placed in jail pending further investigation. They admitted taking money from the passengers but denied any association with the train robbers.

Shorty Dunn's role in the robbery is unknown. Fireman Julette claimed that there were only two robbers, but the passengers said they saw more than two men. The bandits evidently used a boat in their escape, and since lights on the shoreline had been sighted from the train, Dunn had probably been posted at that point to guard the escape boat. The bandits successfully escaped, and Cowboy Jake was back in Sumas the next day.[40]

A night watchman for the Great Northern Railroad had observed the train robbery and hurriedly went by boat to a nearby residence to telephone the railroad company. A train manned by railroad officers was quickly dispatched, but by the time they reached the robbery scene the bandits were long gone. The Pinkertons were then called in. However, they made no investigation and waited to find a stool pigeon who was willing to talk. [41]

Fireman Julette's description of the two bandits identically matched the characteristics of Terry and Miner. Cowboy Jake, however, furnished an alibi through friends in Sumas. On October 5, the brazen desperado gave an interview to *The Seattle Post-Intelligencer* and brashly made these sarcastic and derogatory statements:

> They [the officers of the Great Northern Railroad] lie when they say I did it, and they know they lie. The Canadian Pacific started that story for reasons of its own. . . . It makes me laugh to think of that bunch of incompetents chasing me and Bill Miner through the brush of this state with a lot of bum bloodhounds. They ought to know better than that. I had nothing to do with it, and if they want me here I am, or if they will wire me I'll go down to Seattle and they can operate on me there. They can have me all right enough, but if they want Bill I guess they will have to find him. Bill's up here all right, and I guess he knows even more than I do about that work Monday night, but I'll leave that for Bill to tell. If you want to talk to him, just run up across the line and you'll find him sitting there in the woods. Bill likes the woods.

Ironically, nothing was said about the accurate descriptions of Miner and Terry given by fireman Julette. Terry was described at this time as a man five feet, ten inches in height and stoop-shouldered, with a face much scarred by exposure. [42]

Lem Short was arrested in Chehalis in mid-November because a letter addressed to him was found near the scene of the robbery. Short was constantly pressured and grilled by Seattle officers for two weeks but adamantly refused to divulge any information. His fear of Terry was probably greater than his fear of the police. The frustrated law officers ended up charging him only with grand larceny for the theft of the horse and wagon used in the robbery. [43] No other charges or arrests pertaining to the train robbery were ever made, and the crime remained unsolved.

The actual amount stolen was never disclosed, and this indicates that the loss was substantial. Railroads were inclined to minimize losses, and the Great Northern claimed that the amount did not exceed one thousand dollars. However, rumors soon brought the figure up to thirty-six thousand dollars, most of which was gold bars in transit from the United States Assay Office. Later on, these rumors were supported by the finding of an empty canvas bag on the property of a farmer near Bitter Lake. The bag was stenciled "$35,000," and two frayed holes had been punched into the bag, which showed that it had been carried by two men with a pole. Cowboy Jake Terry and Bill Miner, and perhaps Shorty Dunn, undoubtedly buried the gold, intending to return for it when pressure died down. [44]

PART FOUR: At the End of the Game

*F*ROM OCTOBER UNTIL DECEMBER 1905, Jake Terry made his headquarters at Port Townsend, Washington, continuing his smuggling operations. In December Cowboy Jake was in trouble again, resulting from a chance meeting with his ex-wife, Annie.

After her divorce from Terry, Annie met and married a man named M. S. Kenyon through an advertisement in a lonely-hearts magazine. The union did not last long, and following their divorce, Annie opened a small notions store in Sumas, Washington. She soon began a relationship with A. L. "Gus" Linday, a quiet, inoffensive little man who worked as a postal telegraph lineman. Within a short time the two were married and took up residence in the rear of the notions store.

Annie was described as a trim and winsome woman. According to Roy Franklin Jones, "She had a warm smile and a carriage that suggested pride and quality. Her heavy head of dark hair, piled high, brown eyes and heavy lashes, dainty lace things at the neck and wrist, gave her an attractiveness that complimented her quiet, friendly manner."[45] However, Annie was not quite the sweet, genteel lady that Jones describes, for her subsequent actions prove she was a very cold and callous woman.

On Christmas 1905, Jake Terry returned to Sumas and, upon entering Annie's store for a pair of gloves, chanced to meet his ex-wife again. Apparently the reunion was a welcome one for Annie, who probably had tired of the sedate life she was living, and let Cowboy Jake move in with her. When Linday returned home, Terry ordered him to leave. Linday appealed to Annie, but was coldly told that she could do nothing and that he would have to settle it with Terry. Cowboy Jake then proceeded to beat the little man unmercifully and throw him out the front door. The next night, Linday tried to return to his home, but Terry tossed him out the door again. Linday then went to several saloons in the area and asked his friends for help. Returning to his residence, they gathered outside while Gus Linday attempted to call to Annie.

Angered at Linday's actions, Terry stepped out the door with a pistol and placed a shot between two of the onlookers, scattering the whole crowd. He then proceeded into Sumas, where he shot up the town and terrified the residents and pedestrians by shooting between their feet. He entered several saloons and intimidated the customers. In the U.S. Saloon, he forcibly took a pistol away from the bartender. Terry defied anyone to try to take Annie away from him and returned to the Linday residence. "Terrible Terry" earned his nickname by holding the town at bay for nearly a week while terrorizing the residents.

Meanwhile, Linday obtained the assistance of an attorney, and the two went to Bellingham for aid. Sheriff Williams and a deputy immediately left for Sumas with two warrants for Terry, one for assault with intent to kill and the other for the theft of the gun from the U.S. Saloon. The sheriff had no trouble arresting the notorious desperado, but as they were leaving the Linday house, a crowd of people gathered and began shouting, "Hang him. Let's string him up." Now that Terry was unarmed, the residents regained their courage. Fearing for Terry's life, Sheriff Williams took him across the border and obtained permission from the Canadian authorities to lodge him in the Huntington Hotel until he could take his prisoner aboard the next train for Bellingham.

Terry was held in the Whatcom County jail until April, when he was brought before the Whatcom County Superior Court on assault and robbery charges. Annie mortgaged her store to provide Terry with $250 bail, and he was released pending trial at the next term of court. Cowboy Jake immediately fled across the border into Canada and took up residence at the Huntington Hotel. Now that Terry was gone, Linday dropped his divorce suit and moved back in with Annie.

When Terry's trial came up during the next term of court, he was safely across the border and consequently his bail was forfeited. But, fortunately for Terry, it was too late for him to join in a new scheme cooked up by Bill Miner. [46]

On May 9, 1906, Miner, Dunn, and an itinerant wanderer named Louis Colquhoun, robbed a Canadian Pacific train near Ducks, British Columbia. The trio were quickly caught and brought to trial. Colquhoun was sentenced to twenty-five years while Miner and Dunn received life terms at the penitentiary at New Westminster, British Columbia.

At first, the notorious bandit was kept in close confinement and was put to work in the shoe factory. However, special privileges were soon granted to Bill Miner because negotiations for the return of the bonds and securities were being held between the outlaw and the Canadian Pacific Railroad. His defense lawyer, Alex D. McIntyre, visited any time that Miner wanted to see him. Miner was also allowed to let his hair grow out, to write more than the one letter a month allowed each prisoner, to talk to visitors without a prison officer present, and to have the freedom to leave the prison interior.

During the winter of 1907, a confidential meeting was held in the warden's office among Bill Miner, Warden J. C. Whyte, McIntyre, Canadian Pacific Railroad detective Bullock, and, incredibly, Cowboy Jake Terry, who was still working as Miner's emissary in the negotiations.

After the Linday affair at Sumas, Terry had remained on the Canadian side of the border, working as a logger or engineer whenever he needed money. He no longer had the freedom to cross the border to obtain the spoils from the Seattle train robbery. He realized that Miner, although in prison, was his best chance of obtaining his share of the loot—but only if negotiations were successful. *The Bellingham Herald* outlined Terry's predicament and his involvement in the negotiations:

He often came to the border but never dared venture across as the citizens of Sumas threatened dire vengeance if he did come and it was thought for a time that Mrs. Lindsay [sic] would receive harsh treatment. One morning a sign was found on her door telling her to leave Sumas and the card was adorned with a skull and cross-bones. She failed to go.

Later she went to Minneapolis and there met Jake Terry, first selling out the little store she had in Sumas. [This is in error as later events show that she retained ownership of the store.] After a short sojourn there she returned to Sumas and with her came the notorious Jake, as far as the border. He did not come across.

At the time she went east it was announced that he was negotiating with the Canadian Pacific Railroad for the return of $300,000 worth of bonds that had been taken from an overland train in a holdup two years previous. It was claimed that Terry and the famous Bill Miner, now doing time in Canada for train robbery, turned the trick. Jake returned to Sumas, B.C. [sic] broke. At the time he wanted to betray Bill Miner, his pal, for consideration, but the authorities would not listen to him. . . .

The second time he [Terry] came out of the "pen" [San Quentin] he was a little more careful and took to train robbing. That he was mixed up in the C.P. hold-up at Mission three years ago, there is no doubt. That he was involved in the hold-up only eighteen months ago [Seattle], many believe. He claimed that Bill Miner, who is serving a life sentence across the line, did him "dirt" and that is why he tried to betray him.

In a later edition, *The Herald* continued:

It was believed that Jake Terry . . . was implicated in both robberies, but he was never caught by the authorities.

Terry . . . claimed that Bill Miner played him "dirt" and he tried to "peach" on his former pal, but the officers took no stock in his story.

This clearly indicates that Terry no longer had any bargaining power. Now that Miner was in prison, he did not need Terry's assistance, and he double-crossed him by cutting him out of the negotiations, using the bonds and securities as a bargaining power for himself. Following the meeting at the penitentiary, Cowboy Jake truthfully accused Miner of having done him "dirt." Since he had no idea where the bonds and securities were hidden, he futilely attempted to tell all he knew in exchange for reducing or dropping the charges in Sumas. With Miner in prison, the officers and authorities, who certainly did not trust Terry, were not interested in his statements.

The result of the meeting at the penitentiary was a verbal promise of a pardon for Miner for the return of the securities. Miner would have none of it, and the negotiations floundered. At the same time, Shorty Dunn was visited at the penitentiary by a Pinkerton detective trying to negotiate the return of the $50,000 in U.S. bonds, but Dunn knew no more than Terry. In miner's case, since a pardon could not be guaranteed in writing, other plans were made.[47]

On August 8, 1907, through arrangements between the Canadian Pacific Railroad and the penitentiary at New Westminster, Bill Miner was allowed to escape. Presumably, after Miner successfully crossed the United

States border, the securities and bonds were then returned to C.P.R. officials. [48]

Cowboy Jake Terry was left out in the cold. He would get nothing from the negotiations with the C.P.R. and could not cross the border for the spoils of the Seattle robbery. He had to hope and wait for Miner to get out of prison to get his share. But this was not to be, as Terry met a tragic fate one month before Miner made his escape.

"JAKE TERRY NOTORIOUS DESPERADO SHOT—SMUGGLER IS INSTANTLY KILLED AT SUMAS," screamed the headlines in the extra edition of *The Bellingham Herald* on July 5, 1907. Terry had claimed that he would die with his boots on, and it came to pass. The question is, Why would Cowboy Jake cross the border into the United States for the first time in more than a year? One theory was that he thought it safe since the authorities had relaxed their guard during the Fourth of July celebrations. However, the events that led to his death confirm that he was sick and tired of being separated from Annie, and this was an opportune time to see her.

On July 4 Terry was reported to have had a fight in Huntington, British Columbia, and he slipped over the border that night. He safely hid out somewhere in Sumas until morning, when he entered the U.S. Saloon and had several drinks on credit. He then went to Annie's store and obtained five dollars from her. Returning to the saloon, he paid for his drinks and began bragging about how easy it was for him to get money from Annie Linday. When a patron asked him if he had any trouble with Gus Linday, Terry smugly replied, "Not much. I can turn him over my knee and spank him."

At noon Terry left the saloon, and according to *The Bellingham Herald* of July 6:

> He sauntered up the street and entered the little store owned by Mrs. Lindsey [sic], in the rear of which she and her husband lived. He purchased some cigars from her and then Lindsey entered from the street. He informed Jake that he had better go across the line again. Terry laughed at him, and then the two exchanged angry words. Mrs. Lindsey, scenting trouble, left the store and started for a barber shop a short distance up the street. She says she heard a shot before reaching the place.
>
> According to a story related by one person, Terry started to whip Lindsey and the latter run [sic] into the rear of the building. Jake gave chase, and Lindsey ran into the bedroom and turning fired. Terry must have been close behind, for powder burns were visible where the first shot had entered. As he staggered forward, after the first bullet, he raised his hand and Lindsey fired again. The bullet clipped off a piece of one finger and then entered his head.

The Bellingham Herald of July 5 reported:

> Terry fell lifeless across the threshold of the door. His feet still remain in the bedroom and his head and shoulders rest in the little parlor of the Lindsey home.
>
> Neighbors rushed into the house at the sound of the shooting, and they saw Lindsey with the still smoking revolver, standing by Terry.

Linday was placed under arrest by Marshal Frank Meyers, and the house was locked up after the arrival of Sheriff Williams and Deputy Coroner C. E. Martin. An autopsy was performed, and a preliminary hearing was held in Sumas on the evening of July 5. Linday was charged with first-degree murder and was placed under seven thousand dollars' bond. The sentiment of the townspeople of Sumas was greatly in Linday's favor, and several citizens immediately furnished his bond.

The autopsy on Terry's body revealed that the first bullet entered the right side of his head and entered the brain. The second bullet went through the left temple, also lodging in the brain. Either shot would have proved fatal. Around a dozen sentimental letters from Annie Linday were found on Terry's body and addressed to him as "My Dear Darling." His effects amounted to a few silver coins, a gold watch, and a gold ring. On July 6 Cowboy Jake's remains were shipped to Bellingham for burial.

During Gus Linday's preliminary hearing, Annie Linday slipped over the border to Huntington to escape rebuke from her neighbors. After Linday was released on bond, she returned to Sumas hoping for a reconciliation. As a result of all the publicity, it was disclosed that Annie had previously crossed the border numerous times to see Terry and had even handled smuggling money for him. All this, plus the love letters found on Terry's body, were too much for Linday, and he finally left her and obtained a divorce. Annie soon left Sumas and never returned. Linday's case was held during the September term of Superior Court, and he was found not guilty.[49]

Jake Terry's body was taken to the Maulsby Morgue in Bellingham, where several hundred curious onlookers came to view the remains of the notorious bad man. One of them did more than look, gruesomely cutting off the little finger of Terry's right hand to steal his 14-carat gold ring. Whoever committed the repulsive act was immediately caught, and the ring was turned over to the authorities at Bellingham.

On July 8 Terry was buried at county expense in the Bay View Cemetery. *The Bellingham Herald* of July 8 gave the following report on the fifty-four-year-old desperado's funeral:

TERRY LIES IN UNHONORED GRAVE

Without even a crowd of morbid curiosity seekers in attendance, without a single flower on the rough, wooden box, and followed by not one mourner, Jake Terry, the notorious ex-convict, smuggler, train robber and all around bad man, was buried this morning in the potters field by Undertaker Maulsby. The man who defied the police of two countries and who was shot down by the husband of the woman he wronged, was laid away to rest the way he died. He had the same suit of clothes on and he was clad in "his boots" in which he died.[50]

Thus, the rough and tough brawler known as Terrible Terry was bested by the inoffensive little man whom he had cuckolded. One too many drinks at the U.S. Saloon dulled Terry's senses, and he vastly underestimated what actions mortal fear can induce from a timid and unobtrusive individual. Terry had played the bully once too often, and it cost him his life.

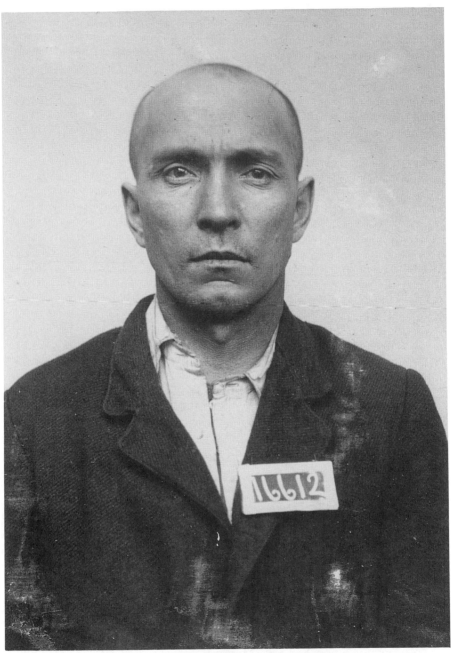

1895 San Quentin Prison photograph of "Cowboy Jake" Terry. CALIFORNIA STATE ARHIVES, SACRAMENTO

United States of America.

IN JUSTICE'S COURT,

BEFORE _D. S. Smith_
Justice of the Peace.

Territory
vs.
J. H. Terry } WARRANT IN ARREST.

TERRITORY OF WASHINGTON, } _ss._
COUNTY OF _King_

To the Sheriff or any Constable of said County, GREETING:

WHEREAS, _H. Atkins & H. Bennton_ has this day complained in writing, under oath, to the undersigned, one of the Justices of the Peace in and for said county, that on the _19th_ day of _July_ 187_3_, at _Seattle_, in said county, _one J. H. Terry did shoot one D. Wright with a calts revolver_

Therefore, in the name of the UNITED STATES you are commanded forthwith to apprehend the said _J. H. Terry_ and bring him before me, to be dealt with according to law.

Given under my hand this _19th_ day of _July_ 187_3_

D. S. Smith
Justice of the Peace.

Arrest warrant for John H. "Jake" Tery for the shooting of Delbert Wright in 1873. Territory of Washington vs. John Terry, Assault with Intent to Murder. DIVISION OF ARCHIVES AND RECORD MANAGEMENT, OFFICE OF THE SECRETARY OF STATE, OLYMPIA

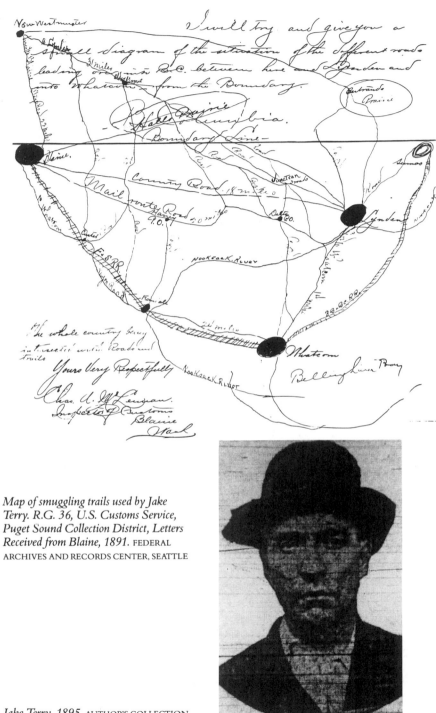

Map of smuggling trails used by Jake
Terry. R.G. 36, U.S. Customs Service,
Puget Sound Collection District, Letters
Received from Blaine, 1891. FEDERAL
ARCHIVES AND RECORDS CENTER, SEATTLE

Jake Terry, 1895. AUTHOR'S COLLECTION

Friday, December 6,1895.

Register of Judgments, Vol. 1, page 109.

United States

959.   v.   Sentence.

Jake Terry.

Comes now this 6th day of December,1895,the said defendant
Jake Terry into open court for sentence,and being informed by the
court of the indictment herein against him and of his conviction
of record herein,he is asked whether he has any legal cause to
show why sentence should not be passed and judgment had against
him,he nothing says save as he before hath said.

Wherefore,by reason of the law and the premises,it is considered by the court,that the said defendant Jake Terry be punished by being imprisoned in the United States Penitentiary at
McNeil's Island,Pierce County,Washington,or in such other place
as may be hereafter designated by the Attorney General of the
United States,for the imprisonment of offenders against the laws
of the United States,for the term of ten years,at hard labor,from
and after this date. And that he pay the costs of this prosecution to be taxed;and that execution issue therefor,and that he be
further imprisoned in the said United States Penitentiary,or in
such other place as may be hereafter designated by the Attorney
General of the United States until such costs are paid or until
he shall be otherwise discharged by due process of law.

And the said defendant Jake Terry is now hereby ordered into
the custody of the United States Marshal,to carry this sentence
into execution.

Register of Judgments, United States vs. Jake Terry *for counterfeiting, Case No. 959,*
Northern Division of District Court, Western District of Washington, FRC 77429.
FEDERAL ARCHIVES AND RECORDS CENTER, SEATTLE

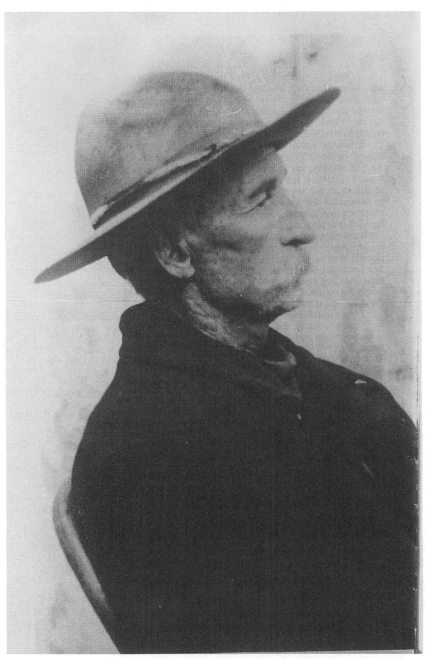

Bill Miner after his capture in May 1906 for train robbery in Canada. BRITISH COLUMBIA PROVINCIAL ARCHIVES, VICTORIA, BRITISH COLUMBIA

Newspaper photos of Gus and Annie Terry Linday. Circa 1907. AUTHOR'S COLLECTION

Jake Terry's grave in the potters-field area of the Bay View Cemetery in Bellingham, Washington. The small protruding rock in right center of photograph marks Terry's grave.
COURTESY BAY VIEW CEMETERY, BELLINGHAM, WASHINGTON

VII. ILLINOIS

WILLIAM S. RUBY

Copperhead Justice

DURING THE CIVIL WAR, Confederate guerrilla warfare and destruction in the state of Missouri reached its peak in the year of 1864. The South realized that it could not defeat the Union in conventional warfare and knew that it was on the verge of losing the war. Confederate commanders in the border states urged guerrilla leaders to step up their activities, pinpointing strike-and-run tactics against field troops, confiscating or destroying enemy supplies, and demolishing railroads and bridges. Most of these raids took place in western and central Missouri by Captain William Quantrill, George Todd, and Bloody Bill Anderson. However, the predominantly Union area around St. Louis was also having problems.

The area in Illinois due south of St. Louis was a secessionist hotbed, and the majority of the residents of Monroe and Randolph counties were southern sympathizers. They were commonly known as Copperheads and belonged to such secret societies as the Knights of the golden Circle and the Sons of Liberty. Their main function was sheltering and aiding Confederate guerrillas, such as Bob Highly, Bob Holmes, and Pres Sweeney, who operated out of Illinois and raided in eastern Missouri. The major leader of the guerrillas on the Missouri side was Sam Hildebrand.[1]

Twenty-eight-year-old Hildebrand was a native of Bonne Terre, Missouri, and had been an active guerrilla since April 1862. Hildebrand survived the war but ran afoul of the law and was subsequently shot and killed in Perry County, Illinois, in March 1872.[2]

The actions of the Illinois guerrillas, Hildebrand's rebel group, and their supporters in Illinois were a thorn in the side of the commanders at Union headquarters in St. Louis. In 1864 they struck back, but the only one who would suffer from their retaliation was William S. Ruby, a United States detective who had been appointed by the provost marshal's office for the Department of Missouri at St. Louis.[3]

William S. Ruby was born in Springfield, Illinois, in April 1837, and during his childhood his parents moved to Decatur in Macon County. He became a harness maker by trade, and before the Civil War he married Emily Widner in Decatur. On September 3, 1861, five months after the Civil War started, Ruby enlisted as a private in Company I, Seventh Illinois Cavalry, in Decatur. He was mustered into service on November 15 at Camp Lyon, Birds Point, Missouri. On January 1, 1862, he was appointed battalion saddler. [4]

Ruby's stint in the army did not last long. Suffering from "chronic nephritis and stricture of the urethra caused by syphilis of long standing," Ruby was reduced to the ranks on April 2, 1862, and was absent without leave in Cairo, Illinois, from April 20 until his disability discharge at Jacinto, near Corinth, Mississippi, on June 27. Wrote Second Lieutenant William Ashmead on June 7, "Said Ruby has not been fit for duty hardley any of the time for three months past, on account of his disease." [5]

Ruby returned to Decatur and, possibly because of his venereal disease, was divorced in 1863. It was likely at this point that he headed for the area around St. Genevieve, Farmington, and Pilot Knob, Missouri. He undoubtedly worked as a saddler for the provost marshals office in St. Genevieve, made friends with Captain Gustavus StGem, the assistant provost marshal, and became interested in applying for an appointment as a U.S. detective. [6]

On August 20, 1864, Ruby wrote the provost marshals department in St. Louis, requesting a position at St. Genevieve as a U.S. detective. On November 18, Captain StGem wrote to Colonel Joseph Darr, Jr., the provost marshal general at St. Louis, recommending Ruby as a replacement for Detective M. R. Taylor. StGem pointed out that the guerrilla bands of Highly, Holmes, and Sweeney had been active that week in the lower portion of St. Genevieve County, robbing St. Mary's merchants of three hundred dollars' worth of goods. Colonel Darr approved a temporary appointment for Ruby on November 25, stipulating that he commence his duties on December 1.

Ruby made his first foray into the field on the day his employment went into effect. Accompanied by five soldiers of StGem's command, he went in pursuit of the guerrillas in St. Genevieve County, only to find they had crossed the Mississippi River into Illinois. On December 3, Ruby also crossed into Illinois, and by the fifth he had gotten wind of a Confederate spy named William Bayles who was being harbored by a southern sympathizer named James in Monroe City. Finding that his quarry had fled, Ruby trailed him to Glasgow City, where he suspected he had been hidden by another Copperhead named Samuel Waddell. Ruby left a soldier on the spy's track and returned to St. Genevieve on the seventh. Ruby's next assignment would be his last. [7]

On December 24, 1864, Captain StGem gave William Ruby orders to arrest one Joshua Burch of Randolph County, Illinois, on the charge of harboring known bushwhackers and rebel soldiers. Following orders, Ruby crossed the Mississippi River, proceeded to Burch's home near

Chester, and arrested him on Christmas Day. He returned with Burch to the provost marshal's office in St. Genevieve and turned his prisoner over to Captain StGem. Burch was subjected to only a good tongue-lashing and was immediately released upon taking an oath of allegiance to the United States.

Joshua Burch was infuriated, and immediately upon his return to Illinois he went before a justice of the peace and made an affidavit against Ruby for kidnapping. Ruby had also returned to Randolph County and was quickly seized and arrested by fifteen southern sympathizers in Kaskaskia and hauled before a justice of the peace, who was also a reported Copperhead. Ruby was bound over for trial for kidnapping under $2,500 bail, which he could not raise, and was lodged in the Randolph County jail at Chester. [8]

Captain StGem received word of Ruby's plight on December 30, and the next day he wrote two letters, one to the provost marshal general, Colonel J. H. Baker, and the other to the officer in command of U.S. forces in Chester, Illinois. StGem outlined the situation, explaining that Ruby was carrying out direct orders, and requested that immediate action be taken to effect Ruby's release.

On January 1, 1865, Emma Taylor, the wife of Detective M. R. Taylor, attempted to visit Ruby in the Randolph County jail, but was refused admittance by the sheriff. She immediately wrote Major G. Abbot, provost marshal at Alton, Illinois, and reported that the citizens would resist any action by the military to free Ruby and that a cannon had been placed in front of the jail.

On January 4 Ruby was allowed to write Captain StGem. His letter was a plaintive appeal for assistance, stating that he was not allowed to have a fire for heat in his cell and that all communication, which would be treated with consideration but not necessarily with compliance, be directed to the sheriff. On January 6 Ruby received permission to write Lieutenant Colonel C. W. Davis of the provost marshal's office in St. Louis with an appeal for assistance.

Apparently stalling for time, Colonel Baker wrote Captain StGem on January 1, requesting the same information StGem sent him on December 31. The captain complied and sent a duplicate report on the twelfth. The only action Colonel Baker ever took was to relieve Ruby of his duties, retroactive to January 1, with this lame excuse: "He [Ruby] having performed no service since that date." Meanwhile, StGem never gave up trying to secure Ruby's exoneration and release. [9]

William Ruby languished in his cold jail cell throughout January and was not allowed to contact his friends, obtain bail, or acquire legal counsel. The jail was guarded by a strong force of southerners who openly defied any U.S. military intervention in the case. Upon the pretense that U.S. forces were being sent by Captain StGem to rescue Ruby, a special term in Randolph County Circuit Court was called on February 1 to try the prisoner. [10]

One grand jury member, staunch Union supporter John Woodside of Coultersville, was outraged by the proceedings of the court. Although

Woodside was semiliterate, his writings give a graphic picture of what transpired:

> The Case I was on the Grand Jury that found the Bill against him [Ruby] — out of 23 there was just 5 union men and that is the way that they got the Bill — for it was not on the Evidence. . . . [11]

Both the grand jury's indictment and Ruby's trial for kidnapping occurred on February 3. The trial transcript reads:

> And now on this day comes the People by Johnson & Thos. G. Allen their attorneys who prosecutes and the defendant by Hood and Wall his attorneys, and the defendant being arraigned enters the plea of not guilty and motion entered by the defendant's Counsel to quash the indictment which motion was by the Court refused. And at the same time presented their petition for a change of venue and counter affidavits by the plaintiffs in Case No. 15 on the docket to apply by agreement in this Cause which application for a change of venue is denied by the Court. Whereupon on the 3rd day of February A D 1865 Comes again said Plaintiffs by their attorneys and the defendant by his attorneys who enters their motion for Continuance on affidavit of Defendant which motion and application by the court refused.

A jury was quickly impaneled, and the trial commenced. Evidence and arguments were presented by both sides, and at the end of the day, the jury retired to reach a verdict. They returned shortly with their decision — guilty. Judge Brian sentenced Ruby to six years imprisonment at the Illinois State Penitentiary at Joliet. [12]

John Woodside gave his colorful version of the court proceedings that day:

> Then what Does old Coperhead Judge Brien [Brian] Doo he Brings him in the same Day for trial and Dose not give him an our [hour] to get Ready for trial — But that was not all he Done — Mr Ruby seen what Kind of trial [he] was Likely to get So he made oath that [he] Did not Believe he could get a fair trial under Old Brian — What Dose the old Scoundrell Doo [you] think to stop that — he got up a paper & sent it Down to the grand jury Room for them to sign that he Could get a fair trial — why your Honer, I never Saw such a mean thing Done in all my Life — they tried him in that way & sent him up for six years — the old fellah new [knew] that nearley all Both the Jurys was Coperheads. [13]

On Valentines Day, William S. Ruby was delivered to the Illinois State Penitentiary. He gave his occupation as harness maker and his habits of life as temperate. He was described as five feet, five and one half inches in height, with dark brown hair, hazel eyes, and a dark complexion. [14]

Now began the furor over a pardon for William Ruby. On February 27 Captain StGem wrote Illinois governor Richard J. Oglesby, requesting that Ruby be pardoned on the grounds that he was acting upon military orders and had no choice but to obey those orders. On February 7 the prosecutor in Ruby's case, Thomas G. Allen, wrote the governor from

Chester, Illinois, that Ruby was an "accomplished scamp" who was guilty of larceny, robbery, and passing counterfeit money"to the great scandal of the Government he professed to represent." The governor also received letters from Major General Grenville M. Dodge and Colonel J. H. Baker of the provost marshal's headquarters in St. Louis, plus Woodside's letter. By April, Governor Oglesby had received three pardon petitions from Randolph County residents and one petition from Ruby's home county of Macon. [15]

Governor Oglesby was faced with a dilemma, being bombarded by supporters of both sides of the Ruby case. On March 3 the beleaguered governor wrote to Major General Dodge:

> The young man Ruby is from my own County, I know the family well, and know him. . . . I have been ready to pardon him and sought for information from Union men in Randolph County whom I know, in the hope of being able to favor the young man, these Union men, so far have all borne evidence against his uniform bad conduct and unsufferable demeanor in the County. . . . Another fact, it is incomprehensible to me that Captain StGem should consider the case of Burch so aggravated as to require him to send Ruby into Illinois to forcibly arrest Burch and carry him out of the State, merely to take his oath and discharge him, so far as taking the oath of a "bushwhacker" or rebel sympathizer is concerned for any good to result from it he might just as well have come over to Illinois and sworn him and returned home, and saved Ruby, and a violation of the "letter of the Law." . . .
>
> It is falling far short of the rule to go as far as StGem did and then simply dismiss the man on an oath, it certainly shows that he acted very indiscreetly in ordering the arrest . . . it was not such a case as would warrant the exercise of such authority, and what is worse embarrasses me in my desire to aid you in hunting out such characters as have forfeited the protection of the Law and deserve the severest punishment. The moment I attempt to act I am to be told the man [Burch] was not guilty at all, was not guilty of anything, and was unjustly arrested, because Captain StGem having him in his hands did not detain him for any offense but at once set him at liberty on an oath. Of course I am unable to sustain any such foolish proceedings.
>
> I hate to arbitrarily pardon a man because he was a Government Detective when our friends say he should not be released, so soon, however, as I can find the time I will more thoroughly investigate the case. . . . [16]

The governor's letter raises the question of Burch's guilt. The only evidence is contained in John Woodside's letter. Woodside knew Burch and questioned him during Ruby's trial:

> I ast Mr Birch what he was arested for—he said Mr St Gem said it was for harboring Returned Rebels—I ast him if he Done it he said thare was 2 Came to his house from Misouri—But sais he went to Chester and ast the . . . Lawyers & he said they told him to keep them of course—They would for they were all strong Coperheads. [17]

While Governor Oglesby was deliberating over the fate of William Ruby, Captain Gustavus StGem again struck out at the Illinois rebels.

Sometime in February, StGem seized some ferry boats at Little Rock Ferry near St. Genevieve. These boats belonged to Illinois resident Felix Mudd, whom StGem accused of being a notorious Copperhead and using his boats to assist rebel guerrillas in crossing the Mississippi River. On February 28 StGem wrote a letter explaining his actions to Captain George C. Tichenor at Headquarters of the Department of Missouri at St. Louis. Major General Dodge, in turn, forwarded the letter to Governor Oglesby as further proof of Copperhead activity in Randolph County.[18]

Colonel Baker again wrote Captain StGem for the facts of the case in lieu of the governor's letter to General Dodge. StGem wrote a letter of rebuttal to Colonel Baker on March 9, stating that Ruby was following direct military orders when he apprehended Burch. The captain defended his actions by stating that with the state of affairs concerning rebel sympathizers in Randolph County, his orders were the only feasible way to get Burch or any others of his ilk. StGem also stated that there were "very few good Union men" in Randolph County. On April 6 he sent Lieutenant Colonel Davis the facts of Ruby's case and wrote:

> I am really grieved to see so much hesitation in his Excellency the Gov. of the State of Illinois to pardon and release said Ruby, as it has been clearly shown by me that Ruby was not personally responsible for the arrest of Joshua Birch [sic] of Randolph County Ills. on the 24th day of Decr. 1864, as he was acting at this time strictly in obedience to my orders. . . . [19]

StGem had no way of knowing that on the same day he wrote this letter, Governor Oglesby had taken decisive action in Ruby's case.

However, the weight that swung the pendulum in Ruby's favor was likely this letter, dated April 3, to the governor from John E. Detrich, a prominent Union supporter and resident of Sparta, Randolph County:

> I have taken some pains to inquire into the facts and believe that Ruby was acting under the orders of the military authorities of the Western Dept. He may have acted erroneously, indeed I think he did, but at the same time do not think he is justly chargeable with any guilt if I have been correctly informed by reliable men. . . . Petitions are now being signed in this County, praying for his pardon and I can assure you that they are signed by loyal men and none others. I may further assure you that the sentiment of the loyal masses of this Co. will sustain you in pardoning him if the evidence before you is as has been represented to me. . . . [20]

On April 6, 1865, Governor Oglesby made his decision and pardoned William Ruby. The penitentiary officials released him the next day.[21]

Following the sobering experience he had suffered during the war, William Ruby decided to better himself. He immediately enrolled at the St. Louis Homeopathic Medical College and graduated in 1867. He returned to Decatur, Illinois, where he practiced medicine for the next twenty-one years.[22]

Years later, when Ruby filed for a Civil War pension, two of his friends in Decatur, John Quinlan and Frank L. Hayes, vouched for his character:

> We knew the above named W. S. Ruby from a time long prior to his enlistment, in the fall of 1861, . . . lived near him and saw him frequently, and knew his reputation in the neighborhood where he lived with his comrades in the army. During all the time of our acquaintance with him he was a sober peaceable man.[23]

On August 5, 1865, William S. Ruby married Eliza A. Ricketts in Decatur, and sixteen years later, on September 22, 1881, their only child, Emma May, was born. In the winter of 1888, the Rubys moved to Riverside, California, where they purchased a home at 182 East Ninth Street. Ruby built up his medical practice and became active in local business affairs. By 1893, Ruby had become the health officer for the city of Riverside as well as the county coroner.[24]

Around the turn of the century Ruby's health began to deteriorate. Unable to work because of a weak heart, eczema of the chest, and a defunct right ankle, Ruby applied for the Civil War pension on August 2, 1900. He was granted a pension of six dollars a month, and he collected it until his death on February 22, 1904, which was more tragic than his ill-fated career as a U.S. detective.[25]

The facts behind William S. Ruby's heartrending demise was reported in *The Riverside Daily Press*:

TIRED OF LIFE HE ENDED IT.

*Dr. Ruby in a Fit of Depression on Account of Poor
Health, Shot Himself Through the Heart.*

> Discouraged by hopeless illness, and in one of the fits of depression to which he had been subject of late, Dr. W. S. Ruby this afternoon placed a pistol over his heart, pulled the trigger, and met instant death.
>
> About 2 o'clock this afternoon, he requested the nurse, Mrs. Woelker, who was caring for him, to go into the yard and get him an orange. She went, but had hardly reached the yard when she heard the report of a pistol. His daughter, Mrs. Ray McCormick, who was the only other person in the house, also heard it and both rushed to the bed room where they found Dr. Ruby dying with a bullet through his heart. Dr. O. C. Darling was summoned by telephone but there was nothing to be done.
>
> Dr. Ruby had been a resident of Riverside for many years and was well known in business and professional circles. For three or four years he had been in feeble health, and since the death of his wife about a year ago, he has had frequent fits of depression. It was one of these, when the burden of living seemed to great, that he committed the terrible act which ended his life.
>
> The coroner's inquest will be held at 10 a.m. tomorrow.[26]

Funeral services for the sixty–seven–year–old Ruby were held at his residence on February 24. Reverend B. S. Haywood officiated at the service, and Ruby was buried in the Evergreen Cemetery.[27]

The unique aspect of Ruby's inglorious career as a U.S. detective was that it made history. William S. Ruby is the only known U.S. military figure during the Civil War to be arrested, tried, convicted, and imprisoned in a Union state for carrying out U.S. military orders. However, this does not answer the question of whether Ruby was a scoundrel who committed unlawful acts under the protection of the U.S. government or a scapegoat who blindly followed the overzealous orders of his commanding officer. This might have been answered had Ruby returned to field duty, but he never got that chance for the Civil War ended five days after his release from prison.

William S. Ruby in 1893. Photo from History and Directory of Riverside County, 1893–1894.

(2)

uniform bad conduct and unofferable demeanor in the County; I do not understand why or good men as these are, who have talked to me on the subject, seem to have such prejudice against him. Another fact, it is incomprehensible to me that Captain Flam should consider the case of Burch as aggravated as to require him to send Ruby into Illinois to forcibly arrest Burch and carry him out of the State, merely to take his oath and discharge him, so far as taking the oath of a "bushwhacker" or rebel sympathizer is concerned for any good to result from it he might just as well have come over to Illinois and sworn him and returned home, and acquit Ruby, and a violation of the "letter of the law."

You know how sensitive our people are——

State of Illinois
Executive Department.
Springfield March 3 1865.

General:

I received to day the petition of Captain Flam for the pardon of W. S. Ruby and have noted the endorsement made by you on his behalf. ——

The young man Ruby is from my own County; I know the family well, and know him. I believe, I have been very anxious to assist him all I am in any reasonable way consistently, and when I have been ready to pardon him and sought for information from Union men in Ran-dolph County whom I know, in the light of being able to favor the young man, these Union men, so far have all borne evidence against his

Above and pages 165 & 166: Illinois governor Richard J. Ogleby's letter regarding the pardon of William Ruby. Executive Clemency Files (RS103.96), W. S. Ruby.

State of Illinois
Executive Department.
Springfield ___ 186_

upon the matter of Military Arrests, whenever therefore an Officer attempts to exercise this sort of authority it should be in a flagrant evil, and one in which public sentiment will uphold the act as a means of certain punishment upon a bad man, and there he should be held and punished. It is falling far short of the rule to go as far as St[?]em did and then simply dismiss the man on an oath, it looks very much like an effort to hunt a case, it certainly shows that he acted very indiscreetly in Ordering the arrest or summarily dismissing the man, it was not such a case as would warrant the exercise of such authority, and what is worse embarrasses me in my desire to aid you, and the State of Missouri in hunting out such characters as have forfeited the protection of

the Law and deems the severest punishment the moment I attempt to ask I am to be told the man was not guilty at all, was not guilty of any thing, and was unjustly arrested, because Captain St[?]em having him in his hands did not detain him for any offence but at once set him at liberty on an oath. Of course I am unable to sustain any such [?] proceedings

I am exceedingly anxious to support your wishes and will go very far to sustain everything the State of Missouri or your authorities may see fit to do to sustain the cause of our country, and dislike to be [?] in a hesitance of summe

Information showing the granting of W. S. Ruby's pardon in April 1865. Executive Clemency Files (RS103.96), W. S. Ruby. ILLINOIS STATE ARCHIVES, SPRINGFIELD

VIII. COLORADO

ALEXANDER McKENZIE

Last of the Wolves

AS LATE AS 1892, STAGECOACHES were still running in the remote areas of southern Colorado to such towns as Spar City, Creede, and Pagosa Springs. All area mail was transported by stagecoaches, or hacks, a carriage or wagonlike vehicle. There had been no stage robberies since 1881, when stages were victimized numerous times by some of the foremost stagecoach robbers in the United States, such as Bill Miner, Billy LeRoy, Charley Allison, and Ham White.[1] After eleven years of placidity, the residents of southern Colorado were shocked when the mail hack from Pagosa Springs to Amargo (Lumberton), New Mexico, was held up by a lone bandit just before daybreak on September 14, 1892.

Seventeen-year-old hack driver Alfred Black was pleasantly conversing with a lone passenger, Pagosa Springs attorney John F. "Frank" Spickard, as he drove the lumbering hack up a hill three miles south of Pagosa Springs. Reaching the top, Black was startled by a command of "Hands up!" which came from a man partially hidden behind a tree and holding a six-shooter. Black immediately halted the hack, and he and Spickard were ordered, "Get out of the wagon, and turn your faces away."

The bandit, who was wearing a long rubber overcoat and a little black slouch hat and whose face was covered with a perforated rubber mask, hurriedly ripped open the mail pouch and took out two registered letters containing fifty-five dollars. He then relieved Spickard of thirty-eight dollars and some bills valued at two thousand dollars, which Spickard was to collect. The robber took one dollar and twenty-five cents from the driver's pocket, thought better of it, and returned the money. Spickard claimed he was going to tackle the bandit but thought he saw a Winchester barrel sticking out of the bushes and gave up the idea. Regardless of what Spickard claimed he saw, there was only one robber.

Having gotten all he was going to get, the bandit went behind some trees while ordering Black, "Lose no time in hitting the road to Amargo." Black didn't; however, after traveling three miles, he turned the hack around and headed back to Pagosa Springs. The young driver was so unnerved by the robbery that he quit his job and left for Arizona.

Upon receipt of news of the robbery, three men left Pagosa Springs in pursuit of the bandit. They trailed him south to the San Juan River, where they stationed guards at all accessible crossings. Because the bandit had a horse, which was shod only in front, and a pony, the posse thought there were two robbers.[2]

Archuletta County sheriff Bill Kern and Joe Chambers tracked two men into New Mexico and arrested them at Tres Piedras. Neither man fitted the description of the bandit, and both were released. For more than a week, no trace of the stage robber could be found, until he committed another holdup.[3]

At 5 p.m., September 28, the stage from Spar City to Creede, driven by George W. Pemberton, was ordered to halt four miles from Spar City by a highwayman hiding behind a willow thicket. The bandit was armed with a six-shooter and a Winchester rifle, masked by a sack with eyeholes, and wearing a black rubber coat. The mail was again rifled but held nothing of value. The lone passenger, William S. Adams, the publisher of *The Creede Candle*, was robbed of two dollars, and Pemberton shelled out around $165. The robber then ordered the driver to wait until he walked up the road to see if anyone was coming. Returning to the stage, he told Pemberton to drive on, and he disappeared into the willows.[4]

When the news reached Creede, Deputy Sheriff James T. "Tom" Delaney immediately started in pursuit and reached the robbery site the next morning. Delaney, a former government scout and a deputy for nine years, was an experienced trailer and soon found horse tracks and indentions made by an unusual type of boot. He followed the tracks for three miles, where he found a willow thicket in which a pack horse with a broken hind shoe had been tied. Heading westward, he followed the trail for seventy miles to Howardsville and discovered that the bandit had left the pack horse with stockman W. J. Arey because it was suffering with a sore back and had a broken shoe on the right hind hoof. Delaney had relentlessly trailed the fugitive for four days and two nights by the time he reached Ouray. On the morning of October 3, he caught up with his quarry walking the streets in town and arrested him, confiscating his six-shooter and Winchester rifle. Before heading back to Creede, the deputy retrieved a black rubber coat from a cabin that the prisoner shared with D. W. Sheidler.[5]

The man Delaney arrested was a twenty-one-year-old Canadian named Alexander A. McKenzie, who adamantly denied committing the holdups. McKenzie was born in April 1871 in Melbourne, Quebec, and was the son of grain merchant Andrew McKenzie and his wife, Janet. Alexander had left Canada for the western U.S. when he was fifteen to work as a cowhand and horse trader. He had been in Colorado for three years and had made staunch friends in the state. He was described as five feet, ten inches in height and weighing 157 pounds, with two or three upper front teeth missing. One report stated he was a hard-looking character while another called him a refined-looking young man.[6]

The Creede Candle gave a summary of the evidence against McKenzie:

> The man is the same one who was about Spur just previous to the robbery. He was suspicioned of it by the citizens soon as it was found out he disappeared at the same time. But Delaney worked on no suspicion, though he came to the same conclusion. McKenzie first denied having left the pack horse at Howardsville, but returning through there and facing the man he left it with, had to confess as much. He wore high-heeled boots which fit the tracks on the Spur road exactly. A black rubber coat, such as the highwayman wore, was found on his saddle [sic]. He had a gun and rifle which tally with the description. It is pretty clear case against him, and Delaney has done some clever work as a sleuth.[7]

On the afternoon of October 6, Delaney returned to Creede with his prisoner in tow, and McKenzie quickly obtained the services of attorney C. J. Gavin. *The Pagosa Springs News* reported:

> The prisoner has since been taken to Creede, and Deputy Delaney says that the prisoner admitted to having been in the Pagosa Springs country about the time that our stage was held up.[8]

Deputy Tom Delaney was a fair man as well as a shrewd lawman. When McKenzie claimed to have witnesses in Creede that would prove him innocent of the Spar City stage robbery, Delaney agreed to take him to question the witnesses. On the afternoon of October 8, Delaney and his prisoner, along with Deputy Sheriff R. P. Buckle and McKenzie's lawyer, went to a restaurant owned by a couple named Busche to interview a four-teen-year-old waitress named Freda Schutz. McKenzie claimed he had eaten dinner at the restaurant with Thomas Cuddahy at the time the stage was robbed and that Freda Schutz would confirm this. Delaney's affidavit reads:

> That the said Freda Schutz in conversation with Alexander McKensie [sic] . . . then stated that she knew that he (McKensie) had eaten at that restaurant, that the last meal he had taken there was breakfast and that was either the morning of the robbery or the morning of the day before the robbery; that she remembered him by him always leaving his horse untied and that she once spoke to him about him leaving his horse untied and it would run away sometime if he did not tie it.

Mrs. Busche also conversed with McKenzie and corroborated the young waitress's statement. This cooked McKenzie's goose, and Delaney took him to the Burnard and Beebe Hotel and turned him over to U.S. Deputy Marshal A. W. Brown.[9]

On October 10 McKenzie's preliminary hearing was held in Del Norte before U.S. Commissioner John B. Haffy. In default of three thousand dollars' bail, McKenzie was remanded to jail and taken to Denver, where his trial was to be held. The prisoner was indicted on December 9 in U.S. District Court on two counts, of robbing the mail and robbing the mail carrier. He pleaded not guilty to both charges. [10]

The Canadian born McKenzie was indigent, and author John M. Motter reported that the court sought funds for his defense from the British Consulate in Denver and that the trial came close to causing an international incident. Motter was partially correct; there was never a hint of an international incident. [11]

Andrew McKenzie received word of his son's plight in November. He immediately took action and appealed to government officials in his province for help. On December 30 several members of the Canadian Parliament and businessmen forwarded a petition to the governor general of Canada, Lord Stanley of Preston. The governor general responded on January 12, 1893, by telegraphing orders to British ambassador Julian Pauncefote in Washington, D.C., to take steps to assure McKenzie a fair trial. The ambassador in turn passed the instructions to Vice Consul Richard Pearce in Denver, who obtained the services of the Denver law firm of Rogers, Cuthbert, and Ellis on January 15, the eve of the trial. In the meantime, Andrew McKenzie went to Denver and hired attorney John W. Hughes of Conejos for $250, all he had to spare. [12]

Alexander McKenzie, now represented by three lawyers, was brought to trial on January 16, 1893, and the jury was sworn. Judge John A. Rivers presided and District Attorney John D. Flemming handled the prosecution. On the seventeenth, evidence from both sides was presented, and the case was turned over to the jury. On January 19 the jury reported that they were hopelessly deadlocked and could not reach a verdict. Judge Rivers immediately discharged the jury. *The Daily News* of January 20 reported:

> It was intimated that the vote showed six for acquittal and six for conviction. The prisoner listened to the report with evident satisfaction. Bail was placed at $5,000 and McKenzie was again marched off to jail. [13]

Judge Moses Hallett now took over as trial judge. In 1881 Judge Hallett had presided over the trials of two notorious stage robbers, Billy LeRoy and Ham White, with disastrous results. LeRoy escaped, and White was released from prison several years later because of trial errors. Judge Hallett intended to make no errors in this trial.

On February 3, Alexander McKenzie appeared in court with his attorney, L. M. Cuthbert, to request that defense witnesses be subpoenaed by the court and that the court bear the expenses. Judge Hallett granted the request. On February 11 court was adjourned because heavy snows had blocked the railroad and detained the witnesses. A new jury was selected on the thirteenth, and McKenzie finally came to trial the next day.

For two days the jury heard the evidence, and by the end of the second day they retired to the jury room to consider the verdict. In one hour the jury filed back into the courtroom with their verdict — guilty. [14]

On March 1 McKenzie's attorneys made a motion for a new trial on the grounds that new evidence had been discovered, that the court erred in admitting certain evidence, and that the evidence presented did not justify a conviction. The motion, however, was denied. Before pronouncing the sentence, Judge Hallett asked the defendant if he had anything to say. McKenzie dejectedly replied that he had nothing to add to what he had stated during his trial. Judge Hallett then passed sentence, giving McKenzie a life term at hard labor in the house of corrections at Detroit. Although this appears to be an exceptionally severe sentence, Judge Hallett had no choice, for revised U.S. Statute No. 4572 reads:

> Any person who shall rob the carrier or Agent of the Mail, and in effecting such robbery, the robber shall wound the person having custody of the mail, or put his life in jeopardy, by use of dangerous weapons, such offender shall be punishable by imprisonment at hard labour for the term of his natural life. [15]

The Daily News covered the trial and commented on McKenzie's reaction to his sentence:

> Alexander McKenzie . . . was sentenced yesterday by Judge Hallett to be confined at hard labor for life in the United States house of correction at Detroit. McKenzie preserved the same stolid and unmoved demeanor that has characterized him since his arrest and did not move a muscle when sentence was pronounced. [16]

Shortly after the trial, an anonymous letter from Denver dated March 9 and titled "An Unjust Sentence" appeared in *The Glengarian*, an Alexandria, Ontario, newspaper. The letter accused the court of convicting McKenzie on circumstantial evidence and of not allowing time for defense witnesses to appear in court and stated that Delaney perjured himself to obtain a reward. Although unsigned, this letter was undoubtedly written by Alexander's father. To prove or disprove these allegations, the evidence presented at the trial must be examined. [17]

D. W. Sheidler, McKenzie's roommate in Ouray and a witness for the defense, stated McKenzie left Ouray the latter part of August. McKenzie testified that by September 8 he was south of Amargo, buying horses, but Nicholas Boston, who was fishing ten miles from Creede, identified the defendant as the man who stopped by his camp that day. When he returned from fishing in the evening, Boston stated, his gun belt and some tobacco and money were missing from his tent. Mr. McArthur, a store owner in Creede, produced the gun belt in court and stated that McKenzie traded it for horse feed in late September.

McKenzie arrived in Pagosa Springs on September 12 with two horses, claiming he was looking for a lost horse. P. A. Deller, a baker in Pagosa Springs, testified that he saw McKenzie buying an unusual type of boots in Johnson's Store on the twelfth, and saloon keeper Charles Shad said the defendant was in his saloon on the evening of September 13, the night before the first robbery. Mail subcontractor W. B. Avery measured the boot tracks at the robbery scene and proved that they were the same size as McKenzie's new boots.

Frank Spickard, the passenger on the Pagosa Springs hack, testified that McKenzie was definitely the bandit. However, defense witness Eudolphus Taylor of Pagosa Springs claimed that Spickard had told him that the person who robbed the hack was J. M. "Ed" Keith of Archuleta County. The defense also had a witness, E. Risenberg of Durango, who stated he overheard Spickard and Keith arguing over the division of money and that Spickard accused Keith of keeping more than his share. D. C. Sargent of Durango countered this by relating that Spickard said only that Keith resembled the bandit in size and build.

On September 25 McKenzie arrived in Creede, and George Williamson claimed he saw the defendant on the road to Spar City that morning. Livery stable owner James Overstreet of Spar City stated he kept McKenzie's sorrel horse until the morning of the twenty-sixth. Spar City postmaster Frank E. Sowards testified that he saw McKenzie in a Spar City saloon on the night of the twenty-seventh and again at six the next morning on the road to Creede. Both Peter Karg and James Overstreet reported seeing McKenzie near the robbery scene on the morning of the robbery.

Although Samuel Adams, the passenger on the Spar City stage, identified McKenzie as the robber, defense witness John Shaw of Del Norte stated that Adams told him that he was too frightened to identify the robber. S. L. Burke of Spar City reported that Adams said the bandit had hands like a woman and wore miner's laced boots, which McKenzie did not own. In his testimony, Adams stated that the bandit's mask had slipped over his face, and he noticed an abrasion on his left cheek. Sheriff Morris Corbitt of Ouray testified that he saw McKenzie in a restaurant in Ouray on October 1, observed him closely, and noticed the abrasion. McKenzie was asked to stand in court and show the left side of his face; the mark of an abrasion was still evident.

McKenzie claimed he left Creede on the day of the second robbery and had trouble with his horse, which forced him to return to town. He further stated he was in Creede when the robbery occurred and left for Howardsville the next day. However, rancher Fred Berry, whose spread was forty miles from Creede, testified he saw McKenzie pass his ranch at 10 a.m. the day after the robbery, a distance too far for McKenzie to travel if he had left Creede as he had claimed.

D. W. Sheidler first claimed that the black rubber coat taken from his cabin in Ouray had not been out of his possession for more than a year but later said he was not sure whether McKenzie had used it or not. McKenzie's lawyers tried to show that the revolver taken from the defendant by Delaney actually belonged to someone else. The attorneys quickly halted this line of defense when the owner, H. C. Smith of Denver, stated that he was a former Denver policeman and that the revolver had been stolen from him on the night of August 23, 1890, when he attempted to arrest three burglars, one of whom bore a striking resemblance to Alexander McKenzie.

As to the accusation that Delaney perjured himself to obtain a reward, the United States government had a standing reward of one thousand dollars for the arrest of anyone robbing the mail. However, it was proven that Delaney had no knowledge of this until after McKenzie's arrest and the deposition and filing of his report.

In desperation, McKenzie's lawyers sent another attorney, named Patton, to Creede to again interview the waitress, Freda Schutz. Whether from pressure or uncertainty, she signed an affidavit on February 23, claiming that she now remembered McKenzie eating dinner in the restaurant with Thomas Cuddahy at the same time the Spar City stage was robbed on September 28. This was the new evidence McKenzie's attorneys tried to introduce in their motion for a new trial. [18]

An aftermath of McKenzie's adjudication involved the convicted man's friend and witness, Thomas Cuddahy. During McKenzie's first trial, Cuddahy was found guilty of contempt of court for not appearing as a witness on January 17 and was fined for the cost of the proceedings. He was more punctual at the second trial. Cuddahy was outspoken in defense of his friend's innocence, and when McKenzie was convicted, he blamed Spickard. *The Pagosa Springs News* outlined what occurred on the day McKenzie was found guilty:

> United States Marshal Brown yesterday arrested Thomas R. Cudahy [sic] on a charge of attempting to intimidate J. F. Spickard of Pagosa Springs. Spickard was an important witness in the prosecution of McKenzie, the highwayman and mail robber convicted yesterday. Cudahy was one of McKenzie's friends, and is almost a giant physically. He appears to attribute his friends conviction principally to the evidence given by Spickard. Twice yesterday he approached Spickard, who, although a large man, is badly crippled, and exclaimed, "You are a perjured cur and have sent an honest man to _____ [hell]. You'll have to settle with me and I just as lief die now as any other time, for I'm fixed [armed].
>
> The bully wilted completely when he discovered what punishment he might receive, and the court reprimanded him and let him proceed his way. [19]

On March 4 the law firm of Rogers, Cuthbert, and Ellis sent a letter to British Vice Consul Richard Pearce outlining the proceedings of McKenzie's trial. The letter was regretful in tone and diplomatically gave the impression that the defense was satisfied that McKenzie was guilty. Excerpted from this letter:

> We believe that every possible defense was made for this defendant and that the trial was in every respect a fair and impartial one. The jury was composed of reliable men of standing in the community, and we do not think that there was any defense on the part of the defendant which was not fully considered by the jury.
>
> The only question involved in the case was as to the identity of the robber, and the jury appeared to have been satisfied from the evidence that the defendant and the robber was the same person.

The law firm also included a bill in the amount of $1,876.82 for services, which the Canadian government considered too high. In May, Vice Consul Pearce requested a reduction of $250, which the law firm agreed to in June. It was paid $1,626.82 on September 25, 1893. [20]

Alexander McKenzie was delivered to the Detroit house of corrections by Marshal A. H. Jones on April 29. On his return to Denver, Jones received $308.27 as his fee for delivering the prisoner. McKenzie's prison record shows that he could read and write, was a laborer by trade, and was in good health. [21]

Unknown to her husband, Janet McKenzie wrote to President Grover Cleveland on December 7, 1893, pleading executive clemency for her son. She enclosed *The Glengarian* article that stated McKenzie received an unjust trial. The letter was forwarded to C. F. Scott, the attorney in charge of pardons in Washington, who requested a statement of facts from the U.S. attorney's office in Denver. On January 6, 1894, U.S. Attorney Henry V. Johnson, who had replaced John D. Flemming, wrote a thirty-one-page unbiased letter to Scott, outlining the entire case. Since the letter was adverse in content, the matter was dropped for the next two years.

Andrew McKenzie, with help from John H. Graham, a personal friend and former principal of St. Francis College in Richmond, Quebec, continued to fight for Alexander's release. On February 26, 1896, two petitions addressed to President Grover Cleveland requesting executive clemency for Alexander McKenzie were circulated in Canada. One was signed by government officials and leading citizens in the townships of Richmond, Melbourne, and Cleveland, while the second went to the Canadian Parliament, where it was signed by twenty-seven members of the House of Commons and Prime Minister Wilfred Laurier. The problem arose when the two petitions were sent separately to U.S. Secretary of State Richard Olney in Washington.

The petition signed by the members of Parliament was sent by Canadian Secretary of State L. A. Catelliers to British ambassador Julian Pauncefote in Washington, who forwarded it to Secretary of State Olney on March 9. The petition was then sent to the U.S. attorney general on March 13. The second petition was sent to Olney by Andrew McKenzie on April 6, who requested that both petitions be attached before presenting them to President Cleveland. This dilemma went on for a year.

To further complicate matters, Joseph Nicholson, superintendent of the Detroit house of corrections wrote the attorney general a letter on March 17 in support of McKenzie's pardon, but U.S. Attorney Johnson in Denver sent another adverse letter on March 30. However, Johnson's predecessor and the prosecutor in McKenzie's trial, John D. Fleming, signed a third petition supporting McKenzie's pardon on August 25. Compounding the situation, John H. Graham continued to bombard the attorney general with letters. In one dated May 25, Graham apologized for the letter and for the Canadian newspaper article Janet McKenzie sent in December 1893. [22]

By December the confusion regarding the petitions had not been cleared up, and Graham wrote Prime Minister Laurier on the thirtieth, outlining the problem. The prime minister forwarded the correspondence to Minister of Justice Oliver Mowat on January 2, 1897, stating, "I would feel much obliged to you if you could find a moment of leisure to give Mr. Graham the information he desires to have."[23]

The issue would never need to be resolved. Around the first of January, Alexander McKenzie suffered an attack of pneumonia that quickly developed into the most dreaded disease that occurred in all prison systems, tuberculosis. In McKenzie's weakened state, the illness progressed rapidly into what was called "galloping consumption." On January 23 Superintendent Nicholson wrote the president, recommending a pardon because McKenzie was dying and his father was in Detroit waiting to take him home. He enclosed supporting statements from two physicians. Four days later Henry Thurber, the president's private secretary, wrote U.S. Pardon Attorney William C. Endicott, Jr., "The President would like to have this case made up and sent over as soon as possible."

The next day, January 28, President Cleveland granted Alexander McKenzie a conditional pardon upon the evidence from Superintendent Nicholson, stating that the convict be released to his father to "summon him to his home to be properly cared for." Nicholson received the warrant for pardon on the thirtieth and released McKenzie to his father's care.

On March 6, 1897, Superintendent Nicholson wrote another letter regarding McKenzie, this time to U.S. Pardon Attorney Endicott, in which he stated, "Now in order that you may know that I base my requests on what I believe to be facts, and so far, I have made no mistake. You will remember the Pardon of Alex McKenzie only a few weeks ago. The enclosed Postal speaks for itself, and shows that my representations as to his physical condition was correct."[24] The postcard read:

Notice of Alexander McKenzie's death, written by John H. Graham of Richmond, Quebec, to Detroit house of corrections superintendent Joseph Nicholson. R.G. 204, Pardon File No. 0-195, Alexander McKenzie. NATIONAL ARCHIVES, WASHINGTON, D.C.

Pagosa Springs in 1889, looking east. AUTHOR'S COLLECTION

Late 1880s or early 1890s stagecoach at the Halfway House stage stop, nine miles south of Pagosa Springs and six miles south of where the September 14, 1892, stage robbery occurred. AUTHOR'S COLLECTION

No. 56   1893.

Department of Justice

CANADA.

From _Privy Council_

Address _____

Date _Jan. 3/11_

SUBJECT: SEC. I SUB. SEC. 4 OF SUBMISSION

Sig. _____

Petition praying that the Gov't will take steps to
insure a fair trial to one Alexander A McKenzie
confined in Denver, Col. accused of stage & U.S. mail
robbery   (y)

ACTION:

Jan 11/11	Report to council	102	785
11/16	OC rec'd		
17 17	Let. to Mr Cleveland etc.	103	38
Feb 4	PC refers despatch 1665 H		
4	U.S. Secy refers despatch	103	447
16	Report to Council		
March 3/6	OC rec'd		
apr 5	PC refers despatch 1799	104	2
6	Report to Council with papers		
28 May	OC rec'd		
June 9/14	PC refers despatch 1934 H	104	651
19/22	Report to Council		
July & aug 26	OC rec'd		
oct 16/18	PC refers despatch 2148 H	105	648
31/31	Report to Council		

*Petition from the Canadian Parliament and Canadian businessmen to ensure Alexander
McKenzie a fair trial. R.G. 13 A2, Vol. 89, File 36/1893.*
NATIONAL ARCHIVES OF CANADA, OTTAWA, ONTARIO

Court met this day at the hour of 10 oclock A. M. pursuant to adjournment

Present: The Honorable Moses Hallett District Judge and other officers as noted on the first day November last past.

United States of America	
924.	vs:
	Alexander McKenzie.

Indictment for robbing mail carrier of mail

At this day comes J. D. Fleming, Esq. District Attorney, who prosecutes the pleas of the United States in this behalf and the said defendant in his own proper person and by L. M. Cuthbert, Esq. his attorney also comes.

And the motion and affidavits for a new trial herein coming on now to be heard is argued by counsel and the Court being now sufficiently advised in the premises, it is ordered by the Court for good and sufficient reasons to the Court appearing, that the said motion be denied.

And thereupon it is enquired of the said prisoner, if anything he hath to say why the judgment of the law should not now be pronounced against him; Whereupon he answers and saith, that his true name is Alexander McKenzie and that his age is twenty two years and further he saith not, except as he before hath said.

And it appearing to the Court, that there is within the District of Colorado, no penitentiary or jail available for the confinement of convicts, who may be imprisoned for a term exceeding one year. And it further appearing that the Attorney General of the United States has, in due form of law, designated and appointed the House of Correction at or near Detroit in the State of Michigan as a fit and proper place for the confinement of such convicts as may be committed by the judgment of any Court, within the District of Colorado, for the term aforesaid.

Wherefore, it is considered by the Court, that the said prisoner Alexander McKenzie be, by the Marshal, from hence removed to the common jail of Arapahoe County, from whence he came, and from there be, by the Marshal,

_____, removed and conveyed, with all convenient speed, to the House of Correction at or near Detroit in the State of Michigan and there delivered to the warden or keeper of the said House of Correction and be by him, the said warden, therein safely kept and confined at hard labor, for the full period of his natural life from this day fully to be completed and ended. To be fed and clothed as the law directs.

It is further considered by the Court, that the said Alexander McKenzie pay the costs of this proceeding to be taxed and let the United States have execution therefor.

Partial transcript of Alexander McKenzie's trial. R.G. 21, U.S. District Court, Denver Division, Criminal Case 924. NATIONAL ARCHIVES AND RECORDS CENTER, DENVER.

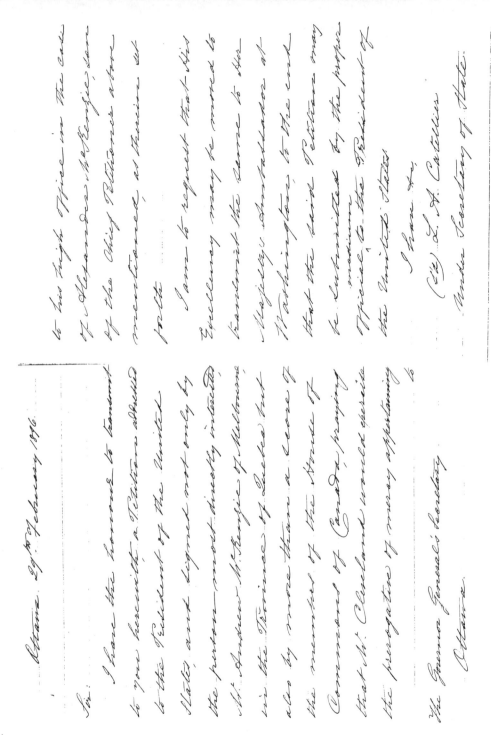

Ottawa 25th February 1896.

Sir:

I have the honour to transmit to you herewith a Petition addressed to the President of the United States, and signed not only by the person most directly interested Mr Andrew McKenzie of Melbourne in the Province of Quebec but also by more than a score of the members of the Strides of Commerce of Canada, praying that Mr Cleveland would exercise the prerogative of mercy appertaining to his high Office in the case of Alexander McKenzie, son of the Chief Petitioner above mentioned, as therein set forth

I am to request that His Excellency may be moved to transmit the same to Her Majesty's Ambassador at Washington, to the end that the said Petitions may be submitted by the proper medium official to the President of the United States

I have &c,
(Sd) L. A. Catellier
Under Secretary of State

The Governor General's Secretary
Ottawa.

Letter from Canadian under secretary of state regarding the pardon of Alexander McKenzie. R.G. 204, Pardon File No. 0-195, Alexander McKenzie. NATIONAL ARCHIVES, WASHINGTON D.C.

Executive Mansion,

Jan 28 , 18 97

Granted. ———

——— This pardon is granted
solely upon the representations of the Superintendent
of the prison where the convict is confined supported
and reinforced by satisfactory
medical testimony, to the
effect that the convict is
in such a precarious con-
dition of health as to
strongly indicate that, under
the most favorable con-
ditions his ~~life~~ death cannot
long be delayed. ———

——— This pardon is however
granted upon the express condition that the friends of
the convict shall upon his
release, receive and remove
him to his home to be
properly cared for

G. C.

IX. MISSOURI

CORA HUBBARD

Bob Dalton in Petticoats

*I*N THE EXTREME SOUTHWEST corner of Missouri, on the western edge of the Ozarks, lies picturesque McDonald County. Nestled in the heart of the county is the quiet little town of Pineville, the county seat; a few miles south is the resort town of Noel. The scenery in McDonald County is breathtaking, especially on the drive north out of Noel on Highway 59, where the road cuts through a huge rock outcrop.

In the late 1880s, not much occurred to disturb the area's peaceful reverie. However, at 10 a.m. on August 17, 1897, Pineville was rocked out of its slumber when the local bank was looted by three bandits. Although bank robbery was no novelty in Missouri at the time, this holdup was unique; the leading spirit of the gang was a woman.

Cora Hubbard was a short, unattractive, and masculine-featured twenty-eight-year-old woman. She had close-cropped black hair combed in a pompadour, a greasy complexion, and a penchant for wearing men's apparel.[1] Her fixation on outlaws led her to boast to friends that she had ridden with the Dalton gang in one or two of their famous raids, a claim which was no more than wishful thinking and idle talk. Cora also erroneously claimed that a six-shooter with Bob Dalton's name and six notches cut into the handle — which was taken from her after her capture — belonged to the famous bandit. It was later proved that a boy had carved Dalton's name on the revolver.[2] Nevertheless, on that August morning in Pineville, Cora Hubbard lived out her fantasies and pulled off a good imitation of her hero.

Cora likely began to develop these fantasies when her family moved from Ohio to Weir City, in the extreme southeast corner of Kansas, not far from where the Daltons committed their acts of outlawry in the early 1890s.[3] Perhaps Cora's rash and reckless actions stemmed from former tragedies suffered by her family and their poverty-stricken condition.

Cora's father, Samuel Hubbard, was born in Madison County, Ohio, on April 5, 1841, and served during the Civil War from September 5, 1861, to October 7, 1864, as a private in Company A, Fortieth Regiment of the Ohio Volunteer Infantry. By the mid-1880s, Hubbard had moved his family to Kansas. Samuel married three times, and his first wife, Cora's mother, died in Ohio. In 1885 he married Rowena Weeks in Spring Hill, Kansas; she died in Weir City on August 19, 1896. On December 5, 1896, eight months before Cora committed the bank robbery, Hubbard married thirty-nine-year-old Nancy Mawson at Columbus, Kansas. Samuel's three marriages fostered a total of seven children. Around Weir City, the Hubbards were known as poor but honest farming people.[4]

In the mid-1890s, Cora Hubbard supposedly married a horse-racer and gambler named J. W. "Bud" Parker. *The Joplin Globe* debunked this report:

> It has been ascertained that Cora Parker was never married to Parker, as has been claimed. It seems she should have been married to him but neglected that formality.[5]

Following her relationship with Parker, Cora returned home, where she remained a year as "a dutiful and helpful daughter." She took over the housework chores when her stepmother, Nancy Hubbard, became ill, and helped her father cultivate and plant two acres of potatoes. In May 1897 Cora left for the Indian Territory to visit two of her sisters. When she returned home, she was accompanied by a twenty-three-year-old cowboy named John Sheets.[6]

Sheets was born in California, Missouri, and had lived with his parents in Dalton, Arkansas, before leaving to work the ranges in Colorado. Heading back east in 1897, he went to work for Cora's alleged husband, Bud Parker, at Allonwell, Indian Territory. Here he met Cora Hubbard and returned with her to her parents' home in Weir City. After a short visit, Cora and Sheets returned to the Indian Territory, where they were supposedly married; however, the *St. Louis Post-Dispatch* stated that Cora had been divorced from a James Russell in April 1897.

While in the Indian Territory they met a tall, gangly thirty-two-year-old widowed farmer named A. Whitfield "Whit" Tennyson, who had come to the Cherokee Nation from Illinois in 1884. In 1890 Tennyson was living in the Delaware District of the Cherokee Nation, and when he lost his wife a few years later, he was living on Cowskin Prairie, a few miles from Southwest City, Missouri.[7]

Both men, no doubt tired of poverty and backbreaking work, fell in easily with Cora's fantasy of staging a Dalton Gang-style bank robbery. Discussing the possibilities, they decided to rob the McDonald County Bank at Pineville, under the assumption that there were fifty or sixty thousand dollars in the vault.[8]

Leaving the Indian Territory, the trio reached Pineville on the night of August 16 and camped on a hill a short distance northeast of town. Early the next morning two of the gang rode into town to look the situation over, leaving the third member at the campsite. Satisfying themselves that it would be an easy haul, the two rode back to camp and packed up. Around 10 a.m., Cora and her two stalwarts mounted their horses and rode into Pineville on the Big Sugar Creek road.

The three decided that there would be less chance of resistance if the two men committed the robbery. So, after hitching their horses in front of Hooper's stable west of the Baptist church, Sheets and Tennyson headed for the bank, leaving Cora, who was dressed as a cowboy, to watch the horses and act as lookout. Just as the two men left, Britt Hooper and a man named Case walked out of the stable into the muzzle of Cora's weapon. She boldly told the two men that it was "no use getting excited at a time like this." Because of Cora's clothing and exposure to the sun, both men took her to be a small part-Indian man. [9]

Bank cashier J. W. Shields and county treasurer M. N. LaMance were sitting under the bank's awning and bank president A. V. Manning was just inside the doorway when the two bandits came around the north corner of the bank. Confronting the two bankers, Sheets stated they wanted the money damn quick. When Shields protested, Sheets struck him in the shoulder with the butt of his Winchester, knocking him down and forcing him to scuttle on all fours after the cash. Following the two bankers into the vault, Sheets handed Manning a sack and, with threats and profanity, told them to fill it up in a hurry.

Tennyson remained in the doorway, guarding LaMance and keeping watch. When two bank patrons, Kin McDonald and a Mrs. Plumlee, drove up in their buggy to the hitching rail, Tennyson warned them, "You just sit still, and you sha'nt be hurt."

LaMance tried to catch Tennyson off guard by keeping up a continuous conversation with him. When Sheets heard Tennyson laugh at one of LaMance's remarks, he sharply ordered him to keep a more careful watch.

Several residents in the hardware store had observed the confrontation at the bank and thought it was only a scuffle. When they realized the bank was being robbed, they quickly rushed off to get their weapons.

Within three minutes of entering the bank, Sheets was out the door with a paltry $529.23 in the sack, $5 of the loot in one-cent pieces. Pushing Shields and Manning in front of them, the bandits hurriedly made their way to their horses. This prevented those citizens who were armed from firing at the bandits and prompted this later remark by Sheets: "There would have been some killing right after the robbery, but the crowd did not push us, and we let them alone."

After quickly mounting their horses, the trio rode out of town the same way they had entered. As they galloped off, one of the three fired a Winchester for a final salute. About a quarter of a mile from where they had camped, the gang encountered Floyd Shields, the young son of the bank cashier. Tennyson forced the boy to trade his valuable mare, Birdie, for the bandit's worn-out horse. The three then took to the hills a mile east of Pineville, crossed Big Sugar Creek, and turned south across Little Sugar Creek, heading for the Indian Territory.[10]

If Cora Hubbard and her companions thought they could swoop down on Pineville, rob the bank, and make a clean getaway, they were sadly mistaken. The residents of McDonald County clearly remembered the May 1894 robbery of the bank at Southwest City, only eighteen miles from Pineville, when Bill Doolin's gang made off with around $4,000 and killed a citizen in the process. News traveled fast, and posses from all over the county organized and quickly took to the trail of the Pineville bandits.

Anticipating the bandits' movements, Noel residents Joe Prickett, Clarence Davis, and Cully Caldwell headed out of town that afternoon and concealed themselves near a ford on Butler Creek, one mile east of town. Another posse from Southwest City, consisting of Charles Bradley, Clark Noel, and Will Farmer, had the same idea and arrived at Butler Creek, only to be taken for the robbers. Fortunately before any tragedy occurred, the two groups recognized each other and joined forces.

In the early afternoon, the three bandits reached the home of William Mosier on Mill Creek and foolishly took time to eat dinner. Around 5 p.m. they reached Butler Creek and were immediately fired on by the concealed posse. Determined not to surrender, the three robbers found themselves involved in a deadly gun battle.

Although a heavy fusillade of lead filled the air, the only fatality was Sheets' horse. However, Cora and Sheets had their guns shot out of their hands, and Sheets was struck with eleven buckshot, one in the forehead, one in the cheek, one in the breast, and the rest in the right arm and wrist. Retrieving his gun, Sheets quickly jumped up behind Cora, and the pair rode eastward into the woods, leaving Cora's gun beside the dead horse.

In the midst of the furious shoot-out, Tennyson became separated from his companions and fled westward across Butler Creek toward the Indian Territory. Tennyson had also been wounded in the melee, struck with several 00 shot, two in the back, two in the neck, two in the left arm, and one in the elbow. The posse also separated and hotly pursued the fleeing bandits. The only casualty the posse suffered was one of the saddle bags got hit by a stray shot.[11]

There were many who pursued the fleeing bandits, including U.S. Marshals Pirmen and Copeland, who trailed the bandits with bloodhounds. However, only one posse would be successful. Around 10 a.m. on the eighteenth, word had reached Southwest City that a heavily armed man had eaten breakfast at the Widow Snail's place, six miles west of town, and had paid the widow for his meal with a handful of one-cent pieces. This information was telephoned to Noel, and bloodhounds were immediately sent to the widow's home. A three-man posse headed by hardware merchant and former U.S. Deputy Marshal Joe D. Yeargain also left Southwest City on the morning of the eighteenth. The experienced former lawman, his brother Scott, and Steve Day relentlessly followed Tennyson's trail into the Indian Territory.

Reaching the hills in the northwest corner of the territory on the afternoon of the eighteenth, the saddle-weary Tennyson stopped at a lonely cabin for supper and rest. Around 6 p.m., Yeargain arrived, saw the cabin, and while reconnoitering, spotted a young Indian girl passing by. Yeargain managed to persuade the girl to go into the cabin and see if a strange man was inside. Within minutes she returned and nodded. The three lawmen took cover and waited for Tennyson to appear.

Steve Day had stationed himself on the hillside and was immediately spotted by Tennyson. When the bandit came out of the cabin and called to the lawman to come down, the Yeargains immediately rose up from behind a fence, covered the bandit with their weapons, and commanded him to give up. Tennyson attempted to use his revolver, but a second warning from the Yeargains changed his mind, and he meekly surrendered. The prisoner was placed in a buggy, tied securely with a rope, and brought to Southwest City around 8 p.m.

Quoting the Southwest City *Enterprise, The Pineville Herald* reported:

> When captured the robber had in his possession a .44-calibre Winchester and a .44-calibre revolver, a bridle and $121.50. The robber acknowledged he was the man that took the horse from the Shields boy at Pineville, and still had the bridle that he took from the horse when he left it at Hazelbaker's Tuesday evening. On arriving in town the robber was taken to Yeargain's hardware store, and was recognized by a number of our citizens as Whit Tennison [*sic*], who lived with his family on Cowskin Prairie, a few miles from town, several years ago. The man is about 35 years old, 6 feet 3 inches tall, and rather intelligent looking. . . . He denies his real name, but talks freely of the robbery and circumstances connected with it, and confessed being one of the robbers. [12]

In the afternoon of August 19, Tennyson was brought to Pineville, where a large crowd had gathered to get a glimpse of the bandit. He readily told where he and his companions had divided and buried a portion of the loot. He also stated that a plat of Pineville, outlining the bandits' escape route to Weir City, Kansas, was buried with the money. Tennyson claimed that Cora's brother, thirty-three-year-old Bill Hubbard, a former resident of Pineville and the son-in-law of Pineville resident S. B. King, had furnished the bank robbers with the plat and had planned the raid. He also revealed that the other two bandits could be found in Weir City. Several men took the prisoner to where the plunder was buried but recovered only $2.62 in change, the bank's tin change box, and the plat. Tennyson was then taken to the Newton County jail at Neosho. [13]

After fleeing into the woods near Noel, Cora and Sheets headed westward toward the Kansas border. Before reaching Kansas, the two split up after making plans to meet later in Weir City. Cora arrived at her parents' home around noon on Saturday, August 21. She immediately discarded her male attire, changed into female clothing, and buried her loot in the garden under a pepper hill and a potato patch. [14]

Leaving Southwest City on the morning of August 21, Joe Yeargain, George Smith, and bank cashier J. W. Shields, who had been humiliated by Sheets during the bank robbery, headed for Weir City. Upon their arrival, Yeargain secured the assistance of City Marshal Hatton. While en route to the Hubbard home at 1 p.m., the lawmen found Bill Hubbard loitering on the streets and promptly arrested him. Arriving at Cora's home, the lawmen had no trouble arresting her.

Fearing the prisoners would be advised of their rights to demand a requisition to convey them to Missouri, Yeargain immediately loaded them into a wagon and drove across the state line to Asbury, Missouri. From there, they took the Frisco train to Joplin. Upon their arrival at 7 p.m., the prisoners were lodged in a third-floor room of the Joplin Hotel. Cora Hubbard was so poorly dressed, having no shoes or hat, that Yeargain went out and bought her a new pair of shoes. At 8:30 p.m. the prisoners were taken to supper in the hotel dining room. [15]

A short time after the prisoners were returned to their room, a reporter from the *Globe* arrived, received permission to interview them, and gave his observations:

> While here the couple [Bill and Cora Hubbard] were interviewed by a GLOBE reporter as they sat side by side manacled together. The man refused to talk, but his sister seemed in the best of spirits and talked freely, laughing the while like a society belle enjoying the leading event of the season. She freely admitted she and her brother had taken part in the robbery of the bank and said the remaining robber had been badly wounded in the battle at Noel. She refused to reveal the whereabouts of this member of the gang, but she had informed Mr. Yeargain and he will use the information to affect his capture.
> When asked if she felt nervous during the robbery of the ban she replied:
> "No, I felt as though I could hold up the whole damn town alone."
> She said her brother would not drink beer because of his being a Hard Shell Baptist.

For dramatics, a Winchester was placed in Cora's hands, and it was reported she handled it like a veteran. Later in the evening, a photographer took flash photographs of the bandits in the hotel room. Bill Hubbard, also poorly dressed in an old colored shirt and trousers, was moody and taciturn, refusing to talk to anyone.

At 12:15 a.m. the officers took their prisoners aboard a Pittsburgh and Gulf train for Southwest City. On Monday, August 23, Yeargain delivered the pair to Pineville. [16]

The news traveled quickly, and the *St. Louis Post-Dispatch* wasted no time in creating a fictitious life for the woman bandit, referring to her as "the Kid" in its sensationalized reporting:

> Though only 25 years of age, Cora has a record as a "bad man" and her performances show her to be possessed of a nerve equal to that of the boldest highwayman that ever lived.
> She was a member of the notorious Dalton gang, with whom she rode in male attire, and after her arrest a revolver was found in her possession inscribed with the name Bob Dalton. How many men she has killed

in her career or how many raids she has been engaged in may never be known. [17]

Upon receipt of the information supplied by Cora Hubbard to Yeargain, McDonald County sheriff Richard Jarrett, bank cashier J. W. Shields, and Pineville merchant J. M. Putnam headed for Weir City to arrest Sheets. As planned, Sheets returned to Weir City on August 26 to meet Cora Hubbard. He had been hanging around Junction City and Parsons, Kansas, before his arrival.

Early on the twenty-sixth, City Marshal Hatton and Constable Dennis went to the Hubbard home in search of the buried bank plunder. Through the efforts of Cora's father and stepmother, they recovered $25 of the loot hidden under the pepper hill and a stocking containing $141 buried in the potato patch.

While the two Kansas officers were recovering the money, Sheets drove up to the Hubbard home at 1 p.m. in a new buggy with a trunk tied to the back. Noting Sheets' arrival, the two officers caught him off guard and arrested him. Sheets was taken to the marshal's office, photographed, and turned over to the Missouri lawmen. Shields identified Sheets as the bandit who had knocked him down with the Winchester. Sheets said that he did not know that Cora had been arrested but had learned of Tennyson's arrest and confession. Later that day, the Missouri lawmen proceeded to the Hubbard home and arrested Cora's father, Samuel Hubbard, on the charge of harboring the bandits. [18]

Not wanting any problems over requisition demands, the Missouri lawmen hustled their two prisoners across the state line to Joplin and lodged them in the same third-floor room in the Joplin Hotel. After supper, a *Globe* reporter showed up to interview the new prisoners. He described Sheets as a good-looking, well-dressed young man of below medium height who did not look like a "bad fellow."

Sheets talked freely about his participation in the robbery but insisted that it was the first criminal act he had ever committed. He claimed to have "blowed in" his two-hundred-dollar share of the loot on the new buggy and horse he drove to Weir City. The reporter gave his observations of the bandit:

> Sheets handled a gun in a way that shows him to be very familiar with that sort of implement. . . . Sheets drank a bottle or so of beer while waiting and got quite jolly along toward the last of his stay here.
>
> An excellent picture of the young bandit was taken by a flash light manipulated by Walker, for the use of the *Globe-Democrat*. Sheets was perfectly at ease during his stay here and did not seem to mind the serious predicament he is in.

If Sheets was calm, cool, and collected, seventy-year-old Samuel Hubbard was a picture of abject wretchedness. Although of large frame, the old man was now bent with age, wearing old, well-used clothing and a wide-brimmed chip hat, grimy and stained with long wear. He showed considerable agitation in regard to his situation and that of his children. The effect that Hubbard's appearance and demeanor had upon the reporter is reflected in his comments:

> Hubbard informed the reporter that he had been sick for the past month, which, he said, unfitted him to a large extent to bear up under the troubles his son and daughter got him into. Hubbard says he did not have a thing to do with the robbery and did not know anything about it except what he had read.
>
> The old man's face is an honest one, and if he is guilty of wrong doing his character is vastly different from what his appearance and conversation indicate.

Amid feelings of sympathy for Hubbard and contempt for the nonchalant attitude of Sheets, the officers took the two men to the Joplin depot that night and boarded the Pee Gee train for Pineville at fifteen minutes past midnight. [19]

It did not take the officials long to realize that Samuel Hubbard and his son Bill had absolutely nothing to do with the bank robbery. On Saturday, August 28, the two men were cleared and released from custody by Sheriff Jarrett, even though Bill Hubbard likely had prior knowledge of the robbery and had given the Pineville plat to the bandits. When Cora and Bill Hubbard were in custody at the Joplin Hotel, Cora, in the presence of her brother, implicated him in the robbery scheme. When questioned about his involvement, he refused to make any comment. Since he did not rob the bank, any testimony against him would be either circumstantial or refutable. Perceiving there was little chance that Bill Hubbard would be convicted, the sheriff released him.

Upon their release, the two Hubbards headed for Joplin to visit Ed Hubbard, another son of Samuel Hubbard. When they arrived that evening, they were interviewed by the *Globe* reporter, who wrote:

> Old Man Hubbard feels sore over his arrest and threatens to bring suit for damages against the officers for taking him from Kansas without a requisition, and against his protest, and that too when he was sick. Lawyers say he has a good case. [20]

On the same day the Hubbards were released from custody, Cora, Sheets, and Tennyson were charged with robbery in McDonald County Circuit Court under Justice of the Peace A. P. Noel. Unable to raise the bail of three thousand dollars each, the three were transferred to the Newton County jail at Neosho, Missouri, where they remained for four months awaiting action by the grand jury. [21]

On Sunday evening, January 9, 1898, the prisoners were returned to Pineville. On the following Tuesday, the grand jury indicted the three bandits on one count of grand larceny and two counts of robbery. That afternoon, all three were tried before Judge Lamson in McDonald County Circuit Court.

Upon guilty pleas to one count of robbery by the three defendants, the charges of grand larceny for the theft of Shields' horse and the second count of robbery were dismissed by the court on a motion by defense attorney Hugh Dobbs. Judge Lamson sentenced Cora and Sheets to twelve years imprisonment in the Missouri State Penitentiary at Jefferson City. Possibly because Tennyson was a recent widower, Judge Lamson showed some leniency in sentencing him to ten years imprisonment. *The Pineville Herald* reported that the prisoners looked extremely well, considering their long confinement, and seemingly were in the best of spirits. [22]

On January 28, 1898, Whit Tennyson, John Sheets, and Cora Hubbard were delivered to the Missouri State Penitentiary by Sheriff Jarrett and were given consecutive convict numbers, 954, 955, and 956. After serving seven and a half years, Tennyson was discharged on July 10, 1905, under "three quarter law," or good time. Three months later, Sheets' sentence was commuted, and he was released on October 13, 1906. [23]

Cora Hubbard fared a little better than her confederates. On December 26, 1904, Missouri State Penitentiary matron Emogean Mackay and assistant matron Leater Sone wrote Governor A. M. Dockery requesting a pardon for Cora on the grounds that she "has been a model prisoner, faithful, even in the smallest detail." On December 31, 1904, Cora was given a New Year's pardon by the governor and was released on January 1, 1905. [24]

If Cora Hubbard intended to set a record when she emulated her tainted hero Bob Dalton, she evidently succeeded. As far as can be determined, this is the only record of an active woman bank robber in Old West history. What ultimately happened to Cora Hubbard is not known, but it seems highly improbable that she ever committed another robbery or resumed the relationship with her so-called husband, John Sheets.

Above: Left to right: Cora Hubbard, Whit Tennyson, and John Sheets after their capture in August 1897. COURTESY McDONALD COUNTY PUBLIC LIBRARY, PINEVILLE, MISSOURI

Right: Cora Hubbard after her capture in August 1897. COURTESY McDONALD COUNTY PUBLIC LIBRARY, PINEVILLE, MISSOURI

CAPIAS.

STATE OF MISSOURI.

COUNTY OF McDonald } ss.

THE STATE OF MISSOURI,
McDonald County, GREETING:

To the Sheriff of McDonald County, GREETING:

We Command You to take *John Sheets A. M. Tennison & Cora Hubbard* if to be found in your County, and him safely keep, so that you have his body before the Judge of our Circuit Court at the Court House in *Pineville* within and for the said County of *McDonald* on *Tuesday the 11 day of January* on the ———— Monday in *March* next, then and there, before our said Judge, to answer an indictment preferred against him by the Grand Jurors of the State of Missouri, empaneled, sworn and charged to inquire in and for the body of the County of *McDonald* aforesaid, for *Robbery*

whereof he stands indicted. And this you shall in nowise omit. And have you then and there this writ. Given under my hand and the seal of our said Court. Done at office in *Pineville* in the County aforesaid, on this *11* day of *January* A. D. 18 *98*

J. J. ——— Clerk.

D. C.

Capias issued in the case of the State of Missouri vs. Whit Tennyson, John Sheets, and Cora Hubbard, *robbery.* McDONALD COUNTY CIRCUIT COURT, PINEVILLE, MISSOURI

X. WYOMING

CATTLE BARONS VERSUS RUSTLERS

Rawhide and Lead

PART ONE: David and Goliath

*W*HEREVER CATTLEMEN ESTABLISHED RANGELAND in the west, rustlers were soon dogging their heels. When conditions became intolerable, the cattlemen took matters into their own hands, lynching these undesirables or exiling them from the rangeland. The Montana vigilantes in the mid-1880s were a prime example of this type of justice. Wyoming, however, attempted to handle this problem in a quasilegal manner, through the Wyoming Stock Growers Association (W.S.G.A.).

In 1973 *The Cheyenne Tribune-Eagle* called the W.S.G.A. the most powerful institution ever organized for the promotion of the range-cattle business. [1] What the newspaper failed to mention was that this organization was founded mainly to curb rustling activities. The first attempt to form an association, at Laramie in April, 1871, was to "organize for mutual protection against depredation against stock." The W.S.G.A. finally got off the ground in October 1872, when five men met in a Cheyenne livery stable and formed the nucleus. The informal meeting was likely responsible for this announcement in the October 17 edition of *The Cheyenne Leader*: "[to] take measures to secure the speedy arrest and punishment of persons engaged in stealing stock or other property."

By 1873 there were 20,000 head of cattle in Wyoming, and in November of that year the W.S.G.A. was formally organized in Cheyenne. In March

1876 the association decided to employ stock detectives at a salary of $150 per month, but not until April of the following year was the first detective, W. C. Lykins, hired. During that summer the association's first cattle roundup was held. From 1883 through 1886, the W.S.G.A. assumed its most extensive police powers, under the leadership of president Joseph Carey and secretary Thomas Sturgis. The method of enforcement proved to be ineffective and costly, one that would further alienate the relationship between the big cattleman and the small rancher.

In October 1883 a special meeting was held in Cheyenne to deal with cattle theft. The membership lined up solidly behind the detective bureau and drew up the controversial Maverick Law, with this definition of a maverick: "Any head of neat cattle regardless of age, found running at large without a mother, and without a brand regardless of any ear mark or wattle that may be upon them." The following provisions gave the W.S.G.A. complete control over all unbranded and stray cattle on the range: (a) disposition of all stray cattle rounded up, (b) calves could not be branded between January 1 and the general roundup each year, (c) all mavericks would be rounded up and sold to the highest bidder, and (d) all cattle with rustler's brands and stray brands were to be treated as mavericks. This law went into effect by legislative action in the spring of 1884 and was unanimously accepted by the big cattlemen. The small ranchers with thirty head of cattle or less were outraged. Their reaction forecasted the violence that would soon follow.

The Maverick Law actually worked against its intentions. The association could not effectively enforce this legislation, and illegal roundups were held across Wyoming. The cost of the association's detective bureau skyrocketed to $15,500 in 1885, and the organization found that the prosecution of rustlers was extremely costly and counterproductive. Rustling continued unabated.

The decline of the W.S.G.A.'s power began in 1885, when the cattle business went into a depression. However, the major reason the association nearly folded was not financial loss or the rustling problem; Mother Nature brought it down. The Wyoming ranchers lost all their winter forage during the devastating summer drought of 1886. The following winter proved to be the worst season in history. Temperatures dropped way below zero and hovered there for weeks at a time. The snow piled up, and herds of cattle froze in their tracks. When the spring thaw arrived, a number of the big ranchers found up to three quarters of their cattle gone, and many went out of business. The small rancher was wiped out.

The W.S.G.A. began losing members at an alarming rate, and its finances quickly dwindled. In 1887 the association decided to close its detective bureau. The big ranchers were now faced with the same dilemma that confronted other ranchers across the west; they would now have to deal with the rustling problem on their own. [2]

The well-known Johnson County War in 1892 was a prime example of the conflict between the big Wyoming stockmen and the small ranchers and the rustlers. Rustling had drastically increased in Wyoming because of the demand for beef to feed the thousands who were working for the Burlington Railroad, which was extending its line from Alliance, Nebraska, across northern Wyoming, to Billings, Montana. Another factor was the increase of homesteaders, or nesters, who had flocked to the west and were settling on rangeland much needed by the cattlemen.

In the spring of 1892, the Wyoming cattlemen and their hired Texas toughs headed north for the Powder River country in Johnson County to put down rustling. The action was ill-planned and resulted in the deaths of two suspected rustlers, Nate Champion and Nick Ray, and the uprising of the citizens who surrounded the invading cattlemen at the T A Ranch near Buffalo. The quick action of President Benjamin Harrison by sending troops from nearby Fort McKinney prevented bloodshed and likely saved the lives of the invaders. [3]

The Johnson County War was not the only action taken by the big cattlemen in Wyoming against rustling activities. The Swan Land and Cattle Company (S.L.C.C.), the largest individual cattle-ranching enterprise in Wyoming, retaliated when it suspected its herds were being raided.

The founder of this gigantic ranching combine was Alexander Hamilton Swan, a native Pennsylvanian born in 1831 who came to Wyoming in 1873 via Iowa, Kansas, and Colorado. Swan and his two brothers started in business near Chugwater, Wyoming, with three thousand cattle and by 1879 had increased their herd to nineteen thousand head. Swan became the second president of the Wyoming Stock Growers Association and continued to expand his business venture. In 1882 Swan had 33,000 cattle on the range and added an additional 31,000 cows by forming a partnership with easterners.

In 1883 the S.L.C.C. had a net worth of $3,300,000, with a reported 108,763 cattle on its range, which bordered on the North Platte River and was more than one hundred miles long and fifty miles wide. However, there was a hitch: Swan based his herd tally on book count, which was not supported by the actual number of cattle on the range. His philosophy was, "Expand, expand, expand," and he bought two additional ranches in 1884 at $250,000 each. In the spring of 1883, Swan traveled to Scotland, where he sold shares of stock for six hundred thousand dollars to well-to-do Englishmen and Scotsmen, who became directors in the firm. Swan was made American manager at a salary of ten thousand dollars a year for five years. This transfer from domestic to foreign control gave the small rancher and the working cowboy further reason for contempt and hatred of the large livestock corporations. Author John Rolfe Burroughs outlined the problem:

> The owners of these outfits, who were in residence in Wyoming only during the pleasant summer and autumn months, comported themselves like princelings among an indigenous population of frontier type American who, in time, came to hate their guts. . . . They, and their haughty guests, seemed to be particularly adept in making themselves obnoxious to Americans.

Burroughs illustrates this with a local story of a visiting Englishman who was looking for a foreign owner and addressed one of the cowboys, "Oh, I say! You there! Can you direct me to your master?" The cowboy, with contempt in his eyes, rode close to the offending Englishman and snarled, "You son-of-a-bitch, I have yet to meet *that* son-of-a-bitch!"

By 1885 the S.L.C.C. was faced with financial loss because of Swan's book count. In spite of this monetary problem, Swan continued to expand and bought more cattle by book count in 1886. By mid-year Swan was in deep trouble with the directors. In May 1887 he resigned, and in March 1888 John Clay took over as manager with a more moderate program. Five years later, the S.L.C.C. retaliated against suspected rustling activities. Its actions would initiate the legend of the alleged hired killer of the big cattlemen, Tom Horn.[4]

All references state that in 1894 Horn arrived in Wyoming and was employed by the S.L.C.C. Even Horn made this claim; however, this is in error, because contemporary newspaper articles and court records show that Horn was in Wyoming and worked for the S.L.C.C. as early as 1893. Before his arrival in Wyoming, Horn had been working for the Pinkerton Detective Agency in Colorado, and he stated in his autobiography, *Life of Tom Horn*, "While Pinkertons is one of the greatest institutions of the kind in existence, I never did like the work, so I left them in 1894. I then came to Wyoming and went to work for the Swan Land and Cattle Company. . . ." Writers from this point on have used Horn's statement as fact and state that Horn was hired by the company as a stock detective. Horn never made this claim, and author Jay Monaghan was likely closer to the truth when he reported that Horn had been hired by manager John Clay to break horses for the S.L.C.C. It was the fall of 1893 before Tom Horn entered the scene as the company's representative of the law. He did not appear as a stock detective but as an official deputy sheriff.[5]

Horn's initial service came as a result of the S.L.C.C.'s suspicion that neighboring ranchers were stealing its cattle. The suspected persons have been referred to as both the Langhoff brothers and the Langhoff gang. Neither is correct—a more fitting sobriquet would be the "Langhoff outfit." Following the Langhoff episode came Horn's alleged assassinations of Wyoming rustlers William Lewis and Fred U. Powell. These three incidents have been mentioned numerous times in other narratives but have never been researched and reported in full, nor has the background information on the involved individuals been related. All of Tom Horn's other notorious acts have been fully reported, including his subsequent trial and hanging in Cheyenne in 1903 for the purported killing of a sixteen-year-old boy. Here, then is the complete story of an arrest and two assassinations credited to Tom Horn.

PART TWO: "Whoever Steals
Any Neat Cattle Shall Be Imprisoned"

*W*HEN THE SWAN LAND AND CATTLE COMPANY suspected the Langhoff Ranch of rustling its cattle in the fall of 1893, thirty-one-year-old Eva Langhoff was struggling to run the ranch by herself while raising her three children: ten-year-old Bessie Frances, eight-year-old Douglas R., and five-year-old Edward F. Subsequent actions would initiate the Wyoming saga of Tom Horn, underplay the S.L.C.C.'s involvement in these actions, and bring notoriety to the Langhoff name.

Eva Langhoff, born Evaline C. Ferrell in Nebraska in 1862, migrated to Wyoming with her parents, Mr. and Mrs. Edward Ferrell, in 1868. They settled on what is now the site of the Laramie city park. Around 1880, Eva met Fredrick A. Langhoff, and the two were married on December 6, 1881, at her parents' home. [6]

Fred Langhoff, also an emigrant to Wyoming, was born in 1859 in Wisconsin and came to Wyoming in 1873 with his mother and older brother, Henry "Hank" Langhoff. In 1879 Fred settled in Albany County, and according to a Works Progress Administration article titled "Sybille Country":

> Fred was well liked, despite the trouble he got into later. He was a good cowman, and a better horse dealer. In fact he delt more in horses than in cattle. His brother Hank and his mother came shortly after Fred located. But there was some personal friction between the two brothers, and Hank and his mother located on the Bluegrass Creek. . . .

In 1882 Fred and Eva established their ranch, the L F Bar, on Sybille Creek, around thirty miles due west of the S.L.C.C. They built a comfortable log house, with substantial stables and sheds. By 1889 the Langhoffs were reported to own thirty-three cattle, thirty-three horses, and farming equipment, for a total value of $1,923. [7]

Whoever wrote or dictated the W.P.A. article apparently knew the Langhoffs and stated, "At first his [Fred's] business seemed to be legitimate enough; but as time went on there were whispers that the Langhoffs' prosperity far exceeded their visible livelihood." The Langhoffs acquired a shady reputation, although that was never substantiated, and their ranch supposedly became a rendezvous for people of dubious character from as far east as Chicago and Omaha. The W.P.A. article also gave this rather lurid description of Eva Langhoff:

> Also, there were rumors of the lure Mrs. Langhoff had for the strangers that came within their gates with horses or cattle to sell. Some of these

strangers falling under her spell, fell so deeply in love with her, they figured they had value received personally, regardless of the profitless deal they may have made on their business arrangements.

Other — bitter and disillusioned — talked — however, there is no gainsaying the fact that, being Fred's wife and the mother of his three children, took nothing away from her charm for other people. She was attractive, and evidently very clever; even the women of the neighborhood that met her, grudgingly admitted she had much personality and charm. [8]

Whether or not the above insinuations are true, the Langhoffs did find themselves in trouble ten years after they moved to the Sybille country. According to the W.P.A. account, they pulled a raw deal on a man named Suggette when he sold them some fancy horses. When Suggette discovered he had been swindled, he complained to the law, which started an investigation of the Langhoffs' operations, and then he hanged himself. This account does not agree with the information in the criminal case brought against the Langhoffs. [9]

On June 10, 1892, in Laramie County, Fred and Eva Langhoff, their ranch hand Louis Bath, and neighboring rancher Thomas Boucher reportedly bought, concealed, and received feloniously eight horses belonging to John Coble, seventeen horses belonging to the Laramie Cattle Company, and one horse belonging to the Royal Horse Association. Allegedly they shipped the horses to dealers McErwin and Kellogg in Owensboro, Kentucky. Prominent area livestock owners constituted the membership of the cattle company and the horse association. Cattle baron John C. Coble, who later became a close friend of Tom Horn, and the S.L.C.C's foreman, Alexander H. "Al" Bowie, were prosecuting witnesses against the Langhoffs. [10]

In Mid-August, *The Laramie Weekly Sentinel* reported:

> Fred A. Langhoff, an old timer and well to do ranchman of the Sabile [*sic*], has been arrested, charged with wholesale horse stealing. He went east a few weeks ago with a train load of horses and sold them and Sheriff Kelley of Cheyenne followed him and arrested him in Wisconsin and brought him back. It is charged that some twenty five or thirty of the horses were stolen from his neighbors. [11]

The charges were filed on August 2, and Fred was arrested on August 9. Bath and Boucher were arrested the next day and released on bail on the thirteenth and nineteenth, respectively. Fred was not released on bail until November 22. Eva Langhoff was never jailed, likely because of her three children. [12]

On December 3 Fred's case was continued until the May 1893 term of court, and on the fourteenth he was again arrested and jailed. The trial of Bath and Boucher was held on the fifteenth, and they were found not guilty. On December 21 Fred's lawyer made a motion to reduce bail from $2,500 to $1,500, and Fred made an affidavit that he had no way of obtaining sureties for his bail and explained his financial situation, which revealed the connection between Suggette and the Langhoffs. He stated that he owned 160 acres but that his wife was the owner of 130 head of cattle, 45 head of horses, and 200 acres of land. He claimed that Suggette had a mortgage of $2,150 on the livestock and all improvements on the land. Fred reported that a great number of the cattle were dead and that the total worth of the holdings was no more than $500, which was now owned by Suggette. There was no mention of Suggette's reported suicide. Bail reduction was denied, and Fred remained in jail for the next six months. [13]

The trial of Fred and Eva was scheduled for June 2, 1893, but was continued because of the absence of defense witnesses. On June 10 Eva Langhoff was tried and found not guilty, but Fred's case was continued, and he was finally released on bail on June 12. Fred apparently figured his chances in court were nil, and he deserted Eva on August 23, 1893, and fled the state. Eva never saw him again. Fred was never brought to trial, and the case was dismissed when the prosecution entered a nolle prosequi on August 28, 1897. [14]

A strange twist in the case occurred around September 30, 1892, when Fred's brother Hank committed suicide by hanging himself at his ranch. No reason was given for his suicide, and his name was not included in the court records in the case against Fred and Eva. [15]

No doubt the Swan Land and Cattle Company was disgruntled over the decision in the Langhoff trial, and it kept a suspicious eye on the ranch. Little more than a month after Fred Langhoff fled the state, the S.L.C.C. was convinced that Eva Langhoff and Louis Bath, who was now foreman, were stealing cattle from them again. [16]

Twenty-four-year-old Louis Bath, who had been indicted with the Langhoffs in 1892, was one of at least eight children of German-born Henry Bath and his wife, Catherine. In the mid-1870s, the Baths arrived in Wyoming via New York and Iowa, and by the 1890s, the entire family was engaged in the ranching business. The W.P.A. article hints that the relationship between Eva and Bath was more than that between employer and employee:

> She operated the ranch alone for some time after that [Fred's desertion], having as a foreman a boy of nineteen [sic] by the name of Lu Bath. He made no secret of his infatuation for his beautiful employer, but it was noticeable that no steadily employed men were hired to work on the ranch after Lu was made foreman. [17]

Determined to take action against the Langhoff ranch, Al Bowie, the foreman of the S.L.C.C. since 1883, had Tom Horn deputized in mid-October by Laramie County sheriff Ira Fredenall. Horn was immediately sent into the Sybille country to watch the Langhoff ranch. He remained hidden in the hills during the day and stealthily made his way to the ranch at night. Horn observed that Eva Langhoff had no cattle of her own and that it would be as late as 9 a.m. before anyone would arise. On October 31 Horn's vigil was rewarded when he observed Eva and Bath loading three calves into their wagon. He followed them to Laramie, and saw the calves delivered to Balch's market. Horn also inspected the Langhoff barn and found what he considered sufficient evidence to take action.

Horn remained in the Sybille hills for nearly two weeks, waiting for his chance to pounce on the Langhoff ranch. On November 10, in the vicinity of the Langhoff ranch, Al Bowie observed unbranded calves following Swan cattle, which carried the two-bar brand. On Sunday, November 12, Horn got the chance he had been waiting for: He spotted Eva and Bath driving a cow and five calves into their barn to be slaughtered and dressed for market.

When the cattle were taken into the barn, Horn took off in search of Al Bowie. Besides Eva Langhoff and Louis Bath, there were three other people inside the barn, Jim Cleve and his wife, Nettie, who lived on the Plaga Fork of the Sybille and had been in the area for only six weeks, and William Taylor, who had lived in the Sybille country for two years and worked for a neighboring rancher. Bath immediately slaughtered the cattle, and the three men and Eva began skinning and dressing the carcasses while Nettie Cleve held the lantern. At 7 p.m. Horn returned with Bowie and two cowboys, Raymond and Rudolph Henke, and entered the barn, catching the suspects still dressing the cattle.[18]

There were two views of what happened next. The W.P.A. article said that Bath lost his head and started "chattering" while defensively holding a knife in his hand. With gun in hand, Horn advanced on Bath and ordered him to drop the knife, giving him until the count of three. Bath complied and surrendered. *The Laramie Boomerang*, however, gave a much different but more plausible account:

> Mr. Horn said he told them they were all under arrest. They asked him if he had a warrant and he told them no, and they replied that they would not go without a warrant and he told them that if they did not it would be a surprise to him. They then took the five prisoners to the house where beds were made on the floor and he says that himself and Al Bowie guarded them there all night. The next morning they were taken to Iron Mountain, on the Cheyenne and Northern [Railroad], and they were brought to Laramie by way of Cheyenne. At Cheyenne warrants were procured from a justice for the parties.

The Henke brothers brought the carcasses of the five calves to Laramie, where they left them at Balch's market as evidence.[19]

The newspaper also outlined the charges against the five defendants:

> The crime for which these parties are arrested is a felony and the information filed against them by the county attorney is drawn in accordance with the chapter of the laws of Wyoming relating to crimes and criminal procedure and is as follows:
> "Whoever steals any horse, mules, or neat cattle, of the value of $5 or upwards, or receives, buys, or conceals any such horse, mule or neat cattle which shall have been stolen, knowing the same to have been stolen, shall be imprisoned in the penitentiary not more than ten years, or may be imprisoned in the county jail not more than six months."[20]

Preliminary hearings for the five defendants were set for November 15 in the Albany County District Court but were postponed until the next day. The defense claimed that the reason the five suspects were taken to Cheyenne and paraded through the streets was for spite because of the malice held against them in that city. The hearing concluded at 11 p.m., and Justice J. H. Hayford set bonds of five hundred dollars each for Taylor and Cleve and one thousand dollars for Bath. They were released on bail the next day. Eva was released on her own recognizance. The charges against Nettie Cleve were dropped, and she was dismissed, only to be arrested on a Carbon County charge of obtaining money under false pretenses. The trial for the cattle theft was set for the January 1894 term of court. [21]

Eva Langhoff's testimony during the prosecution's cross-examination was tinged with sardonic humor, which the newspaper reported:

> . . . she had always been accustomed to stock but she was not an expert at roping stock. Any such report was untrue. She had rode the range some but not much [in] late years. She had not seen any two-legged wolves in that country. [22]

The trial commenced on January 12 under Judge J. W. Blake, and both the prosecution and the defense immediately began to hammer away at their cases. The prosecution, with witnesses Horn and Bowie, attempted to show that two of the calves, worth five dollars each, were the property of the S.L.C.C. and had been taken from their mothers. The defense countered with witnesses Phil and Thomas Bath, brothers of Louis, and rancher Thomas Boucher, who claimed that the calves belonged to them and that Louis Bath had permission to slaughter them for market. It was proven that the cow belonged to Eva Langhoff.

The case came to an end at 11 a.m. on January 17, when the jury returned with their verdict. Dean Krakel states that one defendant was sent to prison while the others were given short jail sentences and small fines. The court records do not agree. The prosecution entered a nolle prosequi for Taylor and Cleve, and they were dismissed with a stern lecture from Judge Blake. Eva Langhoff was found not guilty, but the jury brought in a verdict of guilty for Louis Bath. Defense attorney William H. Bramel filed a motion for a new trial on January 22, but the motion was denied, and Bath was sentenced to eighteen months imprisonment on January 30. The S.L.C.C. might well have lost the entire case if not for the Maverick Law. [23]

Louis Bath entered the Wyoming State Penitentiary at Laramie on January 31. He had served just under one year when he was pardoned by Governor John E. Osborne on January 8, 1895. He returned to spend his life in the Sybille country. [24]

The costly trials left Eva Langhoff nearly destitute, and she lost her ranch. On July 8, 1896, Eva filed for divorce in Laramie, which was granted on August 26, and since she was a Catholic, she never remarried. In her later years she went to live with her daughter, Bessie, and her husband, Harry Green, near Walden, Colorado. In June 1939 she suffered a stroke and was bedridden until her death on July 13. She was buried in the Green Hill Cemetery in Laramie.[25]

The S.L.C.C. had gotten its revenge, but it was a hollow victory at best. Krakel astutely summed up the result: "The joke was on the cattlemen. Horn's employers were stunned by the ineffectiveness of the laws. They knew they would have to contend with the thieves again."[26] If the S.L.C.C. was frustrated by the Langhoff trial, it was in for a real treat one year later, when it had the tables turned by another accused rustler. No longer would the company resort to the legal system; however, it kept close ties with Tom Horn, who would go on to bigger but certainly not better things.

PART THREE: "He Was The Scaredest Son-of-a-bitch You Ever Saw"

A YEAR AND A HALF AFTER THE Langhoff trial, two accused rustlers, William Lewis and Fred U. Powell, were assassinated in the Sybille country. Common consensus is that these killings were committed by Tom Horn for the big cattlemen. This has never been proven one way or the other.

The scenario following the Langhoff trial was that the cattlemen asked Horn to continue his investigations but to make no more arrests. Within a few months he had a detailed report and presented his findings at a cattlemen's meeting in Cheyenne. He also introduced his suggested method of dealing with the rustlers — extermination. Although most of the cattlemen were against this extreme measure, several radicals accepted Horn's proposal, and he was retained and a fee for dead rustlers was set. Horn was given enough cash to tide him over, and he pursued his favorite pastime of carousing in the saloons of Cheyenne until he was needed.[27]

During Horn's trial for the murder of sixteen-year-old Willie Nickell in 1902, several references were made regarding his purported killings of Lewis and Powell. Horn had been indicted on an alleged drunken confession made to lawman Joe LeFors, backed up by witnesses hidden in an adjoining room. During the trial, prosecuting attorney Walter Stoll questioned Horn about his statements to LeFors regarding the assassinations of Lewis and Powell; the following is taken verbatim from the transcript:

> Q. I will ask you if this language was used: "How much did you get for killing these fellows, in the Powell and Lewis case, you got $600 apiece, you killed Lewis in the corral with a six-shooter; I would like to have seen

the expression on his face when you shot him," to which you replied, "He was the scaredest son-of-a-bitch you ever saw," was that language used?

A. I think the language was used; I know to a certainty that something very much like that was said. If he would have asked me if I killed him with a double barreled gun or a gatling gun, I would have said yes.

Q. But it was not a fact that you got $600 apiece for shooting them?

A. Oh no, if he had said I got $17,000 I would have told him yes.

Q. If you got $50.00 you would have told him the same.

A. Yes, or $1.25.

Q. So far as receiving this money is concerned, that is also a falsehood?

A. Yes, that is a falsehood.

Q. As a matter of fact, you didn't kill a man or do a job of this kind?

A. There would have to be an initiation, I never did kill anybody. It would be questionable what I would do, I never killed anybody, nor contracted to kill anybody.

During the cross-examination, Horn claimed that his remarks to LeFors were no more than braggadocio and lies, remarking, "I would not talk to this jury as I did to a man like LeFors. . . . He knew different. LeFors is very much the same kind of a man I am for talk."[28]

On the street, Horn wanted everyone to think of him as a dangerous and notorious killer, but in the courtroom it was a different story. The question still remains: Did Tom Horn kill William Lewis and Fred Powell? For a reasonable conclusion, the life history of both victims must be examined. Startling facts, previously unreported, emerge from this examination.

William Lewis was a native of Wiltshire, England, whose parents were well-to-do and respected. Although his age is unknown, he was likely born in the late 1850s. It is probable that he came to Wyoming in 1882, for he applied for U.S. citizenship on November 6 of that year. His citizenship was granted on February 24, 1888. In August 1895, local rancher George R. Shanton stated he had known Lewis for twelve years. Lewis' ranch was located at Iron Mountain in Laramie County, and in 1894 he was listed as owning fifty-seven cattle, thirty-three horses, and three carriages/wagons at a total value of $1,320.[29]

Lewis' character left much to be desired. He comes across as an arrogant and malicious individual who reportedly stole cattle indiscriminately and bragged about it to his neighbors. After his death, the *Daily Sun-Leader* reported.

> Mr. [John] Whittaker and Mr. Shanton stated this morning that . . . they did not believe he had a friend within many miles of his ranch for he had made himself a very disagreeable neighbor.
>
> It was known among the ranchmen that he had killed their cattle and had brought the carcasses to this city, where he sold them.[30]

The first criminal acts credited to William Lewis occurred on October 6 and 15, 1883, in Albany County, when he engaged a minor named M. T. Alexander to gamble with him at faro. Apparently Lewis took the boy's money, because he was indicted on the twentieth and arrested two days later. On November 9 he pleaded not guilty in both cases but changed his plea in one case on the fifteenth. He was fined twenty-five dollars the same day, and the second case was "dismissed at cost of the defendant." [31]

On September 28, 1886, Lewis was in trouble again when he stole an overcoat and a pair of gloves from Franklin D. Brown in Laramie County. Not satisfied with one coat, he stole another from Gilbert A. Searight the next day. Lewis was indicted on one charge on November 11 and the second charge the next day. Bail was set at two hundred and fifty dollars and one hundred dollars, respectively. On the twelfth, he pleaded not guilty in both cases. Apparently there was a plea bargain, for on November 18 Lewis pleaded guilty to one charge while the prosecution entered a nolle prosequi in the second case. Lewis was sentenced to two months in the Laramie County jail. [32]

It is evident that Lewis was stealing cattle from surrounding ranches, but no one brought charges against him until 1893. On May 28, a scant six months before Horn's raid on the Langhoff ranch, the Swan Land and Cattle Company, Al Bowie, Van Gilford, Samuel Moses, John Coble, and a man named Pierce charged Lewis with grand larceny in Laramie County District Court at Cheyenne. The plaintiffs claimed that Lewis stole one red-and-white calf valued at fifteen dollars. In actuality they set him up by inserting a penny under the hide for identification purposes. The case would backfire right in the face of the Swan Land and Cattle Company. [33]

Lewis was arrested and jailed on May 30. The next day he was indicted and released on five hundred dollars' bond, retaining the services of attorneys Baird and Churchill. Arraignment took place on June 9, Lewis pleaded not guilty, and the case was continued until the next term of court. The case came to trial on November 28, and the next day the jury found Lewis guilty. He was remanded to jail. On December 2 his lawyers filed a motion for a new trial, which was granted on the twelfth. Frank Boehm and James W. Hartsell posted Lewis' bond of seven hundred and fifty dollars on December 13, and he was released from jail. On December 15 the case was continued. [34]

When the court granted Lewis a new trial, the S.L.C.C. became apprehensive about the outcome, so on January 4, 1894, it brought a new charge of stealing livestock against him for the same crime. Lewis quickly retained the services of attorney H. Donzelmann. On the fifteenth, he was arraigned and pleaded not guilty. For the second time Boehm and Hartsell posted Lewis' bond of seven hundred and fifty dollars, and the case was continued. The case was continued again on August 6, a new bond of two hundred and fifty dollars was paid by the same sureties, and trial was set for the following December. [35]

On November 19, 1894, the prosecution made a motion to dismiss the charges of grand larceny against Lewis, which was granted. On December 22 subpoenas were issued, and Lewis' trial for stealing livestock commenced on the twenty-fourth. To the consternation of the S.L.C.C., even with the damning evidence of the penny in the calf's hide, the jury wasted no time in finding Lewis not guilty on the first day of the trial. Apparently the general feeling of the population toward the large livestock owners was antagonistic and defiant, especially when the ownership was in foreign hands. [36]

As did the jury that acquitted him, William Lewis wasted no time in getting his revenge. Immediately upon leaving the courtroom a free man, Lewis, along with attorney Donzelmann, filed these charges against the Swan Land and Cattle Company, Alexander H. Bowie, John C. Coble, Van L. Gilford, Samuel Moses, and one Pierce:

> The said William Lewis, plaintiff, complains of the above named defendants, for that the said defendants, contriving and maliciously intending to injure the said plaintiff in his good name and credit, and to bring him into public scandal and disgrace, and to cause it to be believed that he had been guilty of the crime of stealing one head of neat cattle in the value of fifteen dollars . . .
>
> By means of which the said plaintiff had . . . been put to great expense, to-wit: To the sum of Ten Thousand Dollars in and about procuring to be discharged upon his said trial, and had been greatly hindered in his lawful business for the space of six months to the damage of . . . Five Thousand Dollars.

Fifteen thousand dollars was a great deal of money in the late 1890s, well more than a quarter of a million dollars in today's currency. If Lewis could be acquitted for a crime for which he was proven guilty, then he had an excellent chance of winning this suit against the big cattlemen. And the S.L.C.C. knew it. On January 21, 1895, all the defendants but Pierce answered the charges and denied the allegations. [37]

To add insult to injury, Lewis filed a writ of replevin on January 5, 1895, in Laramie County Justice Court against Sheriff Ira Fredendall for the return of the steer that he had been accused of stealing. The writ stated the value of the now three-year-old steer was twenty dollars, and a replevin fee of twenty dollars was added. On February 5 Sheriff Fredendall appealed the replevin and posted a fifty-dollar surety bond. On March 6 Fredendall entered a judgment against Lewis for the costs. [38]

Although Lewis was now in the driver's seat, he still had problems, and big ones at that. While his lawsuits dragged on throughout the winter and spring and into summer, his life was repeatedly threatened. On at least two occasions, he narrowly escaped an assassin's bullet. Then his ranch house mysteriously burned down, and he moved to the old Montgomery ranch on Horse Creek, one mile east of the Albany County line. Rancher John Whittaker and his foreman, George Shanton, stated to *The Daily Sun-Leader* on August 5, "Lewis had been very suspicious of everybody, and was always accusing his neighbors of designs against his life . . . they knew of no one who had any thought of killing him. . . ."

To compound matters, Lewis was heavily in debt. Frank Boehm of Cheyenne, who had posted Lewis' bonds, held an eight-hundred-dollar mortgage on his cattle. Lewis also owed a good deal of money around the city of Cheyenne.

Time was quickly running out for William Lewis. In mid-July he was seen in Cheyenne, and around the twenty-fourth, he was visited by Cheyenne resident Thomas Roper and his wife and daughter. Lewis told the Ropers that he would be coming to Cheyenne the following week. He never made it.

On July 31, likely in the early morning hours, Lewis loaded a skinned beef carcass into his wagon. While he was hitching up his wagon, a .44-calibre slug slammed into his body, followed by another, and then another. Any of the three shots would have been fatal.

Three days later, ranchers Whittaker, Shanton, and John Harding rode up to the ranch and discovered Lewis' decomposing body. They wrote a quick note to Sheriff Fredendall, which was delivered around 2 p.m. Within the hour, the sheriff, prosecuting attorney J. C. Baird, coroner Theo G. Linton, and Dr. E. P. Rohrbaugh were on their way to Lewis' ranch. [39] The next day, Shanton testified at the coroner's jury:

> On the morning of August 3 I went to the old Montgomery ranch with Mr. John Whittaker and John Harding to look for FT cattle; saw a dead body lying in the corral near the house. We then examined the body and found it to be that of William Lewis. . . . We did not disturb the body, but covered it over. . . . We covered the body with a slicker and a quilt. In the afternoon Whittaker and myself went to Montgomery's ranch, and we found that the body was much more decomposed than it was in the morning. It looked as if the deceased had been dead about three days. The body lay out in the open corral where the sun and the rain had beaten upon it. We examined the ground about the house and corral for tracks, but found none nearer than a quarter of a mile east of the house, where we saw tracks of a horse shod in the front feet, the indications being that the horse had been galloping very rapidly in an easterly direction. Followed the tracks for about a mile when we lost them. We also searched for fresh hide, as we found a carcass of fresh beef in one of Lewis' wagons, covered with a tarpaulin, evidently ready for market. We found no hide but we found apparently fresh offal in a washout about one hundred yards from the house. It had been buried.
>
> When we first found the body we saw a rawhide whip lying about nine feet east of the body and the neckyoke belonging to the wagon in which the beef was loaded, west of the body about four or five feet. The body was dressed except a hat. The remains were encased in a dark coat, blue overalls and a pair of congress gaiters. The body was laying on its left side, the knees drawn up, and facing south. There was a white handkerchief tied around the neck. While there we looked over the body without touching it but could see no evidence of injuries. [40]

Dr. Rohrbaugh examined the body and found two of the slugs had entered the left center of Lewis' back and exited four inches apart near the left breast. The third shot hit Lewis behind the right ear but never exited. Krakel stated that the shots were fired at a range of three hundred yards; this, however, was not mentioned by the coroner's jury, and the following statement by Dr. Rohrbaugh indicates that he had no idea how far away the killer was: "Judging from the position of the body and range of the wounds it was evident that the shots were fired from the west, or uphill from the place where the body lay."

Following the inquest, Lewis' body, now black as coal, was buried near the spot where it was found in the corral. On August 5 a five-hundred-dollar reward for the killer was offered by Wyoming governor William Richards. Frank Boehm was made administrator of Lewis' estate to settle the deceased's debts, but the claims reportedly exceeded the amount received from the sales. Sheriff Fredendall remained in the Horse Creek area until August 6, with no new leads except finding the hides buried by Lewis that did not contain his brand, HKD. On August 8 the sheriff returned to the murder site and doggedly pursued his investigation. *The Boomerang* clearly outlines the futility of his efforts in this sad commentary on the character of Lewis:

> All the people within a radius of fifteen miles of Lewis' place say that they are glad he is dead. He has received no sympathy up there. Even the $500 reward offered will not stir his former neighbors up to action in hunting his murderers. [41]

In regard to Lewis' murder, the questions remain: "Why? Who? How?

In most crimes there is a motive, and no one had a better one than the Swan Land and Cattle Company, John Coble, and the others Lewis had sued. During the prosecution's cross-examination of Horn regarding his confession to LeFors about the Lewis murder, the S.L.C.C. was never mentioned, but John Coble was. The transcript reads:

> Q. Was this language used: "In the Powell and Lewis case, did Coble put in toward your pay?"
> A. I think it was.
> Q. And to which you replied, "No, I wouldn't let him, he fed me and furnished me horses and has done more for me than any man in the country.
> A. Yes sir.
> Q. Was this language: "Did you ever have any trouble to collect your money?" to which you replied, "No, when I do a job of this kind they knew they had to pay me. I would kill a man if he tried to beat me out of ten cents that I had earned," was this language used?
> A. I think it was. [42]

Although Horn denied on the stand that he ever killed a man for money, it is hard to believe that he would have made a statement of this kind to anyone, whether boasting or in jest.

In the four Langhoff and Lewis trials, the S.L.C.C. saw the prosecution gain only a slap-on-the-wrist conviction. Although Lewis was despised by his neighbors, no one was in litigation with him except the S.L.C.C., Coble et al., and they would have to pay out a large amount of money if he won his suit. With William Lewis alive they had a lot to lose; with him dead they had much to gain. On September 3, 1895, the S.L.C.C. et al., along with Sheriff Ira Fredendall, realized the benefits of

Lewis' death when the court ordered the following in both of Lewis' lawsuits, "The death of the above named plaintiff having been suggested to the Court, by order of the Court this case is now dismissed."[43]

Although no rustler had been killed until Lewis' death, rumors had circulated throughout southern Wyoming that Tom Horn had been retained by the big cattlemen to take care of the rustling situation, and he was brought in for questioning. Horn gave his version during his trial for the Nickell's murder:

> Anybody that investigated or knew anything about the killing of that man Lewis knows I was summoned before the Grand Jury here at the investigation of the killing of Lewis. I was in Bates Hole, Natrona County, at the time the killing occurred and the summons was served on me by the sheriff of Natrona County to appear here which I did, and reported to Col. Baird, who was then Prosecuting Attorney. I got an intimation from someone that I was being investigated as to the killing of William Lewis and I told the Prosecuting Attorney . . . where I was and the Grand Jury was adjourned several times until they found where I was, and that was all as far as I was concerned.[44]

Nevertheless, if the S.L.C.C. and the other litigants did away with Lewis, their triggerman undoubtedly was Tom Horn. The method by which Lewis died is a duplicate of that used in the assassinations of Colorado rustlers Matt Rash and Isom Dart in 1900. In all probability, Horn killed those two men.[45]

In Lewis' case, three shots were fired from an undisclosed distance. No evidence could be gathered at the scene of the murder because of the heavy rain that fell the night before the inquest. A likely scenario is that the killer fired two shots into Lewis' back, then approached his victim to make sure of his work and put a coup de grace into the back of his head. Lewis had been running scared for several months, and in that split second after the first slug hit him, his face likely registered the fear he had been anticipating. Only the killer would have seen Lewis' face, which brings back the nagging statement of Tom Horn to Joe LeFors, "He was the scaredest son-of-a-bitch you ever saw."

PART FOUR: Whodunit?

*I*F WILLIAM LEWIS WAS A BAD dream to his neighbors, then Fred Powell was a nightmare to his. With those he liked, Powell was no doubt a friendly man, and he was the only intimate friend that William Lewis had. But the man had a mean streak, and to anyone who incurred his wrath he would stoop to petty reprisals such as destruction of property, arson, and general harassment. He also rustled their stock. To Powell, it was, Do unto others before they do it unto you.

Fredrick U. Powell was born in Virginia and was thirty-seven years old at the time of his death in 1895. He came to Wyoming around the latter part of the 1870s and took a job with the Union Pacific Railroad in Cheyenne. He lost an arm while in service, and the U.P. gave him a job as night watchman. He was later fired when the company discovered that he had taken twenty dollars from a man who was making his way across the country by hopping freight trains. From there Powell moved to the Sybille country.

It was around 1881 when Powell settled on 160 acres on Horse Creek in Albany County, six miles from the Laramie County line and seven miles southwest of William Lewis' ranch. On December 23, 1882, he married twenty-three-year-old Mary N. Wanless in Laramie County. Their only child, William Edwin "Bill," was born in 1885. The life-style of the Powells was one of adversity and chaos from the start, and despite the loss of his arm, Fred Powell was described as a tough and husky man who was looked upon as a rustler from the moment he located on Horse Creek.[46]

On July 24, 1889, Powell reportedly stole four head of cattle in Albany County, one from Hugh McPhee, two from one Hayward, and another from a man named Lannon. On September 7 a criminal warrant was issued, and Powell was arrested. Unable to post a six-hundred-dollar bond, he was remanded to jail. A preliminary hearing was held on September 10, and Powell was ordered to appear before a grand jury on October 16. His bond was reduced to three hundred dollars, which was furnished by his father-in-law, John Keane. Strangely, Powell's brothers-in-law, William and Charles Keane, were prosecuting witnesses. Apparently the grand jury did not find enough evidence to indict him or the plaintiffs dropped their charges, for Powell was never brought to trial.[47]

A year later, on August 16, S. L. Moyer charged Powell with grand larceny in Justice of the Peace Court in Cheyenne. A warrant was issued, and Powell was arrested by Constable B. S. Smith. On the evening of the eighteenth, Powell appeared in court with his attorney, J. C. Baird. The prosecution presented its evidence, and the defense made a motion to dismiss on the grounds that "the evidence did not show that any crime had been committed by the defendant." The motion was sustained, and Justice W. P. Carroll ordered "that the complaint in this case is hereby dismissed and the defendant is discharged from custody."[48]

Fred Powell's troubles took a different turn in January 1892, when his wife sued him for divorce. Mary Powell claimed that for seven years her husband failed to provide for her or their son. She also stated that Powell threatened to shoot her the previous November, chased her with a knife in early December, and abducted their child on December 30. Needless to say, the divorce was granted on February 19. Strange as this may seem, it appears that following the divorce, Mary and her son continued to live off and on with Powell until his death.[49]

Five months later, Powell ran afoul of the law again and continued this pattern every year until his death. On July 15, 1892, he was arrested by Albany County sheriff C. C. Yund for stealing a horse belonging to Josiah Fisher on July 11. The preliminary hearing in Laramie began on the sixteenth, and Powell pleaded not guilty. For four days the evidence was presented, and Powell was bound over for trial during the next court term and released on two hundred dollars' bond. On September 19 the trial commenced under Justice J. H. Hayford, and Powell was found not guilty by the jury.[50]

A year later, Powell ostensibly began his vendetta against his Albany County neighbors. On July 23, 1893, he was charged with malicious trespass and destroying fences belonging to Etherton P. Baker. Apparently Powell feared the brand of adjudication handed out by Justice Hayford, and on July 29 he received a change of venue to Justice M. A. Hance's court. He was tried on the thirty-first, found guilty, and fined fifty dollars plus thirty-nine dollars for court costs. Powell immediately appealed. The appeal was granted on September 12, and he was released on a two-hundred-dollar appearance bond. Four days later he lucked out again, when the jury turned in a verdict of not guilty.[51]

Evidently Powell figured he could get away with anything; however, his luck was running out. On April 24, 1894, he continued his reprisal against his neighbors when he set fire to clothing, bedding, and food products belonging to Joseph Trugillo and Etherton P. Baker. Three days later he was arrested on the charge of incendiarism by Sheriff C. C. Frazer and hauled into court. The case was continued until the thirtieth. Still apprehensive of a ruling under Justice Hayford, Powell requested and was granted a change of venue to Justice Hance's court, and the case was tried that day. The jury had had enough of Powell and found him guilty. He was fined fifty dollars or, if in default, a jail sentence at one dollar per day until the fine was paid. Naturally he appealed, and he was released on one hundred dollars' bond.[52]

Powell could not seem to stay out of trouble. On July 8, 1894, he trespassed on the property of Harry P. Richardson and rode off on one of Richardson's horses without consent. He was arrested on the tenth and, on the thirteenth, again received a change of venue from Justice Hayford's court to Justice Hance's. Trial was held the same day, and Justice Hance, now tired of Powell's antics, quickly found him guilty and fined him forty-five dollars. Again Powell appealed for retrial and was released on one hundred dollars' bond. [53]

Fred Powell's appeal trial for incendiarism came to court on September 12 under Judge J. W. Blake. By this time, everyone was fed up with Powell's shenanigans, and the jury found him guilty the next day. On the eighteenth, Judge Blake sentenced him to four months in the county jail, retroactive to September 14. Because of Powell's conviction, prosecuting attorney W. H. Bramel entered a nolle prosequi on September 15 in the Richardson case. [54]

Following his release from jail, Powell began receiving letters warning him to stop stealing stock and to leave the country or face the consequences. At first, he likely ignored them as idle threats. It was a different story after William Lewis was killed. *The Daily Sun-Leader* grimly summed up the situation:

> The statement was repeatedly heard after the Lewis killing that "One Armed" Powell would be the next to go, and Sheriff Fredendall told Powell at the sale of the Lewis stock that he, Powell, was a fool to stay on Horse Creek and run the risk of losing his life at any moment. Powell appeared to be considerably frightened after the murder of Lewis became known, and it is understood that he was selling out preparatory to leaving the country.
>
> Not long ago Mrs. Powell was in this city [Cheyenne] and called at the Sun-Leader office. She stated that their cattle had all been sold and that they intended going away.

On September 3 Fred Powell reportedly received this last letter:

> Laramie, Wyo., September 2, 1895
>
> Mr. Powell—This is your third and last warning. There are three things for you to do—quit killing other people's cattle or be killed yourself, or leave the country yourself at once.

The letter was written in a disguised hand by a good penman and, of course, was unsigned. [55]

The man did not move fast enough. At 7:30 on the morning of September 10, Fredrick U. Powell died. Here is the statement of Andrew Ross, Powell's hired man:

> I have worked for Fred U. Powell one month. We were alone on the ranch. Mr. Powell and I, we got up about 4 A.M. this morning. We started to haul hay, hauled one load and started for another. We got to a place about 1/2 mile from the ranch down the creek, stopped wagon, got off. Mr. Powell told me to cut some willows so we could fix the rack. [To replace a stick that was missing from a hay rack.] As I was cutting the second willow I heard a shot fired. I looked around and saw Mr. Powell with his hand on his breast. I ran toward him. He exclaimed "Oh! My God!" then fell. I went to him. Examined him and found he was dead. I then went to the ranch of Mr. [Benjamin] Fay and notified Mr. Fay.

> I examined the surrounding vicinity and from what I could ascertain the shot was fired from a ledge of rocks about 250 feet [yards?] distant. I examined the body and found a gunshot wound entering the breast near the center and came out at right of spine near 4th rib. I couldn't see any person when I heard the shot or afterward. [56]

When Ross, a badly frightened man, arrived at the Fay ranch, he encountered Beulah Richardson, who carried the mail between Laramie and Summit. She immediately took the news to Sheriff Grant in Laramie. At the time of the killing, Mary Powell was in Laramie, and when she received the news she left for the ranch with the sheriff and coroner Andrew Miller. The inquest was held later that day with this verdict, "A gun shot wound inflicted with feloneous intent by a party or parties to the jury unknown." [57]

The Daily Sun-Leader gave a more detailed report after Sheriff Grant made his investigation:

> It was supposed that the parties who shot Lewis also killed Powell
> . . . . Powell was shot but once and killed instantly. A rifle ball entered the left side, near the heart, and came out over the right hip. The range was downward. The assassin was concealed behind a ledge of rocks on the opposite side of the creek, and was over 200 yards distant when the fatal shot was fired.
>
> After Ross ran away, the killer walked down to the body, viewed his work and returned to the hill, where he mounted his horse and rode away. His footprints were clearly discernable and careful measurements show he wore a No. 8 boot, and was a man of considerable weight. The officers suspect who the assassin was but have no tangible evidence. [58]

On the eleventh, Mary Powell brought Fred's body to Laramie, where at 4 p.m. the next day he was buried. She adamantly denied that he had received any warning letters to leave the country. [59] This again leaves the questions of who and why.

For the second time, Tom Horn was suspected and brought before a grand jury for questioning. He was never indicted, because of insufficient evidence, and no one was ever arrested for Fred Powell's murder. [60]

In Lewis' death, the evidence shows that the big cattlemen had reason to eliminate him; however, there is no connection between the cattlemen and Powell. All of Powell's court cases and litigations were with his neighbors, who were small ranchers. What reason would the prominent cattlemen have to kill Powell, because he was a known rustler? This is highly unlikely and would have been a foolish move, because loose talk had already linked the cattlemen to Tom Horn in the killing of William Lewis. The plausible solution of who killed Powell is provided by his wife, Mary.

Although Mary Powell led a chaotic and dubious life, she had her good side, which is pointed out by a reliable source provided to the author through the services of the Wyoming Archives. It is also revealed that Mary stated with absolute certainty that she knew who killed her husband, which seems to be the truth. Here is a firsthand account of Mary

Powell's views and convictions; however, the names of those involved are withheld by request:

> Mrs. Powell [Mary] was very alert and recalled many incidents concerning the murder of her husband Fred. She again told us that Tom Horn did not kill Fred Powell. She said that legend had been established and try as she might she would never be able to change the story. And she said, she could not prove the murderer's guilt.
>
> The Powell's were feuding with a neighboring rancher. The rancher was not a very pleasant man. Perhaps his disposition could be attributed to his childhood. He was a "Street Orphan" picked up by the authorities in some city. To save expense of caring for him he was then shipped with others to a point in Iowa where they were chosen by people in the west. He was chosen by a Wyoming rancher, probably for cheap labor.
>
> After the murder of Powell, Mary made life miserable for the rancher. He did not drink and Mary was noted for her alcohol intake. If she had liquor with her when she crossed the rancher's path she insisted he drink with her. Out came her trusty gun and quirt.
>
> She told us one time she accosted him at the Leslie Mine in the hills near her home. She insisted he drink with her. She threatened him with bodily harm and used the quirt on him.
>
> The rancher ran down into the mine to avoid her attack. Mary rolled stones into the mine. The rancher knew he wasn't going to escape so he came up. Mary forced him to drink until he collapsed.
>
> Mary Powell was quite a character but she was not a liar. [61]

Fred Powell's track record leaves no doubt that he had many enemies among his neighbors, and who knows how many others he had provoked who had never taken him to court. If this rancher did kill Powell, he timed his act well. It was only six weeks after the death of Lewis, and the rumors were flying that the cattlemen's hired killer, Tom Horn, had done the deed. The rancher could pull off a copycat killing, and the suspicion would fall on Horn and the big cattlemen. This is exactly what happened. Following Fred Powell's assassination, Mary began her vendetta against the rancher. If he had known that she would take this course of retaliation, he might well have reconsidered his actions. Although the evidence is circumstantial, Mary Powell was likely correct in her presumption.

Mary Powell's life was as colorful and tumultuous as her husband's, and she deserves a few lines of her own. Mary was a strong-willed and outspoken woman, with a character to match Fred Powell's. Born Mary Nora Keane on August 7, 1859, to Irish immigrants John and Mary Keane, she is recorded as the first white child born in Golden, Colorado. The Keanes first arrived in Wyoming in 1868 and in June also fostered the first child born in Laramie. By the time Mary married Fred Powell, her hectic life had led her through two failed marriages and a suicide attempt. [62]

In 1951 Wyoming historian Mary Lou Pence wrote a story about Mary Powell, from which these lines are taken:

> The next years [following Powell's death] were a struggle, and the once wistful and contented girl became a gaunt, raw-boned woman with

sharp crow-footed wrinkles around her eyes. She kept her rifle close at hand. She gathered her stock (and the neighbor's too, some said), and she stacked the wild hay from her fields for the work animals.

"Fight back," she would tell her son Bill. "That's the only way they'll let us live."

"Your horses are over in my corral," she informed one man. "They broke through my fences. If you want them you'd better come after them."

When the rancher arrived to pick up his stock, she said: "Pay me $50, I'm charging board."

But occasionally a cowboy would tell how Mary fixed the cow chip poultice that took the rattler fang's poison out of his leg. [63]

Two years after the death of Powell, Mary found herself in trouble with the law. On May 25, 1897, she and one Richard Colford were charged with committing burglary on May 24 of the house and outbuilding of Laramie resident Joseph Becker. Only Mary was scheduled to be tried the following September 11, but the case was apparently dismissed. [64]

Following the lifestyle of her husband, Mary, with her son Bill, was indicted on two charges of stealing livestock in 1905. In one case, Mary's lawyer made a plea to dismiss the case on the grounds that defendants were refused a jury trial in the preliminary hearing. It was overruled and Mary was found guilty. She was sentenced to three months in jail and the other case was dismissed. Bill was found not guilty. Five years later she was brought to trial for stealing three head of horses; the jury found her not guilty. But Mary wasn't through yet.

Also in 1910 she was charged with arson in the burning of a neighbor's stack of hay. Mary made a motion for a change of venue on the grounds that there was extreme prejudice against her, and she could not receive a fair trial. Her motion was denied, but the jury could not reach a verdict. Her second trial ended the same way, with a hung jury. The case was finally dismissed on a motion by the prosecution. Mary's petty crimes continued: In 1913 she was charged with malicious mischief; in 1914 it was trespass; again in 1914 Mary was charged and brought to trial for striking a neighbor in the face on three occasions. She was fined $15.50. The next year, at age fifty-five, Mary was brought to trial for the last time; for beating up on the same neighbor. Again she was fined for her conduct. The last action against Mary occurred in 1917 when a warrant was issued to search her ranch at Horse Creek for stolen goods, but nothing was found. Fred Powell would have been proud of her. [65]

There was tragedy in Mary Powell's life also. In January 1935 her son Bill, who emulated the actions of his parents with horse theft, bootlegging, and white slavery, was shot to death by his stepson, Alonzo Phelps, in an argument over taking a bath. Mary stepped into the room as the shots were fired and was struck in the left arm. Phelps was later acquitted. On October 23, 1940, Mary's brother, Charles Keane, was struck and killed by a freight train in Laramie. [66]

Mary's turbulent life ended in Cheyenne on January 13, 1941. On the previous December 29, Mary went to visit her daughter-in-law, May

"Billie" Phelps Powell, in Cheyenne. Billie supposedly was working in a house of prostitution, and it was here that Mary suffered a heart attack on January 5 and was taken to a hospital, where she died eight days later. Funeral services were held on the sixteenth in the St. Lawrence O'Toole Catholic Church in Laramie, and Mary was buried in the Green Hill Cemetery.[67]

Tom Horn met his fate on the gallows in Cheyenne on November 20, 1903, for the alleged murder of sixteen-year-old Willie Nickell, who had died in the same manner as Lewis and Powell.[68] It was not Horn's deeds that led him to the hangman's rope—it was his mouth.

Left: Alexander H. Swan of the Swan Land and Cattle Company. COURTESY UNIVERSITY OF WYOMING, LARAMIE

Below: Headquarters of the Swan Land and Cattle Company at Chugwater, Wyoming, around 1900. COURTESY UNIVERSITY OF WYOMING, LARAMIE

Left: Fred Langhoff, circa early 1880s.
COURTESY WYOMING STATE ARCHIVES, MUSEUMS AND HISTORICAL DEPARTMENT, CHEYENNE

Tom Horn while in jail at Cheyenne in 1903. AUTHOR'S COLLECTION

Eva Langhoff at age eighteen.
COURTESY WYOMING STATE ARCHIVES,
MUSEUMS AND HISTORICAL
DEPARTMENT, CHEYENNE

Panoramic view of the Two Bar Ranch (Swan Land and Cattle Company), at Chugwater, Wyoming. COURTESY WYOMING ARCHIVES, MUSEUMS AND HISTORICAL DEPARTMENT, CHEYENNE

The State of Wyoming,)
) ss.
County of Albany.   )   In Justice Court, before M J. H. Hay-
                                  ford, Justice of the Peace.

The State of Wyoming,
                vs.
Louis Bath, Eva Langhoff,
James Cleve, Nellie Cleve
and William Taylor,
              defendants.

INFORMATION.

Comes now William H. Bramel, county and prosecuting attorney
of the County of Albany, in the State of Wyoming, and in the name
and by the authority of the State of Wyoming informs the court and
gives the court to understand, that Louis Bath, Eva Langhoff, James
Cleve, Nellie Cleve and William Taylor, late of the county aforesaid, on the 14th. day of November, A. D. 1893, at the County of
Albany, in the State of Wyoming, then and there, unlawfully and feloniously did kill two calves, the same being neat cattle, of the
value of five dollars each, and of the total value of ten dollars,
of the personal property, goods and chattels of the Swan Land and
Cattle Company, Limited, a corporation, contrary to the form of the
statute in such case made and provided and against the peace and
dignity of the State of Wyoming.

                              William H. Bramel
                              County and prosecuting attorney of
                              the County of Albany, in the State of
                                        Wyoming.

The State of Wyoming,)
) ss.
County of Albany.   )
        I, William H. Bramel, county and prosecuting attorney of
the County of Albany, in the State of Wyoming, do solemnly swear
that I have read the above and foregoing information by me subscri-
bed, that I know the contents thereof and that I have been reliably
informed and verily believe the facts therein stated are true, So
help me God.

                              William H. Bramel
                              County and prosecuting attorney of
                              the County of Albany, in the State
                                        of Wyoming.

        Sworn to before me and signed in my presence this 17th. day
of November, A. D. 1893, and so I hereby certify.

                              J. H. Hayford
                              Justice of the Peace.

*Information from Criminal Case No. 589 against Eva Langhoff for theft of cattle from the
Swan Land and Cattle Company in 1893.* WYOMING STATE ARCHIVES, MUSEUMS AND
HISTORICAL DEPARTMENT, CHEYENNE.

THE TERRITORY OF WYOMING
vs.

William Lewis

Stealing Live Stock

Criminal Appearance Docket 3-421; charges against William Lewis for stealing livestock from the Swan Land and Cattle Company. WYOMING STATE ARCHIVES, MUSEUMS AND HISTORICAL DEPARTMENT, CHEYENNE

View of the terrain of the Sybille Valley. COURTESY WYOMING STATE ARCHIVES, MUSEUMS AND HISTORICAL DEPARTMENT, CHEYENNE.

Docket C   No. 183

In Laramie County District Court.

William Lewis

vs.

The Swan Land and Cattle Company et al

SUMMONS.

CIVIL ACTION FOR THE RECOVERY OF

Money only; amount claimed fifteen thousand dollars

Issued *December 24th* 189 4

Filed *Jan 7th* 189 5

Danl S Swan Clerk.

By_____ Deputy.

SHERIFF'S FEES.

Service,	$	1.25
Return, copies	$	2.00
Mileage,	$	.15
Total,	$	3.40

N Benzelmann

Plaintiff's Attorney.

STATE OF WYOMING, } ss.
COUNTY OF LARAMIE,

I hereby certify that I received the within Summons on the _____ 24th _____ day of _December_ 189 4, at 2.50 o'clock P.M., and served the same at Laramie County aforesaid, on the 24 day of _December_ 189 4, by delivering a certified copy thereof to_gether with all endorsements thereon to A B Bowie as agent for the Swan Land & Cattle Company limited Alexander H Bowie Van Gilford and Samuel Mres, John C Coble and Pierce not found in Laramie County

[signature]

Sheriff of Laramie County.

Summons in the suit for fifteen thousand dollars against the Swan Land and Cattle Company, filed by William Lewis. WYOMING STATE ARCHIVES, MUSEUMS AND HISTORICAL DEPARTMENT, CHEYENNE

Tuesday, September 3, 1895.

William Lewis

vs.   Doc. 6, No. 183.

The Swan Land and Cattle Company. a Corporation
duly organized and existing under an Act of Scotland,
and under the law of the United Kingdom of Great Britain
and Ireland, and doing business within the State of Wyoming,
Alexander H. Bowie, John C. Coble, Wm. G. Gilford, Samuel
Moses, and — Pheres, whose first name is unknown.

The death of the above named
plaintiff having been suggested to the Court, by order of the Court this case is
now dismissed.

William Lewis

vs.   Doc. 6, No 188.

Wm. J. Medendaa.

The death of the plaintiff herein having been suggested to the
Court, it is hereby ordered that this case be dismissed at plaintiff's cost, and
that the defendant go hence without day.

Benjamin F. Gump,

vs.   Doc. 6, No. 154.

Elwood Mead, as State Engineer, et al.

Now on this day, this cause coming on for determination upon the
special appearance of Thomas H. Williams, David A. Bishop and Jacob M. Tomphins, as trustees of the bond holders of the Lake
Voorhees Cattle Company, defendants in the above entitled action, and the court being fully advised in the premises, finds
that no service has been made upon said defendants, as required by law; nor has there been any appearance by
them in this cause, such as to give the court jurisdiction, and that the court is wholly without jurisdiction in said cause as far as
the same relates to the rights of the said Thomas H. Williams, David A. Bishop and Jacob M. Tomphins, as trustees for the bond holders of
the Lake Voorhees Cattle Company.

It is therefore considered and adjudged that the said cause be and the same is hereby dismissed as against the said Thomas H. Williams,
David A. Bishop and Jacob M. Tomphins, as trustees for the bond holders of the Lake Voorhees Cattle Company, to which the plaintiff then and there
duly excepted. And said cause coming on further for determination upon the demurrers of the defendants Elwood L. Usner, and Frank J. Kel-
rich, and upon the separate demurrer of the defendant Charles F. Coffee, defendants in the above entitled action, and the same having been duly

District Court journal showing the charges against the Swan Land and Cattle Company dismissed because of Lewis' death. WYOMING STATE ARCHIVES, MUSEUMS AND HISTORICAL DEPARTMENT, CHEYENNE

JAMES M. FENWICK.

I, ~~J. W. MELDRUM~~, *Clerk of the District Court, within and for said county, in the* ~~Territory~~ STATE *aforesaid, do hereby certify the foregoing to be a true and correct transcript of the judgment entered in the journal of said court in the above entitled action.*

Witness, my hand and the seal of said Court this 18th *day of* September *A. D. 1894*

James M. Fenwick
Clerk District Court.
By Robt. Gale, Dep.

The People of the ~~Territory~~ STATE **of Wyoming:**

To the Sheriff of Albany County, ~~and the Warden and Officers~~ *in charge of the* Jail *at* Albany County *in the State of* Wyoming **Greeting:**

Whereas, *Frederick W. Powell* *has been duly convicted in the District Court of said County and* ~~Territory~~, *of the crime of* Malicious Mischief *and judgment has been pronounced against him that he be punished by imprisonment in the* County Jail *at* Albany County, State of Wyoming *for the term of* Four *months all of which appears of record as is shown by the certified transcript of the judgment endorsed hereon and made a part hereof:*

Now this is to Command You, *the said Sheriff of Albany County, to take and keep* ~~and safely deliver the said~~ *the Said Frederick W. Powell* ~~into the custody of the said Warden or other Officer in charge of said prison, at your earliest convenience.~~

And this is to Command You, *the said* ~~Warden~~ Sheriff *and other Officers in charge of said* ~~prison~~ Jail*, to receive* ~~of and from said Sheriff~~ *the said Frederick W. Powell convicted and sentenced as aforesaid, and him the said Frederick W. Powell keep and imprison in the said* ~~prison~~ Jail *for the term of Four months And these presents shall be your authority for the same* Herein fail not.

Witness, Hon. J. W. Blake *Judge of said District Court, this* 18th *day of* September *A. D., 1894 Attest my hand and the seal of Court, the day and year last above written.*

James M. Fenwick,
Clerk District Court for said District.
By Robt. Gale, Dep.

Judgment in Criminal Case No. 598 against Fred Powell for incendiarism in 1894.

VERDICT OF CORONER'S JURY.

STATE OF WYOMING, } ss.
COUNTY OF ALBANY. {

In the Matter of the Inquest upon the Body of _Fred N Powell_ Deceased.

Before _Andrew Miller_, Coroner.

WE, the undersigned, jurors summoned to appear before _Andrew Miller_, Coroner of the County of Albany, in the State of Wyoming, at _ranch of deceased at Albany County_ on the _10th_ day of _September_, A. D. 189_5_, to enquire into the cause of the death of _Fred N Powell_

having been duly sworn according to law, and having made such inquiry, and having inspected the body, and having heard the testimony adduced, upon our oaths, each and all, do say that we find the name of the deceased was _Fred N Powell_ ; that __he was a native of _the State of Virginia_ aged about _37_ years, and that __he came to h_is_ death on ~~or about~~ the _10"_ day of _September_, A. D. 189_5_, in this County by _a gun shot at 7 30 o'clock a.m. wound inflicted with felonious intent by a party or parties to the Jury unknown_

All of which we duly certify by this verdict of our inquest, in writing, and by us signed, this _10th_ day of _September_, A. D. 189_5_

W J Hills
Benj C Fay
Charles H. Phillips

Right: Charges of burglary against Mary Powell in 1897.
WYOMING STATE ARCHIVES, MUSEUMS AND HISTORICAL DEPARTMENT, CHEYENNE

Left: Mary Powell in the late 1930s.
COURTESY WYOMING STATE ARCHIVES, MUSEUMS AND HISTORICAL DEPARTMENT, CHEYENNE

INFORMATION.—Boomerang Print, Laramie.

STATE OF WYOMING, ⎱ ss: IN JUSTICE'S COURT.
COUNTY OF ALBANY. ⎰   Before _R. E. Fitch_ .... J. P.

THE STATE OF WYOMING,

vs.

Mary Powell and
Richard Colford
Defendant

INFORMATION.

The said _Mary Powell and Richard Colfor_

Defendant..s., _all_ ....accused of the offence of _Burglary_

....for that the said Defendant..s., on the

_24th_ .....day of _May_ ...., A. D. 189_7_

....at the ......

..........................County of Albany, in the State of Wyoming

did break and enter into a dwelling house
....
occupied by Joseph Beeker and did then and there
steal from said premises one oil stove of the vale
of $2.00 the property of said John Beeker
And the said Mary Powell, _and Richard Colford_ and further accused
of breaking and entering into an out ho
situate on said premises No 90 Block 128
in the City of Laramie County of Alb
and State of Wyoming on the 24th d
of May 1897 and therefrom to steal an
carry away 1 drill of the value of $2.00
1 carpenters chisel of the value of 80 cents, 3 M
Wrenches of the value of One Dollar and fifty c.
and one Blacksmiths Punch of the value
50 cents, the Property of Joseph Beeker

contrary to the form of the statute in such case made and provided, and against the peace, and dignity of the

State of Wyoming ...._Moses C Jahren_

..............._County and Prosecuting Attorney_

..............._of Albany County, Wyoming_

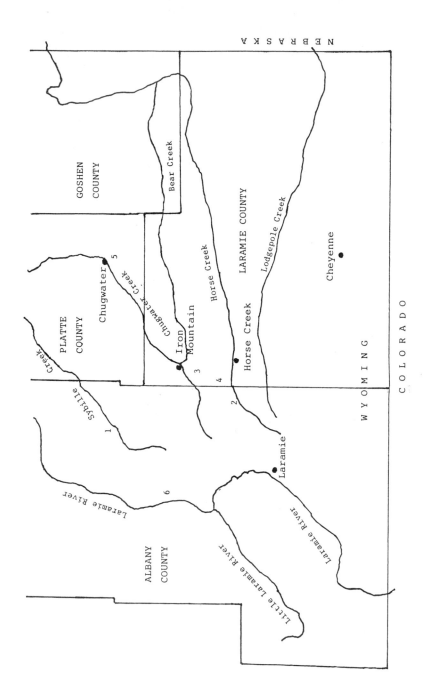

1. *Langhoff ranch; arrest of the Langhoff outfit, November 12, 1893. 2. Fred Powell ranch; Powell shot and killed, September 10, 1895. 3. William Lewis ranch. 4. Montgomery ranch; William Lewis shot and killed, July 31, 1895. 5. Swan Land and Cattle Company. 6. John Coble ranch.*

NOTES

CHAPTER I

1. (a) 1860 Parker County, Texas, Census, Dwelling No. 146, p. 21. (b) H. Smythe, *Historical Sketch of Parker County and Weatherford, Texas* (Lavat Printers, St. Louis: 1877), p. 12. Allen Hill and Jackson Hill are listed as old settlers of 1856. (c) Probate Minutes, Parker County Probate Minute Book I, Estate No. 36, p. 100. Parker County Probate Office, Weatherford. The minutes show that Dusky Hill's correct name was Luduska. (d) Family history of Isabelle Hill Vinyard and letters from Lois Fairman, great granddaughter of Isabelle Hill Vinyard, April 18 and May 19, 1989.

2. (a) Mrs. Clyde Gear Beaty, "Savage Days In Springtown," *The Old West* (Winter, 1966), p. 48. (b) *History of Parker County*, Parker County Historical Commission (Taylor Publishing Company, Dallas, Tex.: 1980), p. 127. (c) *Parker County Frontier Days*, souvenir program, July 28-31, 1954, Weatherford, pp. 11, 63.

3. (a) 1860 Parker County, Texas, Census, Dwelling No. 146, p. 21. All of the Hill family were listed by initials only. (b) Parker County Probate Minute Book I, Estate No. 36, pp. 139-140. The census taker mixed up the ages of Adeline and Allen Junior, listing Allen as the older of the two. The Parker County probate records show that Allen Junior was still a minor in 1875, confirming he could not have been born in 1854. (c) *A List of Fugitives from Justice, Indicted for Felonies in the State of Texas* (issued 1886), p. 74. The list shows that Allen Hill Junior was wanted in Parker and Palo Pinto counties in 1880 and 1881 and was about 25 years old. (d) *The Daily Herald* (Weatherford), January 13, 1920. Weatherford Public Library, Weatherford. This issue contains an article titled Remarkable Document Filed in Weatherford, in which an affidavit signed by two early residents, G. W. Tackitt and A. L. Thomas, gave the history and correct names of the Hill family. (e) Oregon State Board of Health, Certificate of Death, Isabelle Vinyard, State Registered No. 37, Local Registered No. 36. Oregon State Health Division, Salem. (f) Family history of Isabelle Hill Vinyard furnished to author by Lois Fairman and Ellen Hockett, great granddaughters of Isabelle Hill Vinyard.

4. Beaty, p. 48.

5. (a) *The Daily Herald* (Weatherford), January 13, 1920. (b) Ida Lassiter Huckabay, *Ninety-four Years in Jack County* (Austin, Texas: 1949), p. 95. (c) Floyd F. Ewing, "Unionist Sentiment on the Northwest Texas Frontier," *West Texas Historical Association Year Book*, Vol. 33, October, 1957, pp. 66-67.

6. *History of Parker County*, p. 127.

7. (a) *History of Parker County*, p. 127. (b) Beaty, pp. 48-49.

8. (a) *History of Parker County*, p. 128. (b) *The Daily Herald*, January 13, 1920. (c) John W. Nix, *A Tale of Two Schools and Springtown-Parker County* (Thompson and Morrow, Printer, Fort Worth, Tex.: 1945), p. 25.

9. (a) *The Democrat* (Fort Worth), September 6, 1873. Eugene C. Barker Texas History Center, University of Texas, Austin. (b) *History of Parker County*, p. 128. (c) *The Weatherford Democrat*, March 17, 1949. Weatherford Public Library, Weather-

ford. Beginning on March 10, 1949, this newspaper carried a six-week series regarding the Hill tragedy by Robert C. Campbell, titled "When Death Danced with Eleven." Mr. Campbell, a reporter for the *Corsicana Daily Sun*, received his information from Barto Hood, who was a young boy in Springtown at the time of the lynchings. (d) *The Springtown Epigraph*, September 21, 1989. Springtown, Tex.

10. *History of Parker County*, pp. 127–128.

11. Beaty, p. 49.

12. Marvin F. London, *Famous Court Trials of Montague County* (S. J. T. Printers, St. Jo, Tex.: 1974), pp. 20–21.

13. *The Dallas Weekly Herald*, September 27, 1873. Barker Texas History Center, Austin.

14. *The Democrat*, September 6, 1873.

15. *History of Parker County*, p. 128.

16. For the complete history of Texas politics and law enforcement, see T. R. Fehrenbach, *Lone Star, A History of Texas and Texans* (American Legacy Press, New York: 1983) and Walter Prescott Webb, *The Texas Rangers* (University of Texas Press, Austin: 1965).

17. London, pp. 23–24. The county clerk's office in Montague was unable to find the inquest file in its holdings.

18. (a) Beaty, p. 50. (b) *The Weatherford Democrat*, March 24, 1949.

19. Nix, p. 25.

20. (a) *The Democrat*, September 6, 1873. (b) *The Weekly Herald* (Weatherford), May 1, 1913. Weatherford Public Library, Weatherford.

21. (a) Beaty, p. 50. (b) London, p. 21. (c) *The Dallas Weekly Herald*, September 27, 1873. (d) *History of Montague County*, County Series Reader, ERA 1-Immigration, ERA 2-Organization, ERA 3-Progress. Weatherford Public Library, Weatherford.

22. London, pp. 21, 23.

23. (a) *A List of Fugitives from Justice, Indicted for Felonies in the State of Texas* (issued 1886), p. 11. (b) Extradition Papers, No. 852, *The State of Texas vs. Dan Short*, theft of cattle, Department of State, Extradition Service. Texas State Archives, Austin. (c) Maurice Kildare, "The Wilcox Double Robbery," *Real West*, June, 1968, pp. 33 and 50.

24. (a) *The Democrat*, September 6, 1873. (b) *The Weekly Herald*, May 1, 1913. (c) *The Daily Herald*, January 13, 1920. (d) *History of Parker County*, p. 128.

25. (a) *The Daily Herald*, January 13, 1920. (b) *History of Parker County*, p. 128. (c) G. A. Holland, *History of Parker County and the Double Log Cabin* (Herald Publishing Company, Weatherford, Tex.: 1937), p. 88. (d) Huckabay, p. 95. (e) *The Weatherford Democrat*, April 7, 1949, Campbell articles, Part V. (f) *The Democrat*, September 6, 1873.

26. *The Weekly Herald*, May 1, 1913.

27. *The Democrat*, September 6, 1873.

28. *The Springtown Epigraph*, March 21, 1991.

29. (a) London, pp. 23–24. (b)*History of Parker County*, p. 128. (c) Holland, p. 88. (d) *The Weatherford Democrat*, April 14, 1949, Campbell articles, Part VI.

30. (a) Probate Minutes, Parker County Probate Minute Book I, Estate No. 36, pp. 23, 100, 139, 140; Estate No. 39, pp. 301–303. (b) Nix, pp. 25–26. (c) *The Daily Herald*, January 13, 1920.

31. *History of Parker County*, p. 128.

32. Criminal Docket, District Court, Palo Pinto County, 1882, pp. 81–83; Criminal Minutes Book C, District Court, Palo Pinto County, Case No. 543, *State of Texas vs. Allen Hill*, p. 242. Palo Pinto County District Clerk's Office, Palo Pinto.

33. *A List of Fugitives from Justice, Indicted for Felonies in the State of Texas* (issued 1886), p. 74.

34. (a) *The Daily Express* (San Antonio), March 4, 1896. Texas State Archives, Austin. (b) Extradition Papers, No. 1414, *The State of Texas vs. Allen Hill*, murder, Department of State, Extradition Service.

35. (a) Extradition Papers, No. 3005, *The State of Texas vs. Allen Hill*, murder, Department of State, Extradition Service. (b) Monthly Return of Company B, Frontier Forces, State of Texas, month ending February 29, 1896; Service Records, Private Edward F. Connell, Company B, Frontier Battalion, Texas State Archives, Austin.

36. (a) *The Daily Express*, March 4, 1896. (b) *The Fort Worth Gazette*, March 6, 1896. Fort Worth Public Library, Fort Worth.

37. *History of Parker County*, pp. 127–128.

38. *History of Parker County*, p. 128.

39. (a) Family history of Isabelle Hill Vinyard; *The White Hall Register*, October 16, 1869; Greene County, Illinois District Court Records, *People vs. John Vinyard*; furnished to author by Lois Fairman and Ellen Hockett, great granddaughters of Isabelle Hill Vinyard. (b) Power of attorney to D. O. Sullivan from Belle Vinyard, formerly Belle Hill, dated March 12, 1881, Poolville, Parker County, Texas. Weatherford Public Library, Weatherford.

40. *The Lake County Examiner* (Lakeview, Oregon), October 11, 1894. Furnished to author by Ellen Hockett.

41. *The Lake County Examiner*, December 13, 1894. Oregon Historical Society, Portland.

42. *The Lake County Examiner*, May 9, 1895. Furnished to author by Ellen Hockett.

43. (a) Family history of Isabelle Hill Vinyard; *The Lake County Examiner*, December 31, 1925. Furnished to author by Lois Fairman and Ellen Hockett. (b) Oregon State Board of Health, Certificate of Death, Isabelle Vinyard.

CHAPTER II

PART ONE:

1. (a) *The Watauga Democrat* (Boone, North Carolina), October 19, 1988. (b) *The Tomahawk* (Mountain City, Tennessee), December 14 and 21, 1988.

2. (a) McCanles file, furnished to author by Sanna Gaffney, genealogist, of Boone, North Carolina. (b) Interviews with Jessie Williams of Foscoe, North Carolina, February 7, March 2, May 24, and October 25, 1989.

3. (a) Grave marker of Sarah (Shull) DeVald in Shull Cemetery, Shulls Mill, North Carolina. (b) Standard Certificate of Death, Sarah Louisa DeVald, Watauga County Courthouse, Boone. (c) David Leroy Corbitt, *The Formation of the North Carolina Counties, 1663–1943* (State Department of Archives and History, Raleigh, N.C.: 1950), p. 220. (d) Williams interviews.

4. (a) *The Heritage of Watauga County, North Carolina* (Hunter Publishing Company, Winston-Salem, N.C.: 1984), Vol. I, p. 328. (b) John Preston Arthur, *History of Watauga County, North Carolina* (Richmond, Va.: Richard Waddey Company, 1915), pp. 212, 342–343. The rest of Simon Shull's children were Mary (b. March 19, 1793), Sarah (b. March 2, 1795), John (b. March 24, 1799), Joseph (b. April 22, 1801), Temperance (b. October 16, 1804), and a second Elizabeth (b. April 10, 1808). The first Elizabeth died February 15, 1794.

5. (a) Goldene Fillers Burgner, *Carter County, Tennessee, Marriage Records, 1796–1870* (Southern Historical Press, Easley, S.C.: 1987), p. 106. (b) Lois T. Hayes, "Shulls Mills," *The Blue Ridge Stemwinder* (De Soto, Missouri), Vol. 1, No. 3, Winter, 1989, p. 3. (c) Grave markers in various Watauga County cemeteries. (d) 1850

Watauga County, North Carolina, Census, p. 143. (e) 1860 Watauga County, North Carolina, Census, p. 354. (f) *The Heritage of Watauga County, North Carolina*, Vol. I, p. 328. (g) Arthur, p. 343.

6. (a) John Parris, *Roaming the Mountains* (Kingsport Press, Kingsport, Tenn.: 1982), pp. 1–7, 239–241. (b) Arthur, p. 194.

7. (a) Williams interviews. (b) Frank Jenners Wilstach, *Wild Bill Hickok, The Prince of Pistoleers* (New York: 1926), p. 71. (c) William E. Connelley, "Wild Bill, James Butler Hickok," *Kansas Historical Collections*, Vol. 17, p. 5. Kansas Historical Society, Topeka.

8. (a) *The Heritage of Watauga County, North Carolina* (Hunter Publishing Company, Winston-Salem, N.C.: 1987), Vol. II, pp. 134–135. (b) Arthur, p. 194. (c) North Carolina 1830 Census Index, p. 120. (d) North Carolina 1840 Census Index, p. 129.

9. (a) Connelley, p. 1. (b) George W. Hanson, "True Story of Wild Bill, McCanles Affray in Jefferson County, Nebraska, July 12, 1861," *Nebraska Historical Quarterly*, Vol. 49, No. 1, Spring, 1968, p. 5. (c) Frances Terry Ingmire, *Ashe County, North Carolina Marriage Records, 1819–1871* (Ingmire Publications, St. Louis, Mo.: 1984), p. 19. (d) Arthur, pp. 194, 196. (e) 1850 Watauga County, North Carolina, Census, p. 143. (f) 1860 Jones County, Territory of Nebraska, Census, pp. 810–812.

10. (a) *The Watauga Democrat*, February 15, 1894. Belk Library, Appalachian State University, Boone. (b) Arthur, pp. 134, 151. (c) 1852 Watauga County tax receipt to Jesse Council. Furnished to author by Clara Ray of Boone. (d) 1860 Jones County, Territory of Nebraska, Census, pp. 810–812. (e) Charles Dawson, *Pioneer Tales of the Oregon Trail and of Jefferson County* (Topeka, Kansas: 1912), pp. 189–191. (f) Connelley, p. 1.

11. (a) *The Watauga Democrat*, February 15, 1894. (b) Arthur, p. 195.

12. (a) Arthur, p. 194. (b) Williams interviews. (c) Gravestone in Shull Cemetery at Shulls Mill reads, "Martha Allice, Daughter of Sarah Shull, Born May 4, 1856, Died July 2, 1857, Gone to be an Angel."

13. (a) Williams interviews. (b) Arthur, p. 194. (c) Poems of James McCanles (born October 30, 1796, died July 1870). McCanles file. (d) *The Watauga Democrat*, February 15, 1894.

14. (a) Connelley, pp. 1, 2. (b) Dawson, p. 185. (c) Wilstach, p. 61. (d) Glen Chesney Quiett, *Pay Dirt* (Johnsen Publishing Company, Lincoln, Neb.: 1971), pp. 124–125. (e) Williams interviews.

15. Arthur, pp. 195–196.

16. Letters; McCanles file.

17. *Watauga County Deed Book G*, pp. 56–57. Register of Deeds, Watauga County Courthouse, Boone.

18. (a) *Watauga County Deed Book I*, pp. 336–338; Deed Book F, pp. 505–506. (b) *North Carolina Reports, Vol. 88, Cases Argued and Determined in the Supreme Court of North Carolina, February Term, 1883* (Ashe and Gatling, Printers and Binders, Raleigh: 1883), p. 341.

19. *Watauga County Deed Book I*, pp. 333–334.

20. (a) *Watauga County Deed Book I*, pp. 244–245. (b) *North Carolina Reports, Vol. 88*, pp. 340–344.

21. (a) Execution against Property to the Sheriff of Watauga County; J. and J. C. Cowles against D. C. McCanles, John Horton et al., October 25, 1875. Clerk of the Superior Court, Watauga County Courthouse, Boone. (b) Transcript of Judgment, Yadkin County Superior Court, J. and C. J. Cowles against D. C. McCanles and others, November 6, 1875. Clerk of the Superior Court, Watauga County Courthouse, Boone.

22. (a) Letters; McCanles file. (b) Williams interviews. (c) Interview with Bina Teague of Boone, North Carolina, February 27, 1989. (d) *The Mountain Times* (Boone, North Carolina), January 11, 1990. (e) Arthur, p. 134.

23. (a) Connelley, pp. 5–6. (b) Wilstach, p. 62.

24. (a) Ray Stahl, *Greater Johnson City, A Pictorial History* (Donning Company, Norfolk and Virginia Beach, Va.: 1983), p. 35. (b) John Trotwood Moore and Austin P. Foster, *Tennessee, the Volunteer State 1769–1923* (S. J. Clarke Publishing Company, Chicago and Nashville: 1923), Vol. 1, p. 445. (c) Williams interviews. (d) Teague interview.

25. (a) Arthur, pp. 195–196. (b) *The Watauga Democrat*, February 15, 1894. (c) Letters; McCanles file. (d) 1860 Carter County, Tennessee, Census, pp. 167–169.

26. Williams interviews.

PART TWO:

27. (a) Arthur, pp. 195–196. (b) Connelley, pp. 3–4. (c) Dawson, p. 186. (d) Wilstach, pp. 61–62. (e) Quiett, p. 140. (f) *The Fairbury Daily News* (Fairbury, Nebraska, August 13, 1965. Nebraska State Historical Society, Lincoln.

28. (a) Connelley, pp. 4–5. (b) Dawson, p. 186. (c) Joseph G. Rosa, *They Called Him Wild Bill* (University of Oklahoma Press, Norman: 1974), p. 40.

29. (a) Williams interviews. (b) Dawson, p. 195. (c) Rosa, p. 40. (d) *The Fairbury Daily News*, August 13, 1965. (e) Connelley, p. 5. (f) 1860 Jones County, Territory of Nebraska, Census, pp. 810–812. (g) Probate Records from the Estate of D. C. McCanles, July 12, 1861 through January 16, 1863, Docket 2. Gage County Courthouse, Beatrice, Nebraska.

30. (a) Dawson, pp. 187, 189–193. (b) Hanson, pp. 11, 12, 30. (c) Connelley, p. 5. (d) Wilstach, pp. 60 61. (e) Rosa, pp. 41–43

31. (a) Dawson, pp. 193, 194, 197–207. (b) Hanson, pp. 28, 33, 36–37. (c) Connelley, pp. 6–11. (d) Wilstach, pp. 69–73. (e) Rosa, pp. 41–43.

32. Probate Records, D. C. McCanles.

PART THREE:

33. (a) Dawson, p. 212. (b) Hanson, pp. 10–13. (c) Connelley, pp. 11–12. (d) Rosa, pp. 41–42. (e) Letter from William Monroe McCanles, October 1925, "The Only Living Eyewitness," *Nebraska History: A Quarterly*, Vol. 49, No. 1, Spring 1968, p. 47.

34. (a) Dawson, pp. 187, 209, 214–215. (b) Hanson, pp. 13–15. (c) Rosa, pp. 40–44. (d) *The Fairbury Daily News*, August 13, 1965. (e) William Monroe McCanles, "The Only Living Eyewitness."

35. Wilstach, pp. 69–70.

36. (a) Dawson, pp. 193–196. (b) Hanson, pp. 27, 28, 35–37. (c) Connelley, pp. 12–14. (d) Wilstach, pp. 63, 64, 67–72. (e) Williams interviews.

37. (a) Hanson, pp. 14–26. (b) Rosa, pp. 42–52. (c) William Monroe McCanles, "The Only Living Eyewitness." (d) Williams interviews. (e) Teague interview. (f) Dawson, p. 219

38. Hanson, pp. 24 26.

39. (a) Hanson, p. 35. (b) Rosa, p. 52

PART FOUR:

40. Rosa, p. 53.

41. (a) Probate Records, D. C. McCanles. (b) Williams interviews.

42. (a) Williams interviews. (b) Civil War Service Record, Philip T. DeVald, Company A, 1st Regiment Colorado Cavalry. Military Records Branch, National Archives, Washington, D.C.

43. Alvin M. Josephy, Jr., *War on the Frontier,* Civil War series (Time-Life Books, Alexandria, Va.: 1986), pp. 16–37.

44. (a) Civil War Service Record, Philip T. DeVald. (b) War of the Rebellion Pension File, XC-02 692 569, Philip T. DeVald. Veterans Administration Office, Washington, D.C.

45. (a) War of the Rebellion Pension File, Philip T. DeVald. (b) Williams interviews. (c) Harrison County, Iowa, Deed Book 3, pp. 376–377. Harrison County Recorder of Deeds, Logan, Iowa. This deed, dated April 15, 1873, states, "P. T. DeVald and Sarah L. DeVald his wife of the City of Duluth, County of St. Louis, State of Minnesota . . ."

46. (a) Harrison County, Iowa, Deed Book 3, pp. 208, 376–377; Deed Book 18, p. 308. (b) 1880 Harrison County, Iowa, Census, p. 124.

47. (a) Harrison County, Iowa, Deed Book 48, pp. 18, 341, 343; Deed Book 53, p. 275; Deed Book 68, p. 102; Deed Book 69, p. 127. (b) Wilstach, p. 70. (c) Department of Iowa, Grand Army of the Republic records, DeVold [sic], Philip T. State Historical Society of Iowa, Des Moines. (d) *List of Ex-Soldiers, Sailors, and Marines, Living in Iowa*, prepared by Adjutant General William L. Alexander (Geo. E. Roberts, State Printer, Des Moines, Ia: 1886), p. 3. (e) 1885 Harrison County, Iowa, Census, p. 68.

48. (a) *The Heritage of Watauga County North Carolina*, Vol. I, p. 328. (b) Gravestones of Phillip and Phoebe Shull in Shull Cemetery, Shulls Mill. (c) Watauga County Deed Book B, pp. 37–38.

49. Harrison County, Iowa, Deed Book 98, p. 396.

50. (a) Putnam County, Florida, Deed Book 13, pp. 416–417; Deed Book 25, pp. 112, 116, 404, 531; Agreement Book B, p. 590. Putnam County Recorder of Deeds, Palatka, Florida. (b) Williams interviews.

51. (a) Williams interviews. (b) War of the Rebellion Pension File, Philip T. DeVald. (c) 1900 Watauga County, North Carolina, Census (enumerated June 29, 1900), p. 16.

52. (a) 1910 Watauga County, North Carolina, Census, p. 15B. (b) Williams interview, February 7, 1989.

53. Teague interview.

54. (a) Williams interview, October 25, 1989. (b) Teague interview. (c) Standard Certificate of Death, Sarah Louisa DeVald, Watauga Registry of Death Certificates, Vol. 19, p. 200. (d) *The Watauga Democrat*, June 16, 1932.

CHAPTER III

1. "Short Shot," *The State Journal* (Topeka, Kansas), August 24, 1891. Furnished to author by Mary Manship of Osgood, Indiana.

2. *The State Journal*, August 24, 1891. (b) *The Oklahoma Daily Times Journal*, August 26, 1891. Oklahoma Historical Society, Oklahoma City.

3. *The Daily Oklahoman*, February 29, 1920. Oklahoma Historical Society, Oklahoma City.

4. *The Oklahoma Daily Times Journal*, August 26, 1891.

5. (a) *The Versailles Republican*, August 27, 1891. Ripley County Historical Society, Versailles, Indiana. (b) *The Ripley County Journal*, September 29, 1881. Ripley County Historical Society, Versailles, In. (c) Ripley County Marriage Book No. 7, p. 275. Ripley County Clerk's Office, Versailles, In. (d) Short family records, furnished to author by Mary Manship, Osgood, Indiana.

6. *The Versailles Republican*, February 2, 1882.

7. (a) *The Ripley County Journal*, September 29, 1881, and July 21, 1898. (b) Ripley County Deed Book 37, p. 87. Ripley County Clerk's Office, Versailles, In. (c) Proof of Wills, Charles C. Short, dated November 30, 1881. Clerk of the Ripley County Circuit Court, Versailles, In. (d) Short family records.

8. *The Ripley County Journal*, March 23 and April 20, 1882; January 10, 1884.

9. (a) *The Versailles Republican*, December 6, 1883. (b) *The Ripley County Journal*, December 6, 1883. (c) Ripley County Circuit Court Case No. 1231, *State of Indiana vs. Charles E. Short*. Clerk of the Ripley County Circuit Court, Versailles, In.

10. Ripley County Circuit Court Case No. 1231, *State of Indiana vs. Charles E. Short*.

11. *The Ripley County Journal*, June 14, 1883.

12. (a) Ripley County Record of Indictments, 1871–1885, Indictment Nos. 1231 and 1235, p. 535. Clerk of the Ripley County Circuit Court, Versailles, In. (b) Ripley County Jail Keeper's Record, furnished to author by Mary Manship, Osgood, Indiana. (c) *The Versailles Republican*, December 6, 1883.

13. *The Ripley County Journal*, December 6, 1883.

14. (a) *The Versailles Republican*, August 27, 1891. (b) Short family records.

15. (a) Sam P. Ridings, *The Chisholm Trail* (Co-Operative Publishing Company, Guthrie, Ok.: 1936), p.464. (b) Nyle H. Miller and Joseph W. Snell, *Why The West Was Wild* (Kansas State Historical Society, Topeka, Ks.: 1963), p. 4.

16. *The State Journal* (Topeka, Kansas), August 24, 1891.

17. Henry F. Mason, "County Seat Controversies in Southwestern Kansas," *The Kansas Historical Quarterly*, Volume 2, 1933, p. 55.

18. (a) Mason, pp. 45–64. (b) George Rainey, *No Man's Land* (Enid, Ok.: 1937), pp. 198–211. (c) Emerson Hough, *The Story of the Outlaw* (A. L. Burt Company, New York: 1905), pp. 227–255. (d) Henry Bascomb Kelly, "A Tragedy and Trial of No Man's Land," *The Green Bag*, Magazine of attorneys of the U.S., Boston Book Company, Boston, Mass. 8.1, S + 4, Mcs., holdings of the Kansas Historical Society, Topeka. (e) Irma Doster, *Freedom Has a Happy Ring* (Burge Printing Company, Topeka, Ks: 1960), pp. 37–39. (f) *The Oklahoma Daily Times Journal*, August 26, 1891.

19. (a) George Rainey, *The Cherokee Strip* (Co-Operative Publishing Company, Guthrie, Ok.: 1933), p. 255. (b) Ridings, p. 464.

20. (a) Glenn Shirley, *West of Hell's Fringe* (University of Oklahoma Press, Norman: 1978), pp. 3–33. This book has the most comprehensive history of lawlessness in Oklahoma, including the most authentic account of the activities of the Dalton Gang. (b) Rainey, *The Cherokee Strip*, p. 255.

21. *Claims for Services as Deputy Marshals in Oklahoma*, Ex. Doc., No. 144, June 12, 1891, pp. 16, 35–36. Oklahoma Historical Society, Oklahoma City.

22. Shirley, pp. 53–60.

23. (a) *The Oklahoma Daily Times Journal*, August 26, 1891. (b) *The State Journal* (Topeka, Kansas), August 24, 1891.

24. Shirley, pp. 61–63.

25. Rainey, *The Cherokee Strip*, p. 256.

26. Shirley, pp 62–63,

27. (a) Harold Preece, *The Dalton Gang* (Hastings House Publishers, New York, 1963), p. 33. (b) Shirley, p. 42.

28. (a) Thomas B. Ferguson, "Men of the Border," *Harlow's Weekly*, Oklahoma City, Vol. 18, No. 13, March 31, 1920, p. 15. (b) *The Oklahoma Daily Times Journal*, August 26, 1891.

29. C. P. Wickmiller interview by Louise S. Barnes, November 15, 1937, *Indian Pioneer History*, Vol. 49, pp. 342–343. Oklahoma Historical Society, Oklahoma City.

30. *The Hennessey Citizen*, August 28, 1891. Oklahoma Historical Society, Oklahoma City.

31. (a) *The Hennessey Citizen*, August 28, 1891. (b) *The Daily Oklahoman*, February 29, 1920. (c) *The Daily Oklahoma State Capital*, January 24, 1894. Oklahoma Historical Society, Oklahoma City. (d) Rainey, *The Cherokee Strip*, pp. 255–261. (e) Shirley, pp. 62–67. (f) Evan G. Barnard, "A Rider of the Cherokee Strip," *The Daily Oklahoman*, February 10, 1937. (g) Ferguson, p. 15.

32. (a) *The Versailles Republican*, August 27, 1891. (b) *The Ripley County Journal*, September 3, 1891.

33. Shirley, p. 67.

CHAPTER IV

1. (a) *The Albuquerque Evening Democrat*, November 1, 1884. University of New Mexico Library, Santa Fe. (b) *The Black Range* (Chloride, New Mexico), November 7, 1884. University of New Mexico Library, Santa Fe. (c) *The Las Vegas Daily Optic*, November 3 and 12, 1884. University of New Mexico Library, Santa Fe. (d) Jas. B. Hume and Jno. N. Thacker, *Wells Fargo & Company's Robbers Record*, (H. S. Crocker & Company, San Francisco, Ca.: 1884), pp. 26–27.

2. *The Albuquerque Evening Democrat*, November 3, 1884.

3. (a) Record of Convicts, New Mexico Penitentiary, Inmate No. 107, Punch Collins, p. 8. State of New Mexico Records Center and Archives, Santa Fe. (b) Record of Prisoners, Kansas State Penitentiary Book A, Inmate No. 3396, Punch Collins. Kansas State Historical Society, Topeka. (c) *The Las Vegas Daily Optic*, November 12, 1884.

4. (a) *The Trail Drivers of Texas*, originally compiled and edited by J. Marvin Hunter and published under the direction of George W. Saunders (Cokesbury Press, Nashville, Tenn.: 1925), pp. 690–691. (b) *The Las Vegas Daily Optic*, November 12, 1884.

5. (a) Record of Convicts, New Mexico Penitentiary, Inmate No. 107, Punch Collins, p. 8. (b) *The Las Vegas Daily Optic*, November 12, 1884. (c) F. Stanley, *Desperadoes of New Mexico* (World Press, Denver, Co.: 1953), pp. 266–271. (d) Chester D. Potter, Reminiscences of the Socorro Vigilantes, *New Mexico Historical Review*, Vol. 40, No. 1, January 1965, pp. 40–45.

6. (a) Record of Convicts, New Mexico Penitentiary, Inmate Nos. 108, J. W. Pointer; 109, Jefferson Kirkindall; 110, Edwin White; 111, Bill Allen, p. 8. (b) Record of Prisoners, Kansas State Penitentiary Book A, Inmate Nos. 3397, J. W. Pointer; 3398, Jeff Kirkindall; 3407, Edwin White; Book B, Inmate No. 3541, Bill Allen. (c) *The Las Vegas Daily Optic*, November 12, 1884. (d) *The Santa Fe New Mexican Review*, November 12, 1884. New Mexico State Library, Santa Fe.

7. (a) *The Albuquerque Evening Democrat*, November 3, 9, and 10, 1884. (b) *The Las Vegas Daily Optic*, November 12, 1884.

8. (a) *The Albuquerque Evening Democrat*, November 1, 1884. (b) *The Las Vegas Daily Optic*, November 11, 12, and 14, 1884. (c) *The Santa Fe New Mexican Review*, November 12 and 13, 1884.

9. (a) *The Las Vegas Daily Optic*, November 11, 1884. (b) *The Santa Fe New Mexican Review*, November 12, 1884.

10. (a) *The Albuquerque Evening Democrat*, November 12, 1884. (b) *The Santa Fe New Mexican Review*, November 12, 1884.

11. (a) *The Albuquerque Evening Democrat*, November 14, 1884. (b) *The Las Vegas Daily Optic*, November 19 and 21, 1884. (c) *The Santa Fe New Mexican Review*, November 15, 1884.

12. *The Las Vegas Daily Optic*, November 17, 19, and 21, 1884.

13. (a) Socorro County District Court Records, Criminal Case 686. State of New Mexico Records Center and Archives, Santa Fe. (b) *The Santa Fe New Mexican Review*, November 21, 1884. (c) *The Albuquerque Evening Democrat*, November 22, 1884. (d) *The Las Vegas Daily Optic*, November 22 and 25, and December 2, 1884.

14. (a) Record of Prisoners, Kansas State Penitentiary Book A, Inmate Nos. 3396, Punch Collins; 3397, J. W. Pointer; 3398, Jeff Kirkindall; 3407, Edwin White. (b) *Las Vegas Daily Optic*, November 25 and December 8, 1884, and January 3, 1885.

15. (a) Socorro County District Court Records, Criminal Case 686. (b) Record of Prisoners, Kansas State Penitentiary Book B, Inmate No. 3541, Bill Allen. (c) *Las Vegas Daily Optic*, November 21, 1884, March 31 and April 4, 1885. (d) *The Albuquerque Evening Democrat*, April 2, 1885. (e) F. Stanley, *Socorro, the Oasis* (World Press, Denver, Co.: 1950), p. 135.

16. (a) Record of Prisoners, Kansas State Penitentiary Book A, Inmate Nos. 3396, Punch Collins; 3397, J. W. Pointer; 3398, Jeff Kirkindall; 3407, Edwin White; Book B, Inmate No. 3541, Bill Allen. (b) *Informe de la Comision Permanente Especial Sobre la Penitenciaria en el Consejo de la Asamblea Legislativa Vigesimaseptima, Territorio De Nuevo Mexico, Sesion, De 1887*; New Mexico Penitentiary Records, Special Reports, 1887. State of New Mexico Records Center and Archives, Santa Fe.

17. (a) Record of Convicts, New Mexico Penitentiary, Inmate Nos. 107, Punch Collins; 108, J. W. Pointer; 109, Jefferson Kirkindall; 110, Edwin White; 111, Bill Allen, p. 8. (b) *The Albuquerque Evening Democrat*, November 10, 1884.

CHAPTER V

1. *The Texas Criminal Reports. Cases Argued and Adjudged in the Court of Criminal Appeals of the State of Texas*, reported by John F. White (T. H. Flood and Company, Austin: 1911), Vol. 32, p. 365.

2. Pardon request from L. L. Loggins, Texas Penitentiary at Huntsville, to Texas governor Joseph D. Sayers, Austin, dated August 20, 1901. Furnished to author by Mary Alice Winborn of Houston, granddaughter of Pete Loggins.

3. (a) Loggins family records, furnished to author by Linda Pansano of Bridge City, Texas, great granddaughter of Pete Loggins. (b) Jasper County, Texas, Marriage Records, Vol. B, p. 97. Jasper County Clerks Office, Jasper. (c) Pardon request from L. L. Loggins.

4. (a) Jasper County, Texas, Election Returns, 1876–1878, Secretary of State Election Registers. Texas State Archives, Austin. (b) Jasper County, Texas, Election Register, pp. 558–559. Texas State Archives, Austin. (c) Loggins family records.

5. (a) 1880 San Augustine County, Texas, Census, Dwelling No. 75. (b) Interview with Mary Alice Winborn on April 25, 1982. (c) Interview with G. Clyde Lewis of San Augustine, Texas, third cousin of Pete Loggins, on June 7, 1982.

6. (a) *The Texas Criminal Reports*, Vol. 32, p. 366. (b) Texas Department of State Extradition Service Records, Nos. 592 and 2153. Texas State Archives, Austin. (c) Andrew Allen Veatch, "The Autobiography of the Sage of Lone Vale," unpublished manuscript, Sabine County, Texas, 1948/1949, pp. 24 and 25. Furnished to author by Drayton Speights of Hemphill, Texas.

7. (a) Veatch, p. 25. (b) *The Texas Criminal Reports*, Vol. 32, p. 366. (c) Sabine County Criminal Minutes, September 1879–February 1891, p. 4. Sabine County Clerks Office, Hemphill.

8. (a) Texas Department of State Extradition Service Records, Nos. 592 and 2153. (b) *The Texas Criminal Reports*, Vol. 32, pp. 365–366. (c) Veatch, pp. 24–25.

9. (a) Pardon request from L. L. Loggins. (b) Walter Prescott Webb, editor-in-chief, *The Handbook of Texas*, The Texas State Historical Association (Austin: 1952), Vol. II, p. 747.

10. (a) Veatch, p. 25. (b) Interview with Carrol Johnson of Pineland, Texas, nephew of Sterling Eddings, on January 26, 1982. (c) Lewis interview, June 7, 1982. (d) Information excerpted from the author's forthcoming book *Judge Not*.

11. (a) Johnson interview. (b) Executive Clemency Records, Application for Pardon, No. 11822, Wade Noble. Texas State Archives, Austin. (c) *The Texas Criminal Reports*, Vol. 32, pp. 358 and 359. (d) Sabine County Criminal Minutes, September 1879–February 1891, p. 71. (e) Information excerpted from *Judge Not*.

12. (a) Henry C. Fuller, *A Texas Sheriff* (Baker Printing Company, Nacogdoches, Tex.: 1931), p. 56. (b) Veatch, p. 25. (c) Texas Department of State Extradition Service Records, No. 592. (d) Governors Proclamations, Executive Record Book on Rewards, 1883–1887, p. 299. Texas State Archives, Austin.

13. (a) Adjutant Generals Office, General Correspondence: Judge James I. Perkins, Hemphill, Texas, to Governor John Ireland, Austin, Texas, dated February 8, 1886. Texas State Archives, Austin. (b) Adjutant Generals Office, Monthly Return, Company F, Frontier Battalion, State of Texas, month ending March 31, 1886. Texas State Archives, Austin.

14. (a) Lewis interview, June 7, 1982. (b) Loggins family records. (c) *Founders and Patriots of the Republic of Texas* (Daughters of the Republic of Texas, Old Land Office Building, Austin: 1974), Book II, p. 307. (d) Grayson County Marriage Records, Vol. H, p. 418. Grayson County Clerks Office, Sherman, Texas.

15. (a) Information excerpted from the author's forthcoming book, *Judge Not*. (b) White County Marriage Book H, p. 124. White County Clerks Office, Searcy, Arkansas. (c) White County Indictment Book A, *State of Arkansas vs. R. P. Wright*, p. 141. White County Clerks Office, Searcy. (d) White County Criminal Book C, *State of Arkansas vs. R. P. Wright*, Bigamy, p. 184. White County Clerks Office, Searcy. (e) *Register of State Convicts Received at and Discharged from the Arkansas State Penitentiary*, RG 4, Series B, Archival Collections. Arkansas History Commission, Little Rock.

16. (a) Governor's Proclamations, Executive Record Book on Rewards, 1883–1887, pp. 299 and 661; Executive Record Book on Rewards, 1889–1901, p. 24. (b) Texas Department of State Extradition Service Records, No. 1394.

17. (a) Microfilm of Prison Inmate Records, Texas State Penitentiary, No. 10057, L. L. Loggins. Texas Department of Corrections, Huntsville. The records state that Loggins' left eye was artificial. (b) Lewis interview, June 7, 1982.

18. Texas Department of State Extradition Service Records, No. 2153.

19. (a) *Register of State Convicts Received at and Discharged from the Arkansas State Penitentiary*, RG 4, Series B. (b) *The Texas Criminal Reports*, Vol. 32, p. 367. (c) Pardon request from L. L. Loggins.

20. (a) *The Texas Criminal Reports*, Vol. 32, p. 367. (b) Microfilm of Prison Inmate Records, Texas State Penitentiary, No. 10057, L. L. Loggins. (c) *The Galveston Daily News*, October 22, 1893. Texas State Archives, Austin. (d) Pardon request from L. L. Loggins. (e) Pardon Proclamation, No. 6529, Executive Record Book, Pardon and Remissions, 1900–1901, p. 626. Texas State Archives, Austin.

21. (a) Winborn interview. Mrs. Winborn is the daughter of Pete's daughter Myrtie, who told Mrs. Winborn the reason behind the killing of her father. (b) *The Galveston Daily News*, April 3, 1905. (c) Notarized letter to the author from Cindy Jennings, Deputy District Clerk, Conroe, Montgomery County, Texas, dated June 14, 1982. This letter states that D. A. Hooks was never indicted for the killing of Pete Loggins.

CHAPTER VI

PART ONE:

1. (a) 1885 Island County, Washington, Territorial Census. Division of Archives and Record Management, Office of the Secretary of State, Olympia. (b) RG 129, McNeil Penitentiary Register, Volume 1, 1894, Number 117, John E. Terry. Federal

Archives and Records Center, Seattle. (c) Washington State Board of Health Certificate of Death, Jake Terry, Record No. 1, Register No. 1687. Bellingham-Whatcom County District Department of Public Health, Bellingham.

2. *The Olympia Washington Standard*, July 26, 1873. Washington State Library, Northwest Room, Olympia.

3. (a) *Territory of Washington vs. John Terry*, assault with intent to murder. Division of Archives and Record Management, Office of the Secretary of State, Olympia. (b) *The Seattle Weekly Intelligencer*, August 9, 1873. Washington State Library, Northwest Room, Olympia.

4. (a) *The Weekly Pacific Tribune*, August 16, 1873. Washington State Library, Northwest Room, Olympia. (b) *The Seattle Post-Intelligencer Pictorial Review*, September 5, 1965. Division of Archives and Record Management, Office of the Secretary of State, Olympia.

5. (a) Roy Franklin Jones, *Boundary Town* (Fleet Printing Company, Vancouver, Wash.: 1958), pp. 261–262. Jones' book is a history of the town of Sumas, Washington, the scene of Jake Terry's later escapades. This book is extremely well-researched, and Jones, who was a native of Sumas, accurately reported all of Terry's operations that he knew about or had record of. (b) Letter to the author from Forrest Daniel, State Historical Society of North Dakota, Bismarck, January 13, 1986. (c) Letter to the author from Linda M. Sommer, South Dakota Historical Society, State Archives, Pierre, February 7, 1986.

6. (a) Jones, p. 263. (b) 1885 Island County, Washington Territorial Census. (c) RG 129, McNeil Penitentiary Register, Volume 1, 1892, Number 29, John E. Terry.

7. *The Seattle Post-Intelligencer*, July 6, 1907. Washington State Library, Northwest Room, Olympia.

8. (a) Richard W. Markov, "A Decade of Enforcement, the Chinese Exclusion and Whatcom County, 1890 to 1900," August 20, 1972, pp. 1–4, 9–11. Western Washington University, Bellingham, Washington. (b) Jones, pp. 236, 240. (c) Roland L. Delorme, The United States Bureau of Customs and Smuggling on Puget Sound, 1851 to 1913, *Prologue, Journal of the National Archives*, Summer 1973, Volume 5, Number 2, p. 84.

9. *The Bellingham Herald*, July 5, 1907. Bellingham Public Library, Bellingham, Wash.

10. RG 21, Case No. 331, *The United States vs. John E. Terry*, Northern Division of U.S. District Court, Western District of Washington. Federal Archives and Records Center, Seattle.

11. (a) Jones, pp. 239–243. (b) *Illustrated History of Skagit and Snohomish Counties, Their People, Their Commerce, and Their Resources*, (Interstate, 1906), pp 151, 152.

PART TWO:

12. RG 21, Case No. 331, *The United States vs. John E. Terry*.

13. RG 129, McNeil Penitentiary Register, Volume 1, 1892, Number 29, John E. Terry.

14. RG 21, Case No. 331, *The United States vs. John E. Terry*.

15. RG 129, McNeil Penitentiary Register, Volume 1, 1892, Number 29, John E. Terry.

16. Jones, p. 237.

17. RG 36, U.S. Customs Service, Puget Sound Collection District, Box 78, Letters Received from Subports, Inspectors, and Deputies, 1893. Federal Archives and Records Center, Seattle.

18. RG 36, U.S. Customs Service, Puget Sound Collections, Box 79, Letters Received from Subports, Inspectors, and Deputies, 1893–1894.

19. Jones, pp. 237–239.

20. RG 21, Case No. 787, *The United States vs. John E. Terry,* Northern Division of U.S. District Court, Western District of Washington. Federal Archives and Records Center, Seattle.

21. RG 129, McNeil Penitentiary Register, Volume 1, 1894, Number 117, John E. Terry.

22. RG 36, U.S. Customs Service, Puget Sound Collection District, Box 62, Letters Received from Subports, Inspectors, and Deputies, Sumas, 1891–1899.

23. (a) RG 21, Case No. 959, *United States vs. Jake Terry,* Northern Division of U.S. District Court, Western District of Washington, FRC 77429. Federal Archives and Records Center, Seattle. (b) *The Seattle Post-Intelligencer,* December 6, 1895.

24. (a) RG 60, Year File 8289/93. National Archives, Washington, D.C. (b) RG 60, Instruction Book, Volume 59. National Archives, Washington, D.C. (c) RG 60, Miscellaneous Letter Book, Volume 20. National Archives, Washington, D.C.

25. San Quentin Prison Register, Convict No. 16612, Jake Terry, F 3653–9 (VB 113). California State Archives, Sacramento.

26. (a) *The Seattle Post-Intelligencer,* October 5, 1905. (b) San Quentin Prison Register, Convict No. 10191, William A. Miner, F 3653–9(VB 113).

PART THREE:

27. *The Bellingham Herald,* August 9, 1907.

28. (a) *The Seattle Post-Intelligencer,* July 6, 1907. (b) *The Bellingham Herald,* July 5 and August 9, 1907.

29. (a) *The Shoulder Strap, The Official Journal of the British Columbia Police Force,* Tenth Edition, September 1943, p. 42. National Archives of Canada, Ottawa, Ontario.

30. Frank W. Anderson, *Bill Miner . . . Stagecoach and Train Robber* (Heritage House Publishing Company, Ltd., Surry, B.C.: 1982), pp. 5 and 7.

31. *The Seattle Post-Intelligencer,* October 5, 1905.

32. (a) Anderson, pp. 7 and 9. (b) Colin Richards, "Bill Miner—50 Years A Hold-up Man," *The English Westerners Brand Book,* Vol. 8, No. 3, April 1966, p. 1. (c) "C.P.R. Train Hold-up. First Train Hold-up in Canada. Bill Miner." Conversation with Andrew Herbert Mitchell, January 31, 1944. City Archives, Vancouver, British Columbia. (d) *The Seattle Post-Intelligencer,* October 5, 1905.

33. (a) Anderson, pp. 9–11. (b) *The Shoulder Strap,* Tenth Edition, p. 42.

34. *The Seattle Post-Intelligencer,* October 5, 1905.

35. Anderson, p. 31.

36. *The Seattle Post-Intelligencer,* October 6, 1905.

37. *The Seattle Post-Intelligencer,* July 6, 1907.

38. *The Seattle Post-Intelligencer,* October 3, 4, 5, and 6, and November 30, 1905.

39. *The Seattle Post-Intelligencer,* October 5, 1905.

40. *The Seattle Post-Intelligencer,* October 3, 4, 5, and 6, and November 30, 1905.

41. *The Seattle Post-Intelligencer,* October 3, 1905.

42. *The Seattle Post-Intelligencer,* October 5 and 6, 1905.

43. *The Seattle Post-Intelligencer,* November 30, 1905.

44. *The Seattle Post-Intelligencer,* October 3 and November 30, 1905.

PART FOUR:

45. Jones, pp. 252, 262.

46. (a) Jones, pp. 262–265. (b) *The Bellingham Herald,* July 5, 1907. (c) *The Seattle Post-Intelligencer,* July 6, 1907. (d) *The Bellingham Reveille,* July 6, 1907. Bellingham Public Library, Bellingham, Wash.

47. (a) Anderson, pp. 44–48. (b) *The Bellingham Herald,* July 5 and August 9, 1907. (c) *The Atlanta Constitution,* February 28 and March 3, 1911. University of Georgia Library, Athens. (d) *The Atlanta Georgian and News,* February 28, 1911. University of Georgia Library, Athens.

48. For the details of the May 9, 1906, train robbery, Miner's escape, and the repercussions it caused in Canada, see *The Grey Fox: The True Story of Bill Miner, Last of the Old Time Bandits*, by Mark Dugan and John Boessenecker (University of Oklahoma Press, Norman: 1992).

49. (a) *The Bellingham Herald*, July 5 and 6, and August 9, 1907. (b) *The Seattle Post-Intelligencer*, July 6 and 7, 1907. (c) *The Bellingham Reveille*, July 6 and 7, 1907. (d) Jones, pp. 258–271.

50. (a) *The Seattle Post-Intelligencer*, July 7, 1907. (b) Letter to the author from Mr. Dean DeBoer, manager, Bay View Cemetery, Bellingham, March 17, 1986. (c) *The Bellingham Herald*, July 8, 1907. (d) Washington State Board of Health Certificate of Death, Jake Terry, Record No. 1, Register No. 1687.

CHAPTER VII

1. (a) Executive Clemency Files (RS103.96), Executive Section, W. S. Ruby; Letter: Captain Gustavus StGem to Colonel J. H. Baker, Provost Marshal General, Department of Missouri, St. Louis, March 9, 1865. Illinois State Archives, Springfield. (b) RG 110, Records of the Provost Marshal. Civil War (Union), Part I, Entry 36. Military Service Branch, National Archives, Washington, D.C.

2. Henry C. Thompson, *Sam Hildebrand Rides Again. . . .* (Steinbeck Publishing Company, Bonne Terr, Mo.: 1949).

3. (a) Executive Clemency Files (RS103.96), Executive Section, W. S. Ruby. (b) RG 110, Records of the Provost Marshal, Civil War (Union), Part I, Entry 36.

4. (a) RG 15, War of the Rebellion Pension File C 2546255, William S. Ruby. Military Records Branch, National Archives, Washington, D.C. (b) RG 94, C.M.S.R. (Compiled Military Service Records), William S. Ruby, Company I, 7th Illinois Cavalry. Military Records Branch, National Archives, Washington, D.C . (c) Convict Register, Illinois State Penitentiary, Inmate No. 2577, William S. Ruby, p. 9. Illinois State Archives, Springfield. (d) *The Daily Riverside Enterprise*, February 23, 1904. The Riverside Public Library, Riverside, Ca.

5. RG 94, C.M.S.R., William S. Ruby, Company I, 7th Illinois Cavalry.

6. (a) RG 15, War of the Rebellion Pension File C 2546255, William S. Ruby. (b) RG 110, Records of the Provost Marshal, Civil War (Union), Part I, Entry 36.

7. RG 110, Records of the Provost Marshal, Civil War (Union), Part I, Entry 36.

8. (a) Executive Clemency Files (RS103.96), Executive Section, W. S. Ruby; Letters: Captain Gustavus StGem to Colonel J. H. Baker, Provost Marshal General, Department of Missouri, St. Louis, March 9, 1865, and Captain Gustavus StGem to Illinois governor Richard J. Oglesby, February 27, 1865. (b) RG 110, Records of the Provost Marshal, Civil War (Union), Part I, Entry 36.

9. RG 110, Records of the Provost Marshal, Civil War (Union), Part I, Entry 36.

10. (a) Executive Clemency Files (RS103.96), Executive Section, W. S. Ruby; Letter: Captain Gustavus StGem to Illinois Governor Richard J. Oglesby, February 27, 1865. (b) RG 110, Records of the Provost Marshal, Civil War (Union), Part I, Entry 36.

11. Executive Clemency Files (RS103.96), Executive Section, W. S. Ruby; Letter: John J. Woodside, Coulterville, Illinois, to Illinois governor Richard J. Oglesby, February 25, 1865.

12. Executive Clemency Files (RS103.96), Executive Section, W. S. Ruby; Randolph County Circuit Court February Special Term A. D. 1865, *The People vs. William S. Ruby*, indictment for kidnapping.

13. Executive Clemency Files (RS103.96), Executive Section, W. S. Ruby; Woodside letter.

14. Convict Register, Illinois State Penitentiary, Inmate No. 2577, William S. Ruby, p. 9.

15. Executive Clemency Files (RS103.96), Executive Section, W. S. Ruby.

16. Executive Clemency Files (RS103.96), Executive Section, W. S. Ruby; Letter: Illinois governor Richard J. Oglesby to Major General G. M. Dodge, St. Louis, March 3, 1865.

17. Executive Clemency Files (RS103.96), Executive Section, W. S. Ruby; Woodside letter.

18. Executive Clemency Files (RS103.96), Executive Section, W. S. Ruby; Letter: Captain Gustavus StGem to Captain George C. Tichenor, A.D.C., Headquarters of the Department of Missouri, February 28, 1865.

19. RG 110, Records of the Provost Marshal, Civil War (Union), Part I, Entry 36.

20. Executive Clemency Files (RS103.96), Executive Section, W. S. Ruby; Letter: John E. Detrich, Sparta, Illinois, to Illinois governor Richard J. Oglesby, April 3, 1865.

21. (a) Executive Clemency Files (RS103.96), Executive Section, W. S. Ruby. (b) Convict Register, Illinois State Penitentiary, Inmate No. 2577, William S. Ruby, p. 9.

22. *History and Directory of Riverside County, 1893–94*, pp. 134–135; *Riverside City and County Directory, 1897–98*, p. 9C. Riverside Public Library, Riverside, Ca.

23. RG 15, War of the Rebellion Pension File C 2546255, William S. Ruby.

24. (a) RG 15, War of the Rebellion Pension File C 2546255, William S. Ruby. (b) *The Riverside Daily Press*, February 22, 1904. Riverside Public Library, Riverside, Ca. (c) *History and Directory of Riverside County, 1893–94*, pp. 134–135; *Riverside City and County Directory, 1897–98*, p. 9C.

25. RG 15, War of the Rebellion Pension File C 2546255, William S. Ruby.

26. *The Riverside Daily Press*, February 22, 1904.

27. *The Daily Riverside Enterprise*, February 23, 1904.

CHAPTER VIII

1. Mark Dugan, *Bandit Years: A Gathering of Wolves* (Sunstone Press, Santa Fe, N.M.: 1987). This book is a complete history of the careers of the Colorado stage bandits from 1880 to 1881.

2. (a) *The Pagosa Springs News*, September 15, 1892. Colorado Historical Society, Denver. (b) RG 21, U.S. District Court, Denver Division, Criminal Case No. 924, *U.S. vs. Alexander McKenzie*. National Archives and Records Center, Denver. (c) John M. Motter, *Pagosa Country: The First Fifty Years* (Walsworth Publishing Company, Marceline, Mo.: 184), p. 90. (d) RG 204, Pardon File No. 0-195, Alexander McKenzie. National Archives, Washington, D.C.

3. *The Pagosa Springs News*, September 22, 1892.

4. (a) RG 21, U.S. District Court, Denver Division, Criminal Case No. 924, *U.S. vs. Alexander McKenzie*. (b) *The Creede Candle*, October 7, 1892. Colorado Historical Society, Denver. (c) RG 204, Pardon File No. 0-195, Alexander McKenzie.

5. (a) *The Creede Candle*, October 7, 1892. (b) *The Pagosa Springs News*, October 13, 1892. (c) RG 204, Pardon File No. 0-195, Alexander McKenzie.

6. (a) *The Pagosa Springs News*, October 13, 1892. (b) *The Daily News* (Denver), March 2, 1893. Colorado Historical Society, Denver. (c) RG 13 A2, Vol. 89, File 36/1893, Petition for fair trial of Alexander A. McKenzie. National Archives of Canada, Ottawa, Ontario.

7. *The Creede Candle*, October 7, 1892.

8. (a) RG 13 A2, Vol. 89, File 36/1893, Petition for fair trial of Alexander A. McKenzie. (b) *The Pagosa Springs News*, October 13, 1892.

9. RG 21, U.S. District Court, Denver Division, Criminal Case No. 924, *U.S. vs. Alexander McKenzie*: Affidavit of Thomas (James T.) Delaney, February 28, 1893.

10. (a) *The Pagosa Springs News*, October 20, 1892. (b) RG 21, U.S. District Court, Denver Division, Criminal Case No. 924, *U.S. vs. Alexander McKenzie*.

11. Motter, p. 90.

12. RG 13 A2, Vol. 89, File 36/1893, Petition for fair trial of Alexander A. McKenzie.

13. (a) RG 21, U.S. District Court, Denver Division, Final Record Book 5, Entry 35. National Archives and Records Center, Denver, Co. (b) *The Daily News*, December 10, 1892, and January 7, 17, 18, and 20, 1893.

14. (a) RG 21, U.S. District Court, Denver Division, Final Record Book 5, Entry 35. (b) *The Pagosa Springs News*, February 24, 1893. (c) Dugan.

15. (a) RG 21, U.S. District Court, Denver Division, Final Record Book 5, Entry 35. (b) RG 13 A2, Vol. 89, File 36/1893, Petition for fair trial of Alexander A. McKenzie. (c) *The Pagosa Springs News*, March 3, 1893.

16. *The Daily News*, March 2, 1893.

17. RG 204, Pardon File No. 0-195, Alexander McKenzie. *Glengarian* article part of file.

18. (a) RG 21, U.S. District Court, Denver Division, Criminal Case No. 924, *U.S. vs. Alexander McKenzie*. (b) RG 21, U.S. District Court, Denver Division, Final Record Book 5, Entry 35. (c) RG 204, Pardon File No. 0-195, Alexander McKenzie.

19. *The Pagosa Springs News*, February 24, 1893.

20. RG 13 A2, Vol. 89, File 36/1893, Petition for fair trial of Alexander A. McKenzie.

21. (a) General Register of Prisons at Detroit House of Corrections, Volume December 6, 1888–July 26, 1893, p. 335. Detroit Public Library, Burton Collection, Detroit. (b) RG 21, U.S. District Court, Denver Division, Criminal Case No. 924, *U.S. vs. Alexander McKenzie*.

22. RG 204, Pardon File No. 0-195, Alexander McKenzie.

23. RG 13 A2, Vol. 101, File 403/1896, Inquiry regarding pardon of Alexander A. McKenzie. National Archives of Canada, Ottawa, Ontario.

24. (a) RG 204, Pardon File No. 0-195, Alexander McKenzie. (b) General Register of Prisons at Detroit House of Corrections, Volume December 6, 1888–July 26, 1893, p. 335.

CHAPTER IX

1. (a) *The Joplin Daily Globe*, August 22, 1897. The *Daily Globe* office, Joplin, Missouri. (b) *The St. Louis Post-Dispatch,* August 23, 1897. The State Historical Society of Missouri, Columbia.

2. (a) *The Joplin Daily Globe*, August 28, 1897. (b) *The St. Louis Post-Dispatch*, August 23, 1897.

3. Register of Inmates Received, Missouri Penitentiary, January 14, 1898 through September 6, 1899, Vol. W, Record Group 213, p. 8, Inmate No. 956, Cora Hubbard. Missouri State Archives, Jefferson City. The records show that Cora Hubbard was born in Ohio.

4. (a) Hubbard family history, furnished to the author by Robert D. Hubbard, Weir, Kansas. (b) *The Joplin Daily Globe*, August 27, 1897.

5. *The Joplin Daily Globe*, August 29, 1897.

6. *The Joplin Daily Globe*, August 27, 1897.

7. (a) *The Joplin Daily Globe*, August 27, 1897. (b) *The Pineville Herald*, August 21 and September 4, 1897. The State Historical Society of Missouri, Columbia. (c) *The St. Louis Post-Dispatch*, August 22, 1897. (d) Cherokee Nation Census of 1890, Delaware District, Whitfield Tennison [*sic*], p. 70. (e) *Register of Inmates Received*, January 14, 1898–September 6, 1899, Missouri Penitentiary, Inmate Nos. 955, John Sheets; 954, A. W. Tennyson.

8. *The Joplin Daily Globe*, August 27, 1897.

9. (a) *The Pineville Herald*, August 21, 1897. (b) *The St. Louis Post-Dispatch*, August 23, 1897. (c) Clipping from the *Illustrated History of McDonald County, Missouri*, J. A. Sturges. McDonald County Library, Pineville, Mo.

10. (a) *The Pineville Herald*, August 21, 1897. (b) *Illustrated History of McDonald County, Missouri*. (c) *The Joplin Daily Globe*, August 18 and 27, 1897.

11. (a) *The Pineville Herald*, August 21, 1897. (b) *The Joplin Daily Globe*, August 18, 22, and 27, 1897.

12. (a) *The Pineville Herald*, August 21, 1897. (b) *The St. Louis Post-Dispatch*, August 18, 1897.

13. (a) *The Pineville Herald*, August 21, 1897. (b) *The Joplin Daily Globe*, August 22 and 28, 1897.

14. *The Joplin Daily Globe*, August 27 and 28, 1897.

15. (a) *The Pineville Herald*, August 21, 1897. (b) *The Joplin Daily Globe*, August 22 and 28, 1897.

16. *The Joplin Daily Globe*, August 22, 1897.

17. *The St. Louis Post-Dispatch*, August 23, 1897.

18. (a) *The Pineville Herald*, September 4, 1897. (b) *The Joplin Daily Globe*, August 27 and 28, 1897.

19. *The Joplin Daily Globe*, August 27, 1897.

20. *The Joplin Daily Globe*, August 29, 1897.

21. (a) McDonald County Circuit Court Files, *The State of Missouri vs. Whit Tennyson, John Sheets, and Cora Hubbard*, robbery. McDonald County Circuit Court, Pineville, Mo. (b) *The Pineville Herald*, January 15, 1898. Clipping on file at the McDonald County Library, Pineville.

22. (a) *The Pineville Herald*, January 15, 1898. (b) McDonald County Circuit Case Nos. 732, 733, and 734, *State of Missouri vs. John Sheets et al.*, McDonald County Circuit Court Record Book H, pp. 144–148. McDonald County Circuit Court, Pineville, Mo.

23. *Register of Inmates Received*, Missouri Penitentiary, January 14, 1898–September 6, 1899, Inmate Nos. 954, A. W. Tennyson; 955, John Sheets; 956, Cora Hubbard.

24. (a) Pardon file No. 1731, Cora Hubbard, Filed December 31, 1904. Missouri State Archives, Jefferson City. (b) *Register of Inmates Received*, Missouri Penitentiary, January 14, 1898–September 6, 1899, Inmate No. 956, Cora Hubbard. (c) *The Pineville Herald*, December 30, 1904. Clipping on file at the McDonald County Library, Pineville, Mo.

CHAPTER X

PART ONE:

1. *The Cheyenne Tribune-Eagle*, July 22, 1973. Wyoming State Archives, Museums and Historical Department, Cheyenne.

2. The foremost history of the Wyoming cattle industry, from which this information was taken, is John Rolfe Burroughs' *Guardian of the Grasslands* (Pioneer Printing and Stationery Company, Cheyenne, Wyo.: 1971).

3. For a comprehensive history of the Johnson County War, see Helena Huntington Smith, *The War on the Powder River* (McGraw-Hill, New York, London, Toronto: 1966).

4. (a) Burroughs, pp. 50–53, 76–81, 155–156. (b) C. G. Coutant Notes, "Hon. Alexander H. Swan," Wyoming State Archives, Museums and Historical Department, Cheyenne. (c) *The Cheyenne Tribune-Eagle*, July 22, 1973.

5. (a) Tom Horn, *Life of Tom Horn* (University of Oklahoma Press, Norman: 1964), p. 225. (b) Jay Monaghan, *Last of the Bad Men* (Bobbs-Merrill Company, Indianapolis and New York: 1946), pp. 153–154. (c) Dean F. Krakel, *The Saga of Tom Horn* (University of Nebraska Press, Lincoln and London: 1982), p. 4. This is the most comprehensive history of Tom Horn's exploits in Wyoming. (d) Bill O'Neal, *Cattlemen Versus Sheepherders* (Eakin Press, Austin, Tex.: 1989), p. 101.

PART TWO:

6. (a) *The Laramie Republican and Boomerang*, July 14, 1939. Wyoming State Archives, Museums and Historical Department, Cheyenne. (b) 1894 Albany County, Wyoming, Assessment Roles, p. 72. Wyoming State Archives, Museums and Historical Department, Cheyenne. (c) Albany County Marriage Record, Vol. 3, p. 79. Wyoming State Archives, Museums and Historical Department, Cheyenne. (d) Albany County District Court Case D 511, *Evaline C. Langhoff vs. Fred A. Langhoff, divorce,* Wyoming State Archives, Museums and Historical Department, Cheyenne.

7. (a) 1889 Albany County, Wyoming, Assessment Roles, p. 67. (b) W.P.A. article #1367, pp. 5, 6. Wyoming State Archives, Museums and Historical Department, Cheyenne.

8. W.P.A. article #1367, pp. 5, 6.

9. W.P.A. article #1367, pp. 6, 7.

10. Albany County Court Docket No. 3, Criminal Case No. 381, *State of Wyoming vs. Fred Langhoff,* grand larceny; Docket No. 3, Criminal Case No. 382, *State of Wyoming vs. Eva Langhoff, Louis Bath, and Thomas Boucher,* grand larceny; Docket No. 3, Criminal Case No. 397, *State of Wyoming vs. Fred and Eva Langhoff, Louis Bath, and Thomas Boucher,* grand larceny. Wyoming State Archives, Museums and Historical Department, Cheyenne.

11. *Laramie Weekly Sentinel,* August 13, 1892. Wyoming State Archives, Museums and Historical Department, Cheyenne.

12. Laramie County Sheriff's Prison Calendar, pp. 53, 54. Wyoming State Archives, Museums and Historical Department, Cheyenne.

13. (a) Albany County Court Docket No. 3, Criminal Case No. 387. (b) Laramie County Sheriff's Prison Calendar, p. 55.

14. (a) Albany County Court Docket No. 3, Criminal Case No. 387. (b) Laramie County Sheriff's Prison Calendar, p. 55. (c) Albany County District Court Case D-511, *Evaline C. Langhoff vs. Fred A. Langhoff,* divorce.

15. *Laramie Weekly Sentinel,* October 1, 1892.

16. *The Laramie Boomerang,* November 14, 1893. Wyoming State Archives, Museums and Historical Department, Cheyenne.

17. (a) Wyoming State Inmate File No. 165, Louis Bath. Wyoming State Archives, Museums and Historical Department, Cheyenne. (b) 1894 Albany County, Wyoming, Assessment Roles (Bath). (c) W.P.A. article #1367, pp. 6.

18. *The Laramie Boomerang,* November 15, 16, and 17, 1893.

19. (a) W.P.A. article #1367, pp. 7, 8. (b) *The Laramie Boomerang,* November 15, 1893.

20. *The Laramie Boomerang*, November 15, 1893.

21. *The Laramie Boomerang*, November 16 and 17, 1893.

22. *The Laramie Boomerang*, November 17, 1893.

23. (a) Krakel, p. 5. (b) *The Laramie Boomerang*, January 17, 1894. (c) Albany County Criminal Case No. 589, *The State of Wyoming vs. Louis Bath, et al.* Wyoming State Archives, Museums and Historical Department, Cheyenne.

24. Wyoming State Inmate File No. 165, Louis Bath.

25. (a) W.P.A. article #1367, p. 8. (b) Albany County District Court Case D-511, *Evaline C. Langhoff vs. Fred A. Langhoff*, divorce. (c) *The Laramie Republican-Boomerang*, July 14, 1939.

26. Krakel, p. 5.

PART THREE:

27. Krakel, pp. 5, 6.

28. Krakel, pp. 192, 193–195, 197. Tom Horn's entire trial transcript is contained in the book.

29. (a) *The Daily Sun-Leader* (Cheyenne), August 5, 1895. Wyoming State Archives, Museums and Historical Department, Cheyenne. (b) Laramie County Clerk of Court Naturalization Records, Vol. 2, p. 7; Laramie County Clerk of Court Civil Journal No. 6, p. 614. Wyoming State Archives, Museums and Historical Department, Cheyenne. (c) 1894 Laramie County, Wyoming, Assessment Roles, p. 76 Wyoming State Archives, Museums and Historical Department, Cheyenne.

30. (a) Krakel, p. 6. (b) *The Daily Sun-Leader*, August 5, 1895.

31. Albany County Criminal Case Nos. 178 and 179, *Territory of Wyoming vs. William Lewis*, gambling with minor. Wyoming State Archives, Museums and Historical Department, Cheyenne.

32. Laramie County Criminal Case Nos. 101 and 105, *Territory of Wyoming vs. William Lewis*, petit larceny. Wyoming State Archives, Museums and Historical Department, Cheyenne.

33. (a) Laramie County Criminal Appearance Docket 3-412, *State of Wyoming vs. William Lewis*, grand larceny. Wyoming State Archives, Museums and Historical Department, Cheyenne. (b) *The Laramie Boomerang*, November 17, 1893. (c) Laramie County Court Docket No. 6, Case No. 183, *William Lewis vs. The Swan Land and Cattle Company, Ltd., et al.* Wyoming State Archives, Museums and Historical Department, Cheyenne.

34. (a) Laramie County Criminal Appearance Docket 3-412, *State of Wyoming vs. William Lewis*, grand larceny. (b) Laramie County Sheriff's Prison Calendar, pp. 56.

35. Laramie County Criminal Appearance Docket 3-421, *State of Wyoming vs. William Lewis*, stealing livestock. Wyoming State Archives, Museums and Historical Department, Cheyenne.

36. (a) Laramie County Criminal Appearance Docket 3-412, *State of Wyoming vs. William Lewis*, grand larceny. (b) Laramie County Criminal Appearance Docket 3-421, *State of Wyoming vs. William Lewis*, stealing livestock.

37. Laramie County Court Docket No. 6, Case No. 183, *William Lewis vs. The Swan Land and Cattle Company, Ltd., et al.*

38. Laramie County Court Docket No. 6, Case No. 188, *William Lewis vs. Ira Fredendall*. Wyoming State Archives, Museums and Historical Department, Cheyenne.

39. *The Daily Sun-Leader*, August 3 and 5, 1895.

40. *The Daily Sun-Leader*, August 5, 1895.

41. (a) *The Daily Sun-Leader*, August 5 and 8, 1895. (b) Krakel, p. 6. (c) *The Laramie Boomerang*, August 8, 1895.

42. Krakel, p. 195.

43. Laramie County District Court Journal, Vol. 15, p. 34. Wyoming State Archives, Museums and Historical Department, Cheyenne.

44. Krakel, pp. 192, 193.

45. For a comprehensive history of the Brown's Park area of Colorado and the killings of Rash and Dart, see John Rolfe Burroughs, *Where the Old West Stayed Young* (Bonanza Books, New York: 1962).

PART FOUR:

46. (a) *The Daily Sun-Leader*, September 11, 1895. (b) Laramie County Marriage Records, Vol. 2, Book 2, p. 218. Wyoming State Archives, Museums and Historical Department, Cheyenne. (c) Krakel, pp. 7, 8. (d) Verdict of Coroners Jury, No. 133, Albany County, Wyoming, September 12, 1895, Fred U. Powell. Wyoming State Archives, Museums and Historical Department, Cheyenne.

47. Albany County Criminal Case No. 447, *Territory of Wyoming vs. Fredrick U. Powell*, stealing and killing neat cattle. Wyoming State Archives, Museums and Historical Department, Cheyenne.

48. Cheyenne Justice of the Peace Criminal Docket, *State of Wyoming vs. Fred Powell*, grand larceny, pp. 185, 359. Wyoming State Archives, Museums and Historical Department, Cheyenne.

49. (a) Laramie County District Court, Civil Appearance Docket No. 5, Case No. 231, *Mary N. Powell vs. Fredrick U. Powell*, divorce. Wyoming State Archives, Museums and Historical Department, Cheyenne. (b) Laramie County District Court Journal, Vol. 12, pp. 618, 619. Wyoming State Archives, Museums and Historical Department, Cheyenne.

50. Albany County Criminal Case No. 560, *State of Wyoming vs. Fredrick U. Powell*, stealing livestock. Wyoming State Archives, Museums and Historical Department, Cheyenne.

51. Albany County Criminal Case No. 584, *State of Wyoming vs. Fredrick U. Powell*, malicious trespass and destruction of property. Wyoming State Archives, Museums and Historical Department, Cheyenne.

52. Albany County Criminal Case No. 598, *State of Wyoming vs. Fredrick U. Powell*, incendiarism and malicious trespass. Wyoming State Archives, Museums and Historical Department, Cheyenne.

53. Albany County Criminal Case No. 601, *State of Wyoming vs. Fredrick U. Powell*, criminal trespass. Wyoming State Archives, Museums and Historical Department, Cheyenne.

54. Albany County Criminal Case Nos. 601 and 598, *State of Wyoming vs. Fredrick U. Powell*.

55. *The Daily Sun-Leader*, September 11, 1895.

56. Coroner's Inquest and Verdict of Coroner's Jury in death of Fredrick U. Powell, September 10, 1895. Wyoming State Archives, Museums and Historical Department, Cheyenne.

57. (a) *The Daily Sun-Leader*, September 11, 1895. (b) Coroner's Inquest and Verdict of Coroner's Jury in death of Fredrick U. Powell, September 10, 1895.

58. *The Daily Sun-Leader*, September 11, 1895.

59. *The Daily Sun-Leader*, September 12, 1895.

60. (a) T. A. Larson, *History of Wyoming* (University of Nebraska Press, Lincoln: 1965), p. 373. (b) *The Laramie Republican and Boomerang*, January 13, 1941.

61. Letter to the author from a reliable source, dated August 23, 1990, provided through the services of the Wyoming State Archives, Museums and Historical Department, Cheyenne.

62. (a) *The Laramie Republican and Boomerang*, January 13, 1941. (b) For the complete life story of Mary Powell, see Mark Dugan, Family Traditions, *Annals of Wyoming*, Vol. 64, No. 2, Spring, 1992.

63. Mary Lou Pence, "The Woman Who Wouldn't Quit," *The Denver Post-Empire Magazine*, February 25, 1951: Vertical File Collections, Mary Powell. Wyoming State Archives, Museums and Historical Department, Cheyenne.

64. Albany County Criminal Case No. 653, *State of Wyoming vs. Mary Powell*, burglary. Wyoming State Archives, Museums and Historical Department, Cheyenne.

65. (a) Pence. (b) Dugan.

66. (a) *The Wyoming State Tribune-Cheyenne State Leader*, January 7, 1935. Wyoming State Archives, Museums and Historical Department, Cheyenne. (b) *The Laramie Republican and Boomerang*, January 13, 1941. (c) Pence.

67. *The Laramie Republican and Boomerang*, January 13, 1941.

68. Krakel, pp. 260–264.

INDEX

Lord Stanley (Governor General of Canada), 170
Luttrel, Pearl, 61
Lykins, 198
Lynch, Lonnie, 7

McArthur, 171
McCall, S. A. (District Attorney), 120
McCanles, Charles S., 41
McCanles, Clingman, 32
McCanles, David Colbert, 29–30, 32–55
McCanles, Elizabeth, 32
McCanles, Emily Verdinia, 32
McCanles, James, 32, 34–35
McCanles, James Leroy, 32, 36–38, 41, 43–44, 48, 53–55
McCanles, Jennie, 48
McCanles, Julia Elizabeth, 32
McCanles, Julius C., 32
McCanles, Mary C., 32
McCanles, Mary Green, 32, 42, 44, 54
McCanles, Rachel Salina Alexander, 32
McCanles, William Monroe, 32, 49, 51–54
McClurd, Issac, 39
McComas, Charles (District Attorney), 104
McConnell, Capt. A. F., 14
McCormick, Dugan, 9–10
McDonald County, Missouri, 181, 184
McDonald, Kin, 183
McErwin, 198
McGuinis, Emery (U.S. Deputy Marshal), 136
McIntire, Alex D., 145
McKenzie, Alexander A., 168–75
McKenzie, Andrew, 168, 170, 174
McKenzie, Janet, 168, 174
McLean, F. L., 103
McPhee, Hugh, 209
McPherson, Kansas, 103
McQuade brothers, 7

Mackay, Emogean (Missouri Penitentiary Matron), 189
Macon County, Illinois, 156
Manning, A. V., 183
Mannville, Florida, 58
Martin, C. E. (Deputy Coroner), 148
Martin, John A. (Kansas Governor), 85–86
Maulsby, 148
Maupin, Columbus H "Doc," 13
Maury County, Tennessee, 112
Mead Center, Kansas, 84
Melbourne, Quebec, 168
Miller, Andrew (Coroner), 212
Miner, Bill, 127, 137–43, 145–47, 167
Mineral Wells, Texas 14–15
Minot, North Dakota, 128
Mission Junction, British Columbia, 138–39
Mitchell, Herb, 139
Monroe City, Illinois, 156

Montague County, Texas, 3, 7–8
Moorehouse, H., 102
Morrel, Ben, 5
Morrell, J. D., 59
Morris, W. H. "Bud," 10
Morrow, J. L., 17
Moses, Samuel, 204–05
Mosier, William, 184
Mount Vernon, Georgia, 58
Mowat, Oliver (Canadian Minister of Justice), 175
Moyer, S. L., 209
Mudd, Felix, 160
Murrietta, Joaquin, 100
Myers, Frank (Marshal), 148
Myers, Brig. Gen. Murray, 86

Nelson (Deputy Sheriff), 17
Neosho, Missouri, 185, 188
Newman, Joseph, 82
New Westminster, British Columbia, 145
Nichols, Frank (see Bill Allen)
Nicholson, Joseph (Prison Superintendent), 174–75
Nickell, Willie, 202, 208, 215
Noble, Wade, 115
Noel, A. P. (Justice of the Peace), 188
Noel, Clark, 184
Noel, Missouri, 181, 184–86
Norwood, Ed (see Edwin White)
Nye, Jack, 49

Oglesby, Richard (Illinois Governor), 158–60
Oklahoma City, Oklahoma, 89
Olney, Richard (U.S. Secretary of State), 174
Oregon Trail, 41
Osborne, John E. (Wyoming Governor), 201
Osgood, C. W. P., 132
Osgood, Indiana, 79–83, 92
Ouray, Colorado, 168, 171–72
Overland Stage Company, 47–49
Overstreet, James, 172
Overton, R. C., 91
Owensboro, Kentucky, 198

Pagosa Springs, Colorado, 167–68, 171
Palatka, Florida, 57
Paris, Texas, 87
Parker County, Texas, 3–8, 15
Parker, J. W. "Bud," 182
Parsons, Kansas, 187
Patterson, 173
Pauncefote, Julian (British Ambassador), 170
Pearce, Richard (Canadian Vice Consul), 170, 173–74
Pemberton, George W., 168
Perkins, James I. (Judge), 116
Perry County, Illinois, 155
Phelps, Alonzo, 214
Phelps, Sarah May "Billie," 214–15

253

Shull, Rhoda E., 30
Shull, Sarah Louisa, 29–32, 34–37, 39–43, 48–61
Shull, Simon Phillip, 30, 57
Shull, Susan Caroline, 30
Shull, Temperance, 30
Shull, Thomas, 30
Shull, William, 30, 37, 60
Shulls Mill, North Carolina, 30, 32, 34, 37, 40, 49, 59–60
Shumway, John P., 46–47
Sibley, Brig. Gen. H. H., 56
Silverdale, British Columbia, 139
Simkins, E. J. (Judge), 118
Simpson, Pete (Sheriff), 102–03
Sims, B. F., 117
Skuce, James, 99–100, 105
Slack, William H. (Constable), 10
Slough, Col. John, 56
Smith, Abraham, 112–13
Smith, B. S. (Constable), 209
Smith, D. S. (Justice), 128
Smith, George, 185
Smith, H. C., 172
Smith, Newt, 81
Smith, William (Sheriff), 115–16
Snail, Widow, 184
Socorro, New Mexico, 100–04
Sone, Leater (Missouri Penitentiary Matron), 189
Southwest City, Missouri, 182, 184–86
Sowards, Frank E., 172
Spar City, Colorado, 167–68, 172
Sparta, Illinois, 160
Spickard, John F. "Frank," 167, 172–73
Springfield, Illinois, 156
Springfield, Kansas, 86
Spring Hill, Kansas, 182
Springtown, Texas, 4–5, 7–12, 16
Starr, Henry, 100
Stevens County (Kansas) War, 84–88
Steilacoom, Washington, 128
Stiles, Kent, 83
Stocking (Deputy Sheriff), 103
Stockwater, Charles, 45
Stoll, Walter (District Attorney), 202
Sturgis, Thomas, 194
Suggette, 198–99
Sullivan, D. O., 16
Sullivan, P. C., 132
Sumas, Washington, 133–35, 141–42, 144–48
Summit, Wyoming, 212
Swan, Alexander Hamilton, 195–96
Swan Land and Cattle Company, 195–99, 201–05, 207–08
Sweeney, Pres, 155–56
Sybille Country (Wyoming), 197–99, 209

Tackitt, G. W., 13
Tackitt, Pleasant (Reverend), 13

Tarkington, Thomas J., 10
Taylor, Elizabeth, 3
Taylor, Eudolphus, 172
Taylor, Emma, 157
Taylor, M. R. (U.S. Detective), 157
Taylor, William, 200
Teague, Bina, 39, 53, 61
Tennyson, A. Whitfield "Whit," 182–85, 188–89
"Terrible Terry" (see John E. Terry)
Terry, Annie, 128, 131, 133, 144–48
Terry, John E. "Cowboy Jake," 127–48
Terry, Joseph (see John E. Terry)
Terry, J. Y. (Justice), 131
Terry, T. J. (Deputy Sheriff), 102
Texas rangers, 8–9
Thomas, A. L., 12–13
Thomas, Frank, 54
Thompson, Alexander "Al," 13
Thompson, F. A., 102–03
Thorne, Ben, 89–91
Thorne, Jean, 90–91
Thurber, Henry (Secretary to President Grover Cleveland), 174
Tichenor, Capt. George C., 160
Todd (Special U.S. Customs Agent), 133
Todd, George, 155
Tonney, Herbert, 86–87
Topeka, Kansas, 79, 84, 89
Tower, William Sherman, 17–18
Trugillo, Joseph, 210
Tyler, Texas, 118

Valle Crucis, North Carolina, 30
Van Bokkelen, J. A. (U.S. Customs Inspector), 132–33
Vancouver, British Columbia, 133–34, 138
Versailles, Indiana, 82
Vinyard, Alvin, 17
Vinyard, Andrew, 17
Vinyard, Isabelle (see Isabelle Hill)
Vinyard, John Calvin, 15–19
Vinyard, John Wesley, 16
Vinyard, Joseph Allen, 16, 18–19
Vinyard, Martha, 16
Vinyard, Mary, 16
Vinyard, Reta J., 16
Vinyard, Sophia, 16
Vinyard, William, 16, 19
Vorhees, Kansas, 85–86

Waddell, Samuel, 156
Wagner, Fredrick, 81–83
Wagner, Peter, 83
Walden, Colorado, 201
Walker, R. L. (District U.S. Marshal), 88–89
Walker, Samuel C. (U.S. Customs Inspector), 134
Walkersville, Illinois, 16
Wanless, Mary (see Mary Powell)

A Note About the Author

Mark Dugan was raised in Jackson County, Missouri, and has been studying and researching Western American History since he was a child. As a young adult he lived in Europe, mainly Germany for ten years before returning to the United States. He worked for the U.S. Government much of that time. He is a graduate of North Carolina State University and teaches at Appalachian State University at Boone, North Carolina.

He has written several books on bandits in and of the American West.